SAVING OUR
PREPOSITIONS

A Guide for the Perplexed

DAVID THATCHER

Produced by:

Comic reproduced with permission by King Features Syndicate. Reprinted with permission by Torstar Syndication Services.

FriesenPress
Suite 300 – 852 Fort Street
Victoria, BC, Canada V8W 1H8

www.friesenpress.com

Distributed to the trade by The Ingram Book Company

TO
MY SONS
STEPHEN & ANDREAS

(and, of course, to Evelyn who now knows
what a preposition is)

Table of Contents

More and more writers seem to have difficulty using the right preposition in various idioms.

—Bryan A. Garner, *A Dictionary of Modern American Usage*

An observer of the way the English language is being used from day to day cannot avoid noticing an extreme carelessness in the choice of prepositions…. It would not be an exaggeration to say that there is an epidemic of prepositional anarchy around.

—Harry Blamires, *The Penguin Guide to Plain English*

Then comes the thing that can of all things be most mistaken and they are prepositions. Prepositions can live one long life being really nothing but absolutely nothing but mistaken and that makes them irritating if you feel that way about mistakes but certainly something that you can be continuously using and everlastingly enjoying. I like prepositions best of all.

—Gertrude Stein, "Poetry and Grammar"

CHAPTER I

THE PROBLEM

Prepositions may be ubiquitous in the English language but, compared with the legion of nouns, verbs, adjectives and other parts of speech, they are so limited in number (though not in frequency of use) that you'd think they would know their ordained and idiomatic place in an English sentence and remain there not daring to budge an inch.

Not so: these little scoundrels are now scampering around with surprising ease, popping up where you least expect them. It must be fun, if you are a preposition, even a little imp like *on*, to cause mayhem in a sentence like the following: "Shelley was washed up *on* the Italian beach." It invites some snide retort, such as "on the contrary, Shelley was well on his way to being washed up while

> IDIOMATIC: a form of expression natural to a language, person, or group of people: "he had a feeling for phrase and idiom." IDIOM: a group of words established by usage as having a meaning not deducible from those of the individual words (e.g., "over the moon," "see the light").
>
> —*Oxford Dictionary of English*

still in England." The headline "whale-watcher finds peace *in* sea" seems to suggest that the man in question had drowned, whereas the report was less sensational, noting simply that being out in a boat gave him tranquility of mind.

It was Humpty Dumpty's considered opinion that some words, particularly verbs (which he thought "the proudest"), have a temper. Not so prepositions, those cute and deceptively simple words like *at, by, for, in, of, on, to* and *with*, which appear to be little and unassuming, mild-mannered fellows entrusted with the humble task of relating one part of a sentence to another. Yet these "unobtrusive go-betweens" often fall victim to loose or slipshod usage. Diminutive they may be, but errors of commission and omission are perpetrated in their name.

Misuse of prepositions is by no means a new phenomenon. In 1864 Henry Alford, in a somewhat disorganized treatise entitled *A Plea for the Queen's English,* pointed out some common errors of his time, many of which are still being perpetrated today.

No doubt about it: these rebellious runaways are playing leapfrog, copiously spawning statements like "the inhabitants of the island are immune *from* this disease" (*from* should be *to*), "I was discouraged *in* taking a trip to Africa" (*in* should be *from*), "I am indifferent *about* his proposal" (*about* should be *to*). If we look for a pattern in these anomalies of substitution, we discover that several prepositions, like *for, of, to, over,* and *with,* turn out to be aggressive usurpers, tough little cuckoo aliens infiltrating the idiomatic nest, heaving rightful occupants unceremoniously overboard and getting plump from constant feeding.

On the death of former President Gerald Ford in December 2006, George W. Bush (like his father, no stranger to the abuse of English) said that his predecessor had "devoted the best years of his life *in* serving his country." Is it utterly pedantic to prefer "devoted … *to* serving"? Granted, errors made while speaking, especially off the cuff, may be more excusable than ones committed in (and to) writing, but they are errors nonetheless.

Headlines in the newspapers of English-speaking countries often violate conventional usage: "Canadian, Russian pairs rivalry represents a study *of* contrasts." Just a minute, shouldn't that be "a study *in* contrasts," an idiom of emphasis, rather than "a study *of* contrasts" which sounds rather like the subtitle of a routine academic thesis? In "Montenegro shows the way *for* independence" we feel that *for* has usurped the expected place of the preposition *to*.

Errors of omission are much less common, although *from* regularly fails to follow "prevent" and it seems you are hopelessly old-fashioned if you are caught inserting *from* between "graduated" and "Yale," and *of* between "couple" and "things" (or between "short" and "cash"). Cabaret singers "play Las Vegas" and a driver will choose "not to race Monte Carlo" (perhaps because Monte has a faster car). A battered pugilist is now said to "cave" rather than "cave *in*," and troops are "pulled" rather than "pulled *out*." Even a highly respected TV anchor like CBC's Peter Mansbridge is found climbing aboard this linguistic bandwagon when he refers to a colleague "working a story" rather than "working *on* a story." Another newsreader obviously found it too much trouble to insert a preposition between "held" and "London" in the following sentence: "The conference will be held London June 11–20." "He complimented my dress:" well, let's hope the dress was pleased. Would it really be excessively onerous to place *to* between "wrote" and "John" in "she wrote John twice last week"? When we read that a movie star in a troubled marriage has "split his wife *of* seven years," we long to insert the preposition *from* after "split" to make

> When T. S. Eliot complained, in "Burnt Norton," that words "slip, slide, perish, / Decay with imprecision, will not stay in place, / Will not stay still," he may have had English prepositions particularly in mind.

the separation less horrendous, especially for the wife. The exclusion of any preposition from the title of a recent book, *Writing African American Women,* is belatedly remedied by the subtitle: "An encyclopedia *of* literature *by* and *about* women *of* color," which contains no fewer than four. If you want to conflate *by* and *about* in a book title, it would appear, just omit both.

Non-native speakers are understandably flummoxed when we say "close *up*" but "shut *down*," or travel "*in* a car" but "*on* the bus (or train)," further confusing matters by saying "*by* car" and "*by* bus (or train)." Should they happen to be admitted to hospital they might be faced with a phrasal verb (to be dealt with later) asking them either to fill *in* a form or fill it *out*, and drink a medicine *up* or drink it *down*. Should something be their responsibility they will be told that it is *up* to them or *down* to them. To their dismay and puzzlement, their English teachers will "find fault *with* their writing," but "find a fault *in* their writing." It is difficult for such non-native speakers to distinguish between "*with* a view *to*" and "*with* a view *of*," between "*on* the market" and "*in* the market," and between "*in* sight" (as in "keep *in* sight") and "*on* sight" (as in "shoot *on* sight"). The difference between being "*at* home" and being "*in* a home" might also elude them (although anyone unlucky enough to be "*in* a home" could readily explain).

When prepositions, even idiomatic ones, are embedded in clichés, tags and stock phrases, there is less likelihood of a blunder being committed. Constant repetition of the correct version of these phrases has helped to make them resistant to change or modification. We accept the sensed rightness of the preposition we are accustomed to. We are not likely to make the mistake of saying "*about* the twinkling of an eye, "wide *from* the mark" "work my fingers *off* the bone" "worse *through* liquor" or "*under* my dead body" although, given the linguistic anarchy prevailing these days, it would be unwise to wager against this possibility.

However, in many cases of prepositional usage, we can sometimes find ourselves at a loss. Lacking any guidance from logic, grammar, or even from semantics, we can easily and forgivably become confused about (*over?*) which preposition to choose. Where variants exist, are they equally

> Go to, let us go down, and there confuse their language, that they may not understand one another's speech.
>
> —Genesis 11:7

acceptable, or are some preferable to others, and some to be avoided? Is it "obsessed *by*" or "obsessed *with*," "alarmed *at*" or "alarmed *by*"? Do we protest *about* or *against* a perceived injustice or simply omit the preposition altogether? Is a novel centred *around* or *on* a given theme? Is regular attendance required *from* or *of* all potential participants? Do we catch ourselves making a fuss *about*, *of* or *over* a person or thing? Do "careful writers" suffer from a phobia *about*, *against*, *for*, *of*, *over*, or *towards* misused prepositions?

Language is bound to evolve, and our unpretentious prepositions are certainly not exempt from the forces of linguistic change (I'll have more to say on this subject in Chapter 6). But more and more, I've noticed a certain perplexity about, and even a lax and callous disregard for, their accepted idiomatic use. Such violations are worrisome: like canaries down a mine, or polar bears in the Arctic, prepositions are sensitive barometers of grave dangers that may be lurking in their linguistic environment. Because he is the most frequently quoted English author, Shakespeare is also the most frequently misquoted one; by the same token prepositions, constituting the most common part of speech, are among the most commonly misused. Certain quotations from famous writers like Shakespeare are bandied about in mangled form ("in one foul sweep," "gild the lily," "the stuff dreams that dreams are made of"), so much so that the original versions come to be regarded as incorrect. So it is with prepositions: once they gain a foothold in improper usage, they assume a legitimacy both unjustified and hard to dislodge. As the actor Bill Nighy remarked in the *Observer*: "If you spent your life saying 'I'm bored with that', and then a whole generation starts saying, 'I'm bored of it,' it does get to you."

To the regret of many scholars, dictionaries—even the venerable and cumbersome war-horses like the *OED* and Webster's—do not always attach much importance to prepositions. When they do, they are better (like the many internet sites on the subject) at indicating acceptable usage than providing examples of common errors. So, without being a formal and analytic "grammar book," this little volume offers itself as a handy guide to using prepositions idiomatically. It delves into their historical place in the language and investigates, with examples of standard as well as non-standard practice, how and why they seem to be landing themselves, and their users, in more and more linguistic trouble. *Eats, Shoots & Leaves*, says Lynne Truss, was aimed at the small number of British people "who love punctuation and don't like to see it mucked about with" (xvii). This manual is aimed at people who, whether they love prepositions or not, don't like them "mucked about with" either. These people want to see language used well and want to use it well themselves, writing it confidently, speaking it trippingly on the tongue. As Bryan Garner has written in the preface to his *Dictionary of Modern American Usage*: "They want to write effectively; they want to speak effectively. They want their language to be graceful at times and powerful at times. They want to understand how to use words well, how to manipulate sentences, and how to move about in the language without seeming to flail" (Garner ix). Avoiding slipping up on prepositions, those banana peels of modern speech, is an important part of such honourable ambitions, perhaps even a first step to realizing them.

So this book is designed, not specifically for learners of English as a second language (although I hope they will find it helpful) but for native speakers willing to accept the accepted prescripts of good writing as adhered to by the finest practitioners of the language. It is also intended to be of help to teachers of grammar and composition at the high-school and college level. It will be of absolutely no use to those, such as members of the Anti-Queen's English Society, who amuse themselves by rebelling at every opportunity against such prescripts.

It is out of annoyance with the abuse and misuse of prepositions, and perhaps even more out of annoyance with my own annoyance, that I have been prompted, nay, impelled, to embark on a kind of rescue mission. The book is no page-turner, but I have tried to make it informative, instructive, useful and even, wherever possible, entertaining. It can be read by those (bless you all) who prefer to wolf it down more or less from beginning to end, as well as those whose interest might be piqued by a chapter here or there, who prefer to sip or browse, or who want to use it mainly or solely as a reference work or aide-mémoire. My earnest hope is that it will raise awareness and provoke discussion. Like R. W. Burchfield, I have tried to avoid what John Updike called the dogmatism and "stark preachments" of H. W. Fowler in favour of "stating preferences where usage varies, and admitting variation to be valid when opinion is divided among educated adult speakers and writers" (Burchfield 865).

"Prepositions," Sue Coffman writes, "are a lot like mosquitoes: small, annoying, and hard to deal with. But like mosquitoes, they're going to stay around to plague us, so we might as well learn to coexist. Roll up your sleeves, but be sure to use insect repellent" (221).

On a personal note I would like to thank J. C., the anonymous *TLS* columnist, for having generously, if unwittingly, hinted at title of this book at a time I was despairing of ever finding a suitable one. The best I had managed to come up with, *Prepositions for Pleasure and Profit*, seemed, despite its catchy alliterative ring, to lack the requisite note of urgency given the gravity of the crisis facing us. "Save Our Prepositions" is the heading of a column he published in the *TLS* on August 18, 2006. I've just changed "save" to "saving." Thank you again, J. C., whoever and wherever you are.

∾

CHAPTER 2

ENDING A SENTENCE

Most people have heard of two linguistic rules, probably drilled in at school. One, do not split your infinitive, and two, do not end a sentence with a preposition. So what are we supposed to end a sentence with?

Grammarians used to argue that we must not split the infinitive (as in "to boldly go") because, in Latin, the infinitive consists of a single word. If we cannot split the infinitive of a verb, say "amare," we should not split its English equivalent, "to love." Presumably they thought that love was equally indivisible in both languages. Ridiculous as this argument was, it had a kind of twisted logic, as did the rule about not ending a sentence with a preposition, a rule which Fowler calls a "cherished superstition":

> The grammar has a rule absurd
> Which I would call an outworn myth:
> "A preposition is a word
> You mustn't end a
> sentence with."
>
> —Berton Braley, "No Rule to Be Afraid Of"

According to Fowler, both these rules (or "fetishes") are still "misapplied or unduly revered": "The fact is that the remarkable freedom enjoyed by English in putting its prepositions late ... is an important element in the flexibility of the language." He adds: "The power of saying 'people are worth talking to' instead of 'people with whom it is worth while to talk' is not one to be lightly surrendered" (Fowler 1926, 458). Kingsley Amis, in opposing this "fancied prohibition ... dear to ignorant snobs," endorses Fowler's view: "It is natural and harmless in English to use a preposition to end a sentence with." In fact, the familiar construction goes back to Old English times and appears frequently in the Bible as well as in the work of many of the greatest English authors, including Shakespeare. Two occur in Hamlet's "To be or not to be" speech: "fly to others that we know not *of*" and "thousand natural shocks / That flesh is heir *to*." Other plays are rife with them: "the labor we delight *in*" (*Macbeth* 2.3.49), "hasten your generals *after*" (*Antony and Cleopatra* 2.4.2.), "for fear lest day should look their shames *upon*" (*A Midsummer Night's Dream* 3.2.385), "and yours it is *against*" (*The Tempest* 3.1.31). Students who berate Shakespeare for his cavalier attitude towards "proper" grammar are basing their condemnation on an outmoded superstition.

So how did this "superstition" arise? In the seventeenth century it was felt that a preposition, as its Latin name implies ("praepositio," from "prae" meaning "before" and the verb "ponere" meaning "to put") should come before the word it modifies, not after. John Dryden (1631–1700) reasoned that since Latin sentences never end with a preposition English ones have no business doing otherwise. In later life he re-edited his earlier prose in keeping with this attitude: hence "the age I live in" was amended to "the age in which I live." In the eighteenth century, a century marked by a somewhat snobbish or

Mrs Malaprop is speaking to Captain Absolute about Miss Languish: "Long ago I laid my positive conjunctions on her, never to think on the follow again;—I have since laid Sir Anthony's preposition before her; but, I am sorry to say, she seems resolved to decline every particle that I enjoin her."—Richard Sheridan, *The Rivals* hoity-toity emphasis on correctness and good manners, Robert Lowth, a clergyman with rather too much time on his hands, spent much of it dabbling in matters grammatical. In his *Short Introduction to English Grammar* (1762) he recommended that sentences, especially in formal writing, should not end in prepositions. But, to be fair, he wasn't dogmatic about it: he observed that the practice was widespread both in spoken and written English and followed it himself, consciously or unconsciously, in a way that emphasizes his point: "This is an idiom which our language is strongly inclined to." This formal construction is known among contemporary linguists as "pied piping" (some find this term amusing, others can make no sense of it whatsoever).

By precept and example Lowth and Dryden between them carry the can for a misleading doctrine and for its hardening in the work of later influential grammarians. Many generations of students have tied themselves into knots trying to avoid the punishment they would be meted out by not obeying this prescriptive rule. One method was to eliminate the final preposition altogether ("some friends are hard to say goodbye") but that stratagem only landed them in deeper trouble. Another was to resort to pedantic archaism e.g., "whence come you?" for "where do you come *from*?" and "whither are you going?" for "where are you going *to*." So, hence with "whence" and may "whither" wither.

It was an unfortunate slip on the part of the teacher who told his class that "the preposition is a very bad word to end a sentence *with*," but by now the most common response to the commandment "thou shalt not end…" is to turn the whole silly shibboleth into a joke, to ridicule it as humbug. It is clearly a rule up with which many people are fed. Including Winston Churchill, whose name is often brought up in this regard.

In his novel *Everyman*, Philip Roth seems to be deliberately flouting (not flaunting) the "rule" by terminating four consecutive sentences with prepositions: "Many people in America particularly have had the opportunity to abandon origins they didn't want to bother *with*; that they felt imprisoned *by*, that they felt compromised *by*, that they felt ashamed *of*…."

There are several versions of the story (only "attributed" and therefore possibly apocryphal) concerning him. One relates that an officious editor had the audacity to "correct" a proof of Churchill's memoirs by revising a sentence that ended with the outlawed preposition. Sir Winston hurled back at the editor a memorable rebuttal (one of many variants): "This is the sort of arrant pedantry up with which I will not put!"

Strictly speaking, and at the risk of committing an act of "arrant pedantry" myself, Churchill's example does not involve a preposition (or rather two propositions) but a phrasal verb, "to put up with." "Up" looks like a preposition, but syntactically it is an adverbial particle); "with" looks like a preposition and is one. It has been pointed out that in sentences where a phrasal verb is placed at the end it is often impossible to stick the preposition anywhere else but at the end, e.g., "the matter must be seen to."

Fowler's claim that "the legitimacy of the prepositional ending in literary English must be uncompromisingly maintained" might have lodged itself in the mind of the newspaper columnist who responded snappily to the accusation that he was uncouthly violating the terminal preposition "rule": "What do you take me for? A chap who doesn't know how to make full use of all the easy variety the English language is capable of? Don't you know that ending a sentence with a preposition is an idiom many famous writers are very fond of? They realize it's a colloquialism a skilful writer can do a great deal with. Certainly it's a linguistic device you ought to read about."

Ending a sentence with two prepositions is also permissible, but there are limits. Ernest Gowers appeared to be the first to cite the story of a nurse who performed the remarkable feat of getting four apparent prepositions at the end of a sentence by asking her charge: "What did you choose that book to be read to out of for?" Nowadays one can find on the Internet ingenious attempts to improve on this absurdity by adding even more apparent prepositions. A recent search reveals the number has risen to a staggering nine, as in this version about a little boy, deputizing for Gowers' nurse, who had just gone to bed when his father comes into the room carrying a book about Australia. Surprised, the boy asks: "What did you bring that book that I wanted to be read to out of from about Down Under up for?" In fact, in both these versions only the last word, *for*, is strictly speaking a preposition: the rest form part, as in the Churchill citation, of phrasal verbs.

In his novel *Kalooki Nights* (2006) Howard Jacobsen has some innocent fun jamming six prepositions together at the end of a sentence: "For her part my mother ... wouldn't have minded what Shani got up to, so long as she wore something my mother approved of to get up to it in." And surely the poser of the following question was transgressing the rule for comic effect: "Where is this fence that the grass is always greener the other side *of*?"

> I lately lost a preposition;
> It hid, I thought, beneath my chair
> And angrily I cried, "Perdition!
> Up from out of in under there."
>
> Correctness is my vade mecum,
> And straggling phrases I abhor,
> And yet I wondered, "What should he come
> Up from out of in under for?
>
> —Morris Bishop

Let the final word be Fowler's: "Follow no arbitrary rule: if the ... final preposition that has naturally presented itself sounds comfortable, keep it; if it does not sound comfortable, still keep it if it has compensating vigor, or when among awkward possibilities it is the least awkward" (Fowler 459). That kind of advice is not to be sneezed at: it's the kind of advice that many great writers—Chaucer, Shakespeare, Milton, Swift among them—have authorized us to follow. Those who oppose this liberal attitude on the erroneous grounds that good writers avoid ending a sentence with a preposition do not, as one writer has put it, have a leg to stand on.

So let's give the wits free rein, whether they are using prepositions or adverbial particles to conclude their sentences: "Never lend your car to anyone you have given birth *to*," "I have tried in my time to be a philosopher, but cheerfulness always kept breaking *in*," "another victory like that and we're done *for*," "the trouble with doing nothing is that you can never take any time *off*," "the first thing I do in the morning is to read the obituaries in the paper and, if I am not in them, get *up*."

Quiz #1.

In the following sentences, is the preposition (italicized when not missing) correct or incorrect (misused, misplaced, redundant or missing)?

1. "Gloom and sardonic humour is *in* the heart of British comedy."

2. His resignation was received *with* loud and prolonged cheers.

3. Glenn Gould had an affinity *for* Bach.

4. He is reluctant to concur *to* any theory, particularly literary theory.

5. "No philosophy is much good, / If it cannot be understood."

6. This new area of research is a virgin field pregnant *of* possibilities.

∼

Answers: 1. *at* the heart, 2. *by* loud, 3. *for* is correct, 4. concur *with*, 5. is *of* much, 6. pregnant *with*.

CHAPTER 3

ARE PREPOSITIONS BEAUTIFUL?

During the last thirty years or so, surveys have been conducted to determine what people thought were the most beautiful words in the language. In 1980 the *Sunday Times* came up with its top ten: *melody, velvet, crystal, gossamer, autumn, peace, tranquil, twilight, murmur, caress, mellifluous, whisper.* In reporting this competition, David Crystal admits he does not know whether to be pleased or miffed at the result of his surname finishing third (2006, 168). He notes that many of the words seem to have been chosen for their sound, as opposed to words in a 2004 British Council survey among learners which seem indicate a preference for pleasant meaning: *mother, passion, smile, love, eternity, fantastic, destiny, freedom, liberty, tranquility.* Wilfred J. Funk, whoever he is or was, choose the following for *The Book of Lists*: *chimes, dawn, golden, hush, lullaby, luminous, melody, mist, murmuring, tranquil.*

In none of the lists did a preposition achieve anything more than a dismal showing. If truth be told, not one preposition made the top fifty in any poll. Or even the top hundred. Unlikely words performed much better: the word "gonorrhea" was first in one poll, presumably for its sound rather than its meaning, and "if" (the closest to a preposition as a function word) placed forty-third in the British Council list. Perhaps it owed this eminent rank to the abiding influence of Rudyard Kipling.

Why are some words perceived as beautiful? Crystal suggests five criteria, in the light of which prepositions fare extremely poorly. A word must have at least one *l* sound (only four prepositions do); it contains a nasal sound, especially *m* (only *among* and *from* do); it contains other continuant sounds, such as *r* and *s* (prepositions do rather well here); it contains two or three syllables (a third of all prepositions are monosyllables); the consonants and vowels vary from syllable to syllable, as in the word "melody (only five or so prepositions are tri-syllabic). No tri-syllabic preposition comes anywhere close to sounding like "melody," let alone "gonorrhea" with its unfair advantage of an extra syllable.

The word "meconium" meets several of Crystal's criteria superbly. When it was overheard by a woman in the throes of labour pangs, it struck her as the most beautiful word in the language, so she decided to name her baby daughter after it. "Meconium," it turns out, is the medical term for fetal excrement (Pinker 2). And what about "melanoma," so beautiful "you want it to be the name of a tropical wind instead of a tumor" (Nunberg 21)?

For my money, the most aesthetically appealing prepositions are: *above* (the "*v*" is extraordinarily seductive, like the "*v*" in "Guadalquivir"), *among* (a nice twanging effect like a Hawaiian guitar), *down* (perhaps because of the irrelevant associations with eiderdown and dog-training), and *underneath* (a word meeting the criteria which enable "melody" to win popular acclaim).

Henry James (in *A Backward Glance*) thought that "summer afternoon" constituted "the two most beautiful words in

This is what Jane Hirshfield says of *of*: "Its chain link can be delicate or massive. In the human realm, directional: though one thing also connects to another through 'and,' this is not the same." And in regards to *to*: "Your work requires / both transience and transformation: / night changes to day, snow to rain, the shoulder of the living pig to meat."

the English language." His judgement shows that if an abstract preposition is prepared to piggy-back on a more poetic word it can achieve more than passing attention. And though a preposition may not seem beautiful in its own right, we might like to think that, when it appears amid other more gorgeous and evocative words in a line of poetry, like Nashe's magical "brightness falls *from* the air," it can act as a foil, setting off the verbal beauty around it. Sometimes an incantatory effect an be achieved by accentuating the preposition by means of stress patterns, as in Byron's description of his "little isle": "But *in* it there were three tall trees, / And *o'er* it blew the mountain breeze, / And *by* it there were waters flowing, / And *on* it there were young flowers growing" ("The Prisoner of Chillon"). In "Elegy XIX: To His Mistress Going to Bed" John Donne parades five prepositions in strict iambic sequence: "License my roving hands, and let them go / Before, behind, between, above, below."

Christine Brooke-Rose (who died in 2012) wrote three novels with prepositions as their titles: *Out*, *Between* and *Thru*. In 2006 the American poet Jane Hirshfield published a volume of poems named after a preposition. It was entitled *After*: one of these poems commemorates *of*, another *to*. It's hard to imagine these tributes as signalling the beginning of a trend, since our little prepositions are rather unprepossessing and self-effacing. With some memorable exceptions, as in "government *of* the people, *by* the people, *for* the people" in the Gettysburg Address, they are usually unstressed in the rhythm of a sentence. Annoyingly many British and American TV newsreaders have a habit of persistently accentuating prepositions, perhaps in a misguided attempt to give their utterances an added emphasis: thus prepositions containing, say, the vowel "o" (*for, of, to*), do not get elided to "fer," "urv" and "t'" (following the natural stress pattern) but are wrenched into retaining their full strong and open value.

Prepositions seem more at home in the generally utilitarian world of prose than in the more imaginative world of poetry. Unlike some verbs, nouns and adjectives they are not swish, chic, atmospheric, picturesque, flamboyant, evocative, racy or voluptuous. So, dull as they are, at least they run no risk of ever being denounced as vulgar, let alone obscene or pornographic.

That indefatigable expurgator, Thomas Bowdler, had no business messing around with them and knew it. When he emended Mercutio's "the bawdy hand *of* the dial is *on* the prick *of* noon," he left the three prepositions severely alone. He had other fish to fry.

In his OUP blog for August 30, 2007, Ben Zimmer cites a fable by science fiction writer Eleanor Arnason entitled "The Grammarian's Five Daughters." In this story "a mother bestows grammatical gifts to [*on?*] five daughters seeking their fortune in the world. The eldest daughter gets a bag full of nouns, the next gets verbs, the next adjectives, and the next adverbs. The youngest daughter is stuck with the leftovers, those 'dull little words' overlooked by everyone else: the prepositions. But the prepositions ultimately bring order to a chaotic land, serving as the foundation for a strong and thriving nation organized under the motto 'WITH'."

Quiz #2.

In the following sentences, is the preposition correct or incorrect (misused, misplaced, redundant or missing)?

1. When you're done squabbling *into* politics, I'd like you to help me in the kitchen.

2. The Christmas tree caught *on* fire.

3. The psychiatrist helped him battle his illusions.

4. The President has a commitment *to* law and order.

5. He claimed to be getting closer *with* Jesus every day.

6. How many calories should you consume a day?

~

Answers: 1. squabbling *over*, 2. (delete *on*), 3. battle *against*, 4. *to* is correct, 5. closer *to*, 6. *in* a day

CHAPTER 4

FACTS AND FIGURES

Prepositions may not rank as beautiful, nor are they deemed important enough—unlike nouns, verbs and adjectives—to be capitalized in titles of books and articles, but I submit they are worth caring about.

WHAT IS A PREPOSITION? A preposition is that part of speech which connects or relates one part of a sentence, usually a noun, a pronoun, a verb form ending in "-ing" or some equivalent complement (which the preposition is said to "govern"), to another part of the sentence or to the sentence as a whole. Many prepositions establish a spatial or temporal link between two aspects of a sentence (some do double duty, being used to signify place as well as time: *around, at, before, past, toward, up*). So essentially a preposition is a linking device,

Just as we might speak about a "portraiture" of adjectives, a "substantiality" of nouns, an "intensity" of verbs, a "togetherness" of conjunctions, a "deputizing" of pronouns, or perhaps even a "shortage" of articles, we might refer to a "relativity of prepositions."

constituting the connective tissue of language. An anonymous eighteenth-century writer used an apt simile: "As the members of the body are knit together by *nerves, tendons,* and *ligaments,* without which they would be useless and no way serviceable, either to themselves or to one another, so, prepositions are the *nerves* and *ligaments* of all discourse" (cited in Yagoda 160–61). Prepositions have also been compared to the mortar that holds together the bricks (nouns, verbs, adjectives) in a building (sentence or paragraph). The sentence "I went the cinema my friend the evening the twenty-fifth" resembles a pile of loose bricks: "When the prepositions are added ('I went *to* the cinema *with* my friend *on* the evening *of* the twenty-fifth') the bricks are fastened together in a meaningful fabric" (Blamires 2000, 158). Clearly, omitting connectives simply leads to "barrenness and confusion" (Fernald vii).

BREVITY—THE SOUL OF PREPOSITIONS. The first thing to notice about prepositions is how short many of them are. This is true of prepositions in many languages: Russian, for instance, has four prepositions ("b," "k," "c," "y") consisting of one simple alphabet letter, and even these are frequently elided into the next word at the cost of their own singularity. But English prepositions are the true champions of minimalism, often having evolved from longer forms. A good third of them are strictly monosyllabic. Those that aren't have an irresistible urge (especially in old-fashioned verse) to become so: some get beheaded (*'gainst, 'neath, 'pon, 'tween* and *'twixt*), others either eviscerated (*o'er*) or curtailed (*fro* and even *fra,* a contraction of *fram* meaning *from*). "O'clock" is a contraction we are all familiar with, and the very modern (and American) *thru* is a colloquial instance of this tendency (Robert Browning's poetry is full of archaic contractions like *o'* and *i'*). Prepositions are apparently prepared to go to any lengths to get shorter, even to the point of emulating Russian ones by reducing themselves, as in Shakespeare's time, to a single letter (a', i', o', t', w') or even, especially today, vanishing altogether from sentences where you might have a legitimate expectation of finding them.

A Comparison

Paragraph with prepositions deleted: "Breakfast Uncle Percival used walk, especially spring, Auntie Mabel his wife twenty years the towpath. His opinion these walks were very good his health, and he did them good spirits, wishing he'd exercised he had met her the dance-hall the war. Percival would talk his wife these walks. Them reigned a harmony description. If they got tired their exertions fresh air they used look a convenient bench and sit it. When the clock the church tower the river showed a quarter twelve, they had enough a day. They got and started, making sure they had left nothing the bench."

Same paragraph with prepositions restored: "*After* breakfast Uncle Percival used *to* walk, especially *in* spring, *with* Auntie Mabel his wife *of* twenty years *along* the towpath. *In* his opinion these walks were very *for* good his health, and he did them *in* good spirits, wishing he'd exercised *before* he had met her *at* the dance-hall *during* the war. Percival would talk *at* great length *to* his wife *on* these walks. *Between* them reigned a harmony *beyond* description. If they got tired *from* their exertions *in* the fresh air they used *to* look *for* a convenient bench and sit *on* it. When the clock *on* the church tower *across* the river showed a quarter *to* twelve, they had enough *for* a day. They got *up* and started *off*, making sure they had left nothing *under* the bench."

HOW MANY PREPOSITIONS ARE THERE IN ENGLISH? There are about seventy simple prepositions in English. The class of pronouns and the class of conjunctions contain even less, the classes of verbs, nouns, adjectives and adverbs considerably more. The stock of English prepositions, pronouns and conjunctions is finite: it is extremely unlikely any more will ever be invented. The language is continually adding to its hoard of verbs, nouns, adjectives and adverbs, many of which we could well dispense with. As Mark Twain said of the adjective, and Ernest Hemingway of the adverb, "When in doubt, strike it out." On the other hand, the entire corpus of prepositions, to which can be added the corpus of pronouns and conjunctions, represents an essential component of the language, a component which was established centuries ago and has hardly changed since. This claim cannot be made of any other class as a whole.

WHERE ARE THEY? Everywhere. In clichés: "make no bones *about* it," "*against* the grain," "fall *between* two stools," "circumstances *beyond* our control," "elephant *in* the room," "get *into* trouble," "belle *of* the ball," "*off* the beaten track," "jump *on* the bandwagon," "let the cat *out of* the bag," "keep it *under* your hat," "help the police *with* their enquiries." In works of fiction: "*Away* from Her," "Staring *at* the Sun," "*Behind* the Scenes *at* the British Museum," "*For* Whom the Bell Tolls," "*From* Here *to* Eternity," "One Flew *over* the Cuckoo's Nest," "*Through* the Looking-Glass," "A Passage *to* India," "Coming *up* for Air." In witticisms: "I didn't get too many women running *after* me—it was their husbands who'd be *after* me" (Charlie

Despite the frequency of prepositions in everyday speech children seem not to take an immediate interest in them. According to Alison Gopnik, author of *Scientist in the Crib*, the following are the first words they speak: 1. Mama; 2. Dada; 3. Juice; 4. Ball; 5. Doggie; 6. Gone; 7. There; 8. Uh-oh; 9. More; 10. What's that? One way to avoid making blunders with prepositions is not to use them.

George). "I married *beneath* me—all women do" (Nancy Astor). "Sex *between* a man and a woman can be wonderful—provided you get *between* the right man and the right woman" (Woody Allen). "I took up a collection *for* a man in our office, but I didn't get enough money to buy one" (Ruth Buzzi) "*Outside* every thin woman is a fat man trying to get *in*" (Katharine Whitehorn). "Anybody who says he can see *through* women is missing a lot" (Groucho Marx). "A woman *without* a man is like a fish *without* a bicycle" (Gloria Steinem).

COMMON BUT NOT VULGAR. The most common word in the English language is the one that starts (and pops up six times in) the sentence I trust you are reading—the definite article "the." Of the first twenty-five most frequent words in written English nine, according to the *Oxford English Corpus*, are prepositions. Hats off then to *to* (third position), *of* (fifth), *in* (seventh), *for* (twelfth), *on* (fifteenth), *with* (sixteenth), *as* (eighteenth), *at* (twenty-first), *by* (twenty-fifth). Making the first eighty (but bear in mind that some of these may also be adverbs) are: *from, up, out, about, into,* and *over*). *After* is in eighty-fourth position (results in the WordCount website differ only slightly from those in the *OEC*). Bryson (150) reports a 1923 study which found that only forty-three words account for half the words in daily use, and only nine account for one quarter of all the words in any representative sample of written English: *and, be, have, it, of, the, to, will, you.* Such a finding helps to explain why *of* and *to* place so high. Even in Middle English *of* and *in* were the most common prepositions.

WHAT ARE THE MOST COMMON PREPOSITIONS? Prepositions that consist of one word are known as simple prepositions. Here is a list of the most common ones: it excludes Scottish dialect prepositions like *anent* (*about*), *athort* (*athwart, across*), *fornent* (*near, opposite, alongside*), *outwith* (*beyond, outside*) and prepositions which are spelt differently, as in Irvine Welsh's dialect novel *Trainspotters* (1993), e.g., *efter, fir, fa, oot, tae* and *wi.*

- *aboard, about, above, absent (American English), across, after, against, along, alongside, amid(st), among(st), apart from, around, as, astraddle, astride, at, athwart, atop*

- *before, behind, below, beneath, beside(s), between, beyond, but, by*

- *chez, concerning*

- *despite, down, during*

- *ere, except, excepting, excluding*

- *following, for, from*

- *in, inside, into*

- *like*

- *minus*

- *near, notwithstanding*

- *of, off, on, onto, opposite, out, outside, over*

- *pace, past, pending*

- *regarding, round*

- *since*

- *than, through, throughout, till, to, toward(s)*

- *under, underneath, until, up, upon*

- *via*

- *with, withal, within, without*

A list of less frequently used prepositions would include *abaft* (=*behind*), *abeam* (= "*opposite* the middle of a ship"), *afore, anti, aslant, bar, barring, cum, fore, given, granted, midst, per, plus, post, pro* and *save.* Some "-ing" prepositions (e.g., *concerning, excepting, regarding*) look like present participles but are classified as "participle prepositions."

WHERE DO PREPOSITIONS COME FROM? With the notable exception of *chez*, every one of the hundred basic, most common words is Germanic, or at least Anglo-Saxon, in origin. Germanic tribes (Angles, Saxons, Jutes) settled in England in the 5th and 6th centuries bringing with them their own native dialects. English is a name derived from the tribe of the Angles Otherwise we would be speaking Saxonian or Jutish. Many German and English prepositions are cognate, that is, they reveal common derivation or ancestry: *bei/by, fuer/for, rund/round, vor/ before, seit/since, mit/with, vor/from, ein/in, unter/under.* In modern Danish some are identical (*for, over, under*) and others very close (*efter/after, fra/from, i/in, til/till, af/of* and *off, ad/at, langs/along*). As a general rule, prepositions (like pronouns, conjunctions, irregular verbs and some crude four-letter words) are of Germanic, Old Norse or Anglo-Saxon lineage. They are therefore among the most ancient and venerable words in the language: aged to perfection, they deserve our respect for both their immaculate pedigree and their sheer longevity. Very few prepositions ever become obsolete. Even those that do, suffering the opprobrium of being regarded as archaic, are still recognizable: *amidst, anenst (alongside of), athwart, betwixt, bove (above), fore, withal*

Table showing how the spelling of prepositions has changed:

Old English	Middle English	Modern English
onbutan	aboute(n)	about
aefter	efter	after
aet	aet	at
beforan	beforen	before
betweonum	betwenen	between
be/bi	be/bi/by	by
fram	fram	from
ofer	ofer	over
til	untill	until

ARE ALL PREPOSITIONS SIMPLE? No. There are creatures known as complex (or compound) prepositions that consist of combinations of two or three words acting as a single unit. Examples of two-word phrases are: *according to, ahead of, all over, apart from, as for, as from, as from, because of, close to, contrary to, except for, near to, next to, out of.* Also common are three-word phrases: *by dint of, by means of, in charge of, with reference to, in accordance with, in front of, in spite of, on top of.* By combining prepositions it is possible to signify a relationship or meaning beyond the capability one poor preposition alone. In the sentence "the sounds are coming *from under* the porch" the sounds do not come *from* the porch, and they do not come *under* the porch—they come *from under* the porch (Strumpf 206). And *down under* is widely understood as referring to Australia. Not so widely known is "*from away*," a term used in eastern Canada to refer to someone not "*from* here," i.e., from nowhere further than the next village.

WHAT CAN PREPOSITIONS EXPRESS? Jonathan Aaron has written a poem entitled "Prepositions". It begins: "They're supposed to help you talk about here and there—/ In your pocket, on the street, under the table. / About then and now—It's finished between us. / Come back to me. What will I do without you? / when and where—The day before yesterday. / Down by the riverside. Over my head" (*TLS* October 28, 2011, 23). Prepositions are indeed helpful, playing "a key role in the expression of other notions every bit as important as those expressed though the workings of the verb system" (Lindstromberg 25). They can express cause ("die *of* cancer"), agency ("composed *by* Bach"), instrumentality ("*with* a spade"), manner ("*in* style"), means ("*through* effort"), function ("lamp *for* reading") and purpose ("*in order to* succeed"). A preposition like *with* is highly versatile in this respect: compare "walk *with* a lady, *with* difficulty, *with* a limp, *with* a cane, *with* a sprained ankle" (cited in Fernald 9).

Prepositions can often surprise by virtue of their antithetical expressiveness: "The tradition in the islands is that a man lives *on* his land but *by* what he gets out of the sea." "Prostate cancer is often harmless—a disease that men die *with*, not *of*." "If you have a troubled past you have to live *with* it, but you don't have to live *in* it." "I think it's terrible what nursing homes do *to* the old, when they claim that they are doing something *for* them." "I walk *about*, not *to* and *from*" (a retiree describing his empty, purposeless days). "In his youth a man lives *through* his body; in old age he lives *against* it." In classical times Spartan mothers would tell their sons before battle: "Come back *with* your shield, or *on* it."

CAN PREPOSITIONS HAVE MORE THAN ONE MEANING? Yes. A good dictionary will reveal that many prepositions are what linguists call "polysemous," i.e., not limited to a single meaning. The *OED*, for example, gives ten different definitions of *with* and any dictionary will provide multiple entries for *about, above, after, before, for, from, in, into, of, up,* etc. (for a handy and up-to-date overview see "Guide to the Particles" in the *Oxford Phrasal Verbs Dictionary for Learners of English*). Coded meanings of prepositions are a staple of cryptic crosswords: *about, for, in, from, out* and *round* point to an anagram; *among, below, by, during, from, in* and *inside* to a hidden word; *about, in, outside, round* and *without* to a position on either side of another word; *back, down, over* and *up* require a word to be spelt backwards. *For* often means "to obtain the solution" as in this recent clue: "Tories pop in *for* part of speech." Answer: "preposition" (anagram of the first three words). In the clue "launderette concealed below" the answer is hidden in the word "la*undere*tte." "Round" is a preposition, but confusion is deliberately sown because, like many other words in these clues, it could also be another part of speech, in this case a verb, a noun or an adjective.

In the following eight cryptic crossword clues, there are eleven different prepositions: 1. One who dreams *about* going places (5-6). 2. A month *at* work *with* American creature (7). 3. Chart needed *by* the French *to* find tree (5). 4. Ruler has measure *for* every alternative (7). 5. Knowledge *of* teeth? (6). 6. Give *out* old newspapers (7). 7. Neighbourhoods may get me *into* music (11). 8. King *in* crooked lane, on foot (5).

Answers: 2. Sleep-walker. 2. Octopus. 3. Maple. 4. Emperor. 5. Wisdom. 6. Express. 7. Communities. 8. Ankle.

PREPOSITIONS AND THE QUESTION OF IDIOM.

Only phrases and expressions ("go Dutch," "quit cold turkey," "be nobody's poodle," "scream blue murder") can be termed idioms. In these cases either the meaning cannot be deduced from the constituent words or the meaning is metaphorical rather than literal. The statement "he is *on* his fifth wife" does not, one assumes, invite a literal understanding of *on.* Many cliches ("the green light," "*in* the bag," "*at* a loose end") and euphemisms ("answer nature's call, "spend a penny," "powder one's nose") are idioms. Like other single words, prepositions may form part of an idiom ("pull the rug *from under* someone's feet," "put someone's nose *out of* joint," "feel *off* colour," "be *in* the pink"), but standing on their own they are not idioms—they can only be used idiomatically or unidiomatically. To confess you are "bored *by* (or *with*)" the subject of prepositions is to speak idiomatically, to say "bored *of*" is not. This book is largely about the frequently unidiomatic use of prepositions in contemporary speech and writing.

DO FOREIGN SPEAKERS MAKE PREPOSITIONAL ERRORS IN THEIR OWN LANGUAGES? A large topic, and not one to be covered in a single paragraph. The short answer is: "Apparently not, and certainly not to the same degree." Spaniards, for their part, declare stoutly they never make such mistakes, even with *para* and *por*, prepositions which cause such headaches for learners of their language. The French have been known to confuse *dans* (concrete) with *en* (abstract), and to say "je vous remercie *pour* votre aide" (on the model of "merci *pour*") instead of "je vous remercie *de* votre aide," but insist that most mistakes they make are the result of contamination from other languages, especially English. Germans are aware that other Germans tend to confuse *nach* with *zu*, both of these with *bei*, and say *bei* when they should be employing *in*. It's said that young Turkish immigrants in Germany skirt the problem of incorrect usage by avoiding prepositions altogether.

LIKES AND UNLIKES. Most words do not have opposites. A third of all prepositions consist of opposite pairs: *above/ below, after/ before, beneath/over, down/up, from/to, in/out, inside/outside, like/unlike, (up)on/under(neath), with/without.* Many prepositions adore the company of their likes: *down and out, out and away, over and above.* Some are identical twins: *by* and *by, on* and *on, out* and *out, over* and *over, round* and *round, through* and *through.* Some seek out their opposites: *ins* and *outs, off* and *on, to* and *fro, ups* and *downs.*

In May 2012 Bizarro published a syndicated cartoon showing two Roman senators (as we guess from their togas) encountering each other. One asks: "Are you going to the forum or againstum?"

CAN PREPOSITIONS BE INVENTED? Yes, they can, but only in artificial or "auxiliary" languages like Esperanto or Ido (just the best known of several hundreds of constructed languages specially devised to facilitate global communication). Even then such invented languages borrow heavily from existing ones. Diego Marani's delightful pan-European language Europanto takes its vocabulary from English, French, German, Spanish, Italian, Dutch and, occasionally, Latin (yes, his prepositions also reflect this catholicity of taste). Esperanto and Ido adopt, verbatim, Latin equivalents for many of their prepositions: apud (*beside*), dum (*during*), inter (*between*), sed (*but*), sub (*under*), super (*above*), trans (*through*), trans (*across*). Esperanto has an indefinite preposition ("je") that can be pressed into service when employing another preposition would result in confusion. Having such a preposition in English would be a godsend.

Klingon, as everyone knows by now, is the official language of the Klingon Empire invented by Marc Okrand for the 1984 film Star Trek III. It has a grammar, a dictionary, an enthusiastic internet following but very few prepositions: these are formed mostly by means of noun and verb suffixes.

CAN PREPOSITIONS BE PLACED ANYWHERE? Nearly all prepositions can begin a sentence. A preposition can be placed before or after any other preposition, often giving rise to a highly idiomatic expression, e.g., "he knows he is *in for* it now," "they are not *up to* such a difficult job," "I don't feel I am *up for* a long hike." It can also be situated before or after any verb, any adverb, any adjective, any noun (or gerund). It can be compared to a nomad, a victim of wanderlust or a star soccer player with a roving commission. But it is not completely at liberty to go where it likes: it can come only before an article (a, an, the) and possessive pronouns (him/his, her/her, it/its). It cannot be placed either before or after subject pronouns (I, he, she). But it bears repeating that it is quite legitimate (see Chapter 2) to put any preposition you like at the end of any sentence.

CAN PREPOSITIONS BE OMITTED? Yes and no. In cases where the meaning of the preposition is taken as implied in the preceding verb, it can be omitted, e.g., "to climb (*up*) the mountain," "pass (*by*) the forest," "turn (*round*) the corner." It is also sometimes dropped before a conjunction (e.g., where, what, whether, who, how): you can say "I'm not certain *of* where she went" or "I'm not certain where she went." Often (see the list provided in Part II of Chapter 11)) a preposition is inserted where one is not needed ("abdicate *from* the throne," "catch *on* fire," "plummet *down*").

In the sentence "Peter Mandelson has no special knowledge or interest in Northern Ireland," the omitted preposition *of* should be placed after "knowledge": "You cannot have knowledge *in* something, but only knowledge *of* something" (Trask 189). Some verbs can take a preposition or omit it without much change in meaning (e.g., "approve *of* / approve," "offend *against* / offend," "repent *of* / repent," but in some cases the meaning does alter. "To know a suitable candidate" is not the same as "to know *of* a suitable candidate" (the first implying personal acquaintance, the second implying second-hand information). Rowe and Webb (207) offer further examples of semantic change: "We escape detection, injury etc., but we escape *from* prison, custody, etc. We meditate (= purpose) revenge, but meditate *upon* (= consider) the shortness of life. We remark (= notice) a person's conduct, and may remark *upon* (= make remarks upon) it. We admit an excuse, but a thing admits *of* excuse."

"*With*" was once regarded as redundant as in "to commiserate *with* someone," but now most people would never dream of omitting it.

Tom Cole notes that prepositions are sometimes optional. He offers these examples: "When I'm at home, I feel safe" and "when I'm home, I feel safe." But *at* would be strange if inserted into "I'll be home by six," and its loss would be felt if omitted from "make yourself *at* home."

We can say "*in* the pouring rain," but we must say "it's pouring *with* rain," not "it's pouring rain." Some omissions are a matter of fashion: people in Britain are now increasingly fond of using the simple verb "sort" rather than the phrasal verb "sort *out*." In America you are permitted to drop the *out* from "hang *out*" (thus leaving "hang" hanging), and to shorten "pass *away*" to "pass" (suggesting, not death, but rather a bad hand at bridge). "Exit," as a verb, used to be followed by *from*; nowadays you can read headlines like "President Obama has made a promise to exit Iraq and Afghanistan." A TV news programme gets "wrapped" rather than "wrapped *up*."

CAN PREPOSITIONS BE IRRITATING? In 2004 the Plain English Campaign canvassed its supporters to nominate expressions that most irritated them. Garnering most of the votes was the phrase "*at* the end *of* the day," while the tautological "*at* this moment *in* time" took second place (tied with the excessive use of "like"). Next was "*with* all due respect." Among other popular bugbears: "*in* the final analysis," "when push comes *to* shove," "*between* a rock and a hard place," "sing *from* the same hymn-sheet (or song-book)."

WHEN IS A PREPOSITION NOT A WORD? As Ben Yagoda (181–82) tells us, when it's a symbol, "specifically the @ sign. It is the one common component of every e-mail address on earth, and it has generated an abundance of cute nicknames": "roll mop" or "pickled herring" (Czech), "monkey's tail" (Dutch), "little snail" (French), "little duck" (Greek), "strudel" (Hebrew), "*a* with an elephant's trunk" (Swedish), "the wiggling wormlike character" (Thai). The @ sign was included on the first typewriter keyboard as a commonly understood symbol for "at the price of," and in 1972 was chosen by an American engineer named Ray Tomlinson as a way of indicating where the generator of a computer message was located, i.e., "at." "If you look at the keyboard, there really aren't a whole lot of choices," Tomlinson said. "It's the only preposition on the keyboard."

WHEN IS A PREPOSITION NOT A PREPOSITION?

It is important to note that what looks and acts like a simple preposition can happily function also as another part of speech, for instance, as a noun (*behind, inside, over*), as a verb (*down, near, out*), as an adverb (*along, beside, by*), as an adjective ("short pants are *in*," "driving all that way just isn't *on*") or as a subordinating conjunction (*after, before, since*). Some words like *out, round* and *up* are particularly versatile in this respect. This process, variously known as "functional shift" or "word-class conversion," has been described as one of the most distinctive features of the English language. It is particularly prominent in Shakespeare.

Very frequently prepositions mask themselves as particles (a particle being a preposition or an adverb used to construct a phrasal verb). And the mention of particles leads us to the absorbing topic of phrasal verbs.

CHAPTER 5
PHRASAL VERBS

The following witticisms clearly violate the "rule" about not ending a sentence with a preposition: "A verbal contract isn't worth the paper it's written *on*," "I don't understand why people insist that marriage is doomed—all five of mine worked *out*," "television is for appearing *on*, not looking *at*," "outside every thin person is a fat one trying to get *in*," "death is nature's way of telling you to slow *down*." But these witticisms are also examples of phrasal verbs.

Phrasal verbs consist of a verb and a particle that may be either an adverb or a preposition. In "he put the book *down*" the word "*down*" is an adverb (sometimes called an "adverbial particle"), but in "he climbed *down* the mountain" it is a preposition.

The most celebrated concatenation of phrasal verbs must be Timothy Leary's clarion call to the young in the sixties: "Turn on, tune in, drop out."

Howard Jacobson's prize-winning novel *The Finkler Question* (2010) has this exchange about an invitation to dinner: "'Come over,' he said. 'I'll order in Chinese.' 'You speak Chinese now?'" Clever wordplay: "order *in*" is a phrasal verb, the second *in* is a preposition. Similarly, in Mae West's famous (but often misquoted) invitation, "Why don't you come *up* sometime and see me," "come *up*" is a phrasal verb with "*up*" as an adverbial particle; but had she said "Why don't you come *up* the stairs sometime and see me," *up* would be a preposition.

In a letter to the *Reader's Digest* in 1969, it was pointed out that "we've got a two-letter word we use constantly that many have more meanings than any other." The letter continues: "The word is *up*. It is easy to understand *up*, meaning toward the sky or toward the top of the list. But when we waken, why do we wake *up*? At a meeting, why does a topic come *up*? And why are participants said to speak *up*? Why are officers *up* for election? And why is it up to the secretary to write *up* a report?" (cited in Burchfield 812) The letter goes on to offer twenty more instances of *up* forming part of a phrasal verb.

A clever cryptic crossword clue for an eight-letter word runs as follows: "It's always used *up* when needed." At first sight this looks like a conundrum, even an irresolvable paradox, but then you realize that "used *up*" is not, as you've rashly taken it to be, a phrasal verb (in the sense of "exhausted" or "used *up* until nothing is left") but consists of a verb employing *up* as an adverb (in the sense of "in an upright position"). The answer to the clue is, of course, an umbrella."

To stick with *up*: the stark difference in meaning between "What's *up, * Doc?" and "What's *up* Doc?" is not only dictated by the presence or absence of the comma, but by *up* used first as adverbial particle and then as preposition.

Frequently, phrasal verbs are idiomatic, implying that the meaning cannot be determined by looking at the verb and the particle separately. For example, it is impossible to guess that, among other alternative meanings, "fall *through*" means "not happen" and "put *off*" means "postpone." Anyone unfamiliar with British university parlance would not know what to make of an undergraduate "going *down*" once term had ended, or, in a less pleasant scenario, being "sent *down*" before it had reached that point.

John Mortimer, in his autobiographical *Clinging to the Wreckage*, recalls his barrister father saying to him: "I think we might run *to* Oxford, provided you fall *in* and read the law." Sentences such as these are virtually incomprehensible to anyone not thoroughly at home with the quirks of English idiom evident in phrasal verbs like "run *to*" and "fall *in*." The *Oxford Phrasal Verbs Dictionary for Learners of English* lists over thirty verb-plus-preposition locutions for "run" (including "run *across*," "run *down*," "run *on*," "run *through*" and "run *up*") and around fifteen for "fall" (e.g., "fall *for*," "fall *into*," "fall *on*," "fall *over*" and "fall *under*").

As defined in this dictionary, the phrase "fool *around*" has two meanings: to waste time or behave in a silly way, and, especially American English, to have a casual sexual relationship with someone not your partner. "Fooling *around*" with one's wife is better, and safer, than fooling *around* without her. A recent news gossip columnist reported that a rock star had "fooled *around on*" his actress wife, leading to their divorce. Did she perhaps object to him not taking her seriously enough in bed? In this case the phrasal verb "cheat *on*" seems to have insinuated itself into "fool *around on*."

"Ours is a Copious Language," intoned Mr. Podsnap, "and Trying to Strangers." Indeed, what a nightmare all these phrasal verbs must be for learners of English as a second language—no wonder they need the help of a specialized dictionary! "It is curious to reflect," writes Bill Bryson, "that we have computers that can effortlessly compute pi to 5,000 places and yet cannot be made to understand that ... to make up a story, to make up one's face, and to make up after a fight are all quite separate things" (193). Computers would also be challenged to recognize that "coming *out*" can be applied to flowers, books, photographs, exam results and, sporadically in England, the sun, and was something once done by strikers and debutantes but is now performed by homosexuals. Even native speakers have trouble explaining to themselves why, in computer terminology, it is "log *on*" rather than the seemingly more logical "log *in*."

New phrasal verbs (and compound nouns derived from them like "let-up," "frame-up," "hand-out," "take-over") are being invented all the time, especially in informal spoken language (for examples see Yagoda 174–81). A striking demonstration of the predominant and versatile role played by prepositions is the phenomenon of "psychobabble" which took root in California in the 1960s. David Lodge, in a perceptive essay, has described "psychobabble" as "the slang that is spoken there by the educated middle classes, and carried, by a kind of cultural gulf-stream, to every part of the world where English is spoken" (Michaels 504). Even the British are now familiar with phrases like "*off* the wall," "laid *back*," "*up*front," "spaced *out*," "*with* it," as well as with a host of phrasal verbs. Some of these verbs take a preposition as the particle ("dump *on*," "be *into*," "get *behind*") and some an adverb ("blow *away*," come *from*," get *down*") and some an adverb and a preposition ("get *off on*"). Lodge points out that these metaphors "are usually drawn from the movement or organization of matter in space," noting that psychobabble "is predominantly verbal rather than nominal in emphasis, and relies heavily upon the deviant use of adverbs and prepositions to give commonplace verbs a new figurative force" (Michaels 506).

This is especially true of the highly popular preposition *out* which, according to Lodge, usually connotes "the breaking of some conventional limit or boundary, a dangerous but exhilarating excess, e.g., to *munch out* (to gorge oneself), to *mellow out* (relax as a result of taking dope), to *wig out* (to get very excited, a variant of the older 'to flip one's wig'), to *freak out* (to go or cause to become very excited), to *gross out* (to disgust) and to *luck out*, which means not to run out of luck, but to find permanent good fortune" (Michaels 511).

By relying on Cyra McFadden's "wickedly knowing satire" *The Serial* as the main source of his examples, Lodge has, as it were, lucked out big time. He does not conceal his relish at the comical effect produced when a character happens to get two tropes combined, as in "I can't exactly get behind where you're coming from." What Lodge terms the "unintended collision of the metaphorical with the literal" results when another character insists on sending her husband's socks to the laundry because she "couldn't get behind ironing boards." In another instance the psychobabble question "Where are *you* coming from?" is answered by the bathetically literal "I'm coming from the bank" (Michaels 507, 508).

Several of these phrasal verbs have more than one meaning. It would be tempting to commend Lodge for "getting it together" in his stimulating essay had not the phrase a second but inappropriate meaning, in psychobabble, of "having a romantic or sexual relationship with somebody."

Quiz #3.

In the following sentences, is the preposition correct or incorrect (misused, misplaced, redundant or missing)?

1. I can't take my eyes *from* you.

2. The child died *of* injuries received from being run over.

3. I'd rather enter the grave than *into* Parliament.

4. They had no hesitation *to* sign on to the declaration.

5. She traded on his weakness *for* women.

6. The movements of important people are veiled *with* secrecy.

~

Answers: 1. *off* you, 2. *from injuries*, 3. (delete *into*), 4. *in* signing, 5. *for* is correct, 6. veiled *in*.

CHAPTER 6

CHANGE AND (IN) CORRECTNESS

Almost all languages, except safely dead ones like classical Greek and Latin, are subject to continual flux. Unlike, say, Icelandic, which has changed relatively little in a thousand years, English has undergone radical transformations since its Anglo-Saxon beginnings: "Almost any untrained person looking at a manuscript from the time of, say, the Venerable Bede would be hard pressed to identify it as being in English—and in a sense he or she would be right. Today we have not only a completely different

"On 3 October 1957, ask anyone what a 'sputnik' was, and they would have been mystified. A day later, the word was on everyone's lips. These days, of course, the Internet can send a new word around the world in a matter of minutes. *Ground zero* obtained a new global lease of life by the evening on September 11, 2001" (Crystal 2006, 3–4). Until recently no one was aware of leaving a "carbon footprint," or talked about "sustainable" this or that, or had heard of, let alone demanded, "closure."

[40]

vocabulary and system of spelling, but even a different structure" (Bryson 38–39). Gender is gone from English (although retained by German, French, Italian and many other languages), verbs and adjectives are much less inflected than they used to be, and nouns are no longer declined. Words change or accrue in meaning and in the value (positive or negative) assigned to them. A word like "academic" can retain its respectable connotations but acquire a new sense of "pedantic" or "without real or practical significance."

Theorists talk about the interplay between dominant, emergent and residual ideologies, and a similar dynamic operates in the field of linguistic as well as ideological change: some forms which were "accepted as a part of standard English in the recent past are constantly falling into disuse and disappearing, while others are coming into use and becoming accepted as part of the standard. As a result, there is at any moment a measure of uncertainty about which forms should be accepted as part of standard English" (Trask 271). Linguistic transgression, if persisted in by enough people over a long enough time, might be likened to treason in politics. As Sir John Harington (1561–1612) said in a famous epigram: "Treason doth never prosper: what's the reason? / For if it prosper, none dare call it treason." In ten or twenty years' time even the expression "bored *of*" may no longer seem treasonable.

It could be argued that the faster the changes occur (especially in the area of idiomatic usage) the greater will be the resistance to them. Recent neologisms, including compounds with an adverb or preposition (e.g., "update," "ongoing," "input"), as well as verbs suddenly becoming transitive (e.g., "grow a business," "disappear an opponent") can expect to meet with a measure of hostility. Gradual changes, like those established over a century or two, tend no longer to create

> But in this ghastly patois 'meet up with' is most gooey—
> in those innocent far-off days
> they said 'Meet me in St. Louis!'
> and it was always 'meet me' in
> those old-fashioned conditions,
> but communal self-
> importance has added two
> needless prepositions.
>
> —Gavin Ewart, "More Is Better—Or Is It?"

a feeling of outrage or fear that the language has been irremediably corrupted. For good or evil, British (and Canadian) English is constantly being influenced by American usage.

In addition to the familiar differences in spelling (honour/honor), vocabulary (lift/elevator), and pronunciation (bath/bath), there are differences in the British and American use of prepositions. We might compare "he had the advantage *of* a weaker opponent" (British), and "he has the advantage *over* a weaker opponent" (American), or "she is nervous *of* strangers" (British) and "she is nervous *around* strangers" (American). In Britain parents might name their child *after* a relative, whereas in the US they would name the child *for* a relative (although *after* is also possible). In Britain prepositions are often used, for the sake of emphasis, in cases where they are not strictly needed, like adding *up* to "cheer," "clean," "finish," "hurry" and "wake." Americans go one better (like Samuel Goldwyn with his "include me *out*"): they will add *up* to "listen," "open" and "wait," *with* to "meet," "speak" and "visit," *out* to "close," "win" and "lose." Such usages strike the British as odd and sometimes confusing (does "visit *with*" mean you visit someone on your own or in the company of another person?) Some current locutions, e.g., "defend *of*," seem both confusing and plain wrong to British ears. On occasion Americans will tack on two prepositions in forming a phrasal verb, e.g., "to beat *up on*," or will omit a preposition in cases where the British would retain it, saying "the dog jumped *out* the car" instead of "the dog jumped *out of* the car," simply "show" for "show *up*, and "walk" for "walk *out*."

Off of is quite acceptable in American speech and even writing, but considered a barbarism in England. *Through* in the sense of "up to and including," as in "Monday *through* Friday," is a handy American usage well on its way to

> The British tend to say "*at* school," "*at* college," "oblivious *of*," and prefer "*towards*," the Americans favour "*in* school," "*in* college," "oblivious *to*" and curtail "*towards*" of its final letter. In America you can be angry *at* somebody, in Britain you would be angry *with* him or her. In New York you would talk about a building *on* Wall Street, in London about one *in* Fleet Street.

acceptance in Britain. The British "chat *up*" meaning to "talk flirtatiously to (a person) in the hope of seducing him or her" has no US equivalent" (Trask 27–28). Trask cites another phrase which "can produce giggles and confusion": "In Britain, if you *knock up* a woman, you awaken her in the morning by banging on her bedroom door. In the USA, if you knock up a woman, you make her pregnant. The American use is now beginning to be heard in Britain" (168). This slang usage dates from the early nineteenth century and can be found in Hemingway, Henry Miller and the movie *Knocked Up* (2007); Trask wisely refuses to speculate on why it is gaining currency, but he might have advised English tennis players to refrain from asking their American opponents whether they want to knock up at the start of a game. Perhaps he had in mind that unfortunate line of dialogue in Somerset Maugham's 1931 play *Breadwinner*: "Why don't you and Dinah go and have a knock-up?"

As Bryson says, English has the virtue of being "a fluid and democratic language in which meanings shift and change in response to the pressures of common usage rather than the dictates of committees. To interfere with that process is arguably both arrogant and futile" (145). The extreme forms of the prescriptivist view of language, which insists on strict adherence to fixed rules, are gradually giving way to the descriptivist approach, which limits itself to documenting how language is actually used. Yet, as Bryson points out, "even the most liberal descriptivist would accept that there must be *some* conventions of usage" (146), especially in the interests of clear and unimpeded understanding.

All parts of speech, including prepositions, are subject in their uses to the continuous process of change. There was a time when people said "afoot" not (or as well as) "*on* foot," "*on* sleep" not "asleep," "*on* live" not "alive." They also used to believe (or trust) *on* rather than *in* something. Today we say "*on* earth" not "*in* earth," and "*for* long" (as in "I won't stay *for* long") not "*at* long." And we also prefer "aversion *to*" and "abhorrence *of*," whereas 250 years ago Laurence Sterne could write of Tristram Shandy's father having an "aversion *from*" and an "abhorrence *to*" the name of Tristram.

Let's take the phrase "slow (or quick) *on* the uptake." Two hundred years ago the preferred preposition was not *on* but *at* or *in*:

at has almost disappeared from modern uses of this expression, and, although *in* seems still clings to life, *on* has replaced both of them as the norm. Grammarians preferred "slow *of* speech" to "slow *in* speech," and ordinary speakers still do; however, "blind *of* one eye" (once thought the "correct" form) has been overwhelmingly replaced by "blind *in* one eye." Again, in the pitched battle between "receptive *to*" and "receptive *of*," a grammarian asserted, in 1927, that *to* was incorrect: one search engine registers nine million hits for *to* and only 130,000 for *of*, a clear victory for *vox populi*. Now common phrases "greedy *for*" and "congruous *with*" were once frowned upon, but the previous "correct" forms ("greedy *of*" and "congruous *to*") now look quaint. It's gratifying to report that "centred *on*," the currently approved form, has nearly 80 million hits, whereas its denigrated rival "centred *around*" has only three million. Even so, that number is three million too many. The same might be said of "proud *of*" and "proud *about*": those who write "proud *about*" (or, worse, "proud *at*") are in a minority, and have nothing to be proud *of*.

> Occasionally one will hear the phrase "too close *to* comfort." Is this a lapse for the much more common "too close *for* comfort," or does the change in preposition signal a change in meaning?

A search engine may be a rough-and-ready guide, one to be used with great caution, but an assiduous trawl may well give some indication of general linguistic preferences. "Cynical *about*" is much preferred to "cynical *toward*" (or *towards*). "Overwhelmed *by*" is three times as common as its competitor "overwhelmed *with*," although it might be argued that there is a slight difference in meaning between the two phrases. Four out of five opt for "put the finishing touches *to*" (rather than *on*). "Chat *with*" is ten times more popular that "chat *to*," but that may reflect a largely American preference. Also used ten times more often is the conventional expression "make love *to*" which is still preferred to its recent challenger "make love *with*." Yes, we can indeed "make love *with*" our eyes, our hands, our hearts etc., no problem there, but the phrase seems to reflect a change in sexual mores: "make love *to*" has, for many, come to define love as exploitation or objectification, a one-sided exercise along the lines of Baudelaire's victim and executioner, whereas "make love *with*" (which seems to owe its origin to pop lyrics) seems to convey a feeling of caring mutuality (as in Larkin's use of the phrase in a December 1954 letter to Monica Jones). While happily in the amatory realm, let me note that "love *of*" and "love *for*" appear to be equally favoured; however, the time-honoured "beloved *of*" is slowly yielding to "beloved *by*," and the colloquial "being crazy *about* somebody" seems to be giving way to "being crazy *for* somebody." "I can't take my eyes *from* you" (again from a pop song lyric) is scarcely making a dint in the traditional "I can't take my eyes *off* you."

The older school of pundits (like Boyd, Bierce, Furnald, Nesfield, Rowe) were sticklers for what they deemed "proper" usage: addicted to classifying and listing prepositions as right or wrong, correct or incorrect, they prescribed or proscribed accordingly. Their desire to uphold the integrity of the language was laudable, but these hardliners did not take sufficiently into account the awkward fact that no usage, almost by definition, can be regarded as fixed and permanent. We change our laws to reflect changing social mores: the laws banning, say, marijuana use and same-sex marriage have been, or are being, changed in response to protests that these laws are ill-founded or discriminatory. When grammarians lay down laws regulating prepositions, they seem to exhibit little or no awareness that such laws might well be repealed at some later date. Boyd, for example, categorically declares the following usages to be wrong: "angry *at*, " compare *to*," "continue *with*," "disappointed *by*, "identical *to*," and "solution *to*," though no one would, at least in specific cases, object to them now. Using *at* instead of *by*, as in "she was shocked *at* his conduct," was, according to Bierce, a solecism both "very common" and "without excuse" (13), but nowadays both prepositions are acceptable. Rowe and Webb advised their readers not to substitute one preposition for another ("incorrect") one: they declared that such words as "apprehensive," "boast," "certain," "complain," "dubious," and "sanguine" should be followed by *of*, not *about*, but nowadays *of* and *about* are used interchangeably with these words. The general tendency has been for some words and phrases to accommodate more than one preposition: prepositions once outlawed in specific phrases become, over time, gradually legitimized.

"Aim *for*" was once thought incorrect—"aim *at*" was the recommended form. Nowadays they are equally favoured. The same is true of "embarrassed *at*" and "indispensable *for*" (regarded as incorrect) as opposed to "embarrassed *by*" and "indispensable *to*"— either preposition is acceptable now. Speakers are equally divided between "lease *on* life" and "lease *of* life," "knack *for*" and "knack *of*," "danger *to*" and "danger *for*," "name *after*" and "name *for*," "evidence *for*" and "evidence *of*," "put closure *on*" and "put closure *to*," "disregard *for*" and "disregard *of*." Twice as many speakers say "*for* all intents and purposes" rather than "*to* all intents and purposes," both prepositions being allowable (the mishearing "intensive purposes" is not).

As with variations in pronunciation (words like "advertisement," "either," "garage," and route"), there is no basis for asserting that one variation is correct. Hence certain words can be followed by a number of different prepositions with little or no change of meaning: "analogy" can be followed by *between, of, to* and *with,* "authority" by *for, on, over* and *to,* "disappointed" by *about, at, by, in, of, over,* and *with,* and "hatred" by *for* and *of.* "Conform," like "identical," can take either *to* or *with* (many other examples of free variation will be found in Part I of Chapter 11). We can take our choice between "*of* my own accord" and "*on* my own accord" (though some authorities, e.g., Burchfield 15, decree that *on* is now obsolete). Whether we continue to use the traditional *to*, instead of *for*, to partner "crucial," "en route," "essential" and "vital" might well be either a matter of personal taste or a lingering conservatism or nostalgia on the part of the older generation.

Variations are partly attributable to differences in the speaker's age, locality and educational background (Levin 94). A recent study has shown that children in the US are increasingly tending to say "*on* accident" (perhaps by analogy with "*on* purpose") rather than the established "*by* accident." Young adults can be found employing both *on* and *by*, but people over fifty use *on* hardly at all—to their ears "*on* accident" sounds very strange.

In their category entitled "Different Prepositions—Same Meaning," Rowe and Webb offer "abound *with* (or *in*) fish," "careless *about* (or *of*) the consequences," and twenty similar examples of equivalence. But several items in their list have not withstood the forces of historical change: we now much prefer to say "borrow *from*" not "borrow *of*," "lenient *to(wards)*" not "lenient *with*," and "recover *from*" not "recover *of*."

A change of preposition can signal or accompany a change in meaning. Such changes are especially marked in connection with phrasal verbs of motion like "run," "walk" and "jump." "Jump," for example, can be followed by *at, beyond, for, into, onto, over* and *through*. Other parts of speech can exhibit a similar shift: some people may not be "comfortable *with* the theory of evolution" but may be quite "comfortable *in* heavy hiking boots." Consider the distinctions between "asking *about* the mayor," "asking *for* the mayor," and "asking *of* the mayor." "Concerned" can take *about, at, for, in, over, with,* "divided" *against, among, between, by, for, into,* "give" *for, of, into,* "live" *at, by, for, in, off, on, through, with*. Such differences can sometimes lead to confusion about which preposition to use (e.g., adapted *for* / adapted *to*, anxious *for* / anxious *about*, compare *to* / compare *with*, distinguished *by* / distinguished *for*).

If language is in constant flux, it might be argued, how can there be any basis for fixed standards? "At what point," wonders Trask (3), "can we safely say that a vanishing form is no longer part of the standard language, or that an emerging form is now uncontroversially part of our standard language? There are no simple answers to these questions." Perhaps what it boils down to is not so much a set of hard-and-fast grammatical rules but a question of clear or unclear communication. As Michael McCarthy has said, the lesson we should be teaching our children is that grammar "weaves threads into the tapestry of meaning" and that those threads "can easily become snagged." Standard English is English which is both idiomatic and clear. It is the English which is recommended because it reflects the contemporary practice of the best and most careful writers.

We can go a step further and argue that standard English is English that shows respect for the decorum, tradition and integrity of the language. As W. H. Auden has said: "Writers cannot invent their own language and are dependent upon the language they inherit so that, if it be corrupt, they must be corrupted" (cited in

Crystal 2000, 36). An enemy of vulgarization, good English shows courtesy towards readers (or listeners) by not imposing on them, as do many slapdash e-mail exchanges these days, barriers to under-standing. Such barriers compel unnecessary expenditure of both time and energy or what David Foster Wallace has called "extra cognitive effort, a kind of rapid sift-and-discard process" involv-ing "extra work": "It's debatable just how much extra work, but it seems indisputable that we put *some* extra neural burden on the recipient when we fail to follow certain conventions" (49).

In summary, if standard English be deemed "correct," it is "correct" in the sense of being "proper," i.e., courteous, consider-ate and well-mannered as opposed to "permanently right." We are talking about a desirable linguistic etiquette, an etiquette based on consistency and uniformity. In the words (cited on the Internet) of Raymond Rhinehart: "Non-standard use of English is the commu-nications equivalent of spinach in one's teeth or the open zipper: it's distracting and, incidentally, reflects poorly on you, your school, and even your parents." And, besides exemplifying considerateness, standard English possesses the practical virtue of convenience: "It is simply convenient to have a standard form of the language which is agreed on by everybody. If all of us, wherever we are born, learn and use standard English, then we can all speak and write to one another with practically no uncertainty, confusion or misunder-standing" (Trask 272).

An increased effort on the part of all of us to use prepositions idiomatically would go a long way to achieving such a desir-able goal.

~

CHAPTER 7

USE AND MISUSE

All words can be problematic, but prepositions are particularly so because their use and meaning often seem, and indeed often are, so arbitrary and "peculiar" (the word "idiom" derives from the Greek for "peculiar"). We might say that the idiomatic preposition tends towards the figurative, the non-idiomatic towards the literal, as in this well-known jingle: "The bird is *on* the wing / But that's absurd / The wing is *on* the bird." We can sense the difference between "the dog jumped *at* the man's throat" and "I jumped *at* the chance," or between "she looked *into* the mirror" and "she looked *into* the problem." Familiar prepositions like *after, by, for, of* and *on* can veer towards the figurative when found in phrases the meaning of which cannot be determined by their constituent parts alone. Examples are not far to seek: "*after* all" (all things considered), "*by* far" (to a great extent), "*for* good" (permanently), "*of* course" (certainly), "*on* edge" (nervous).

One explanation for misused prepositions may lie in a hybrid phenomenon we might call "crossover" or, following Brians (129), "cross-pollination." This is essentially a problem of transposition, rather like the verbal confusion that produces spoonerisms, malapropisms and the "portmanteau" words like "slithy" ("lithe" plus "slimy") in Lewis Carroll's "Jabberwocky." When he asks, "What do you mean by that insinuendo?" Archie Bunker has conflated "innuendo" and "insinuation" and created high verbal comedy. My niece, as a young slip of a girl, did the same when she once asked me to fetch her an ice-cream from the "reshiverator."

The semi-literate "irregardless" was probably spawned by "irrespective."

It's been pointed out that you can "hone *down*" the edge of a knife, or a point in an argument, and you can "home *in on*" a radar beam but you definitely cannot "hone *in on*" anything. At my local tennis court there is a notice: "*In* consideration *of* other players do not enter the court until your time to play." I think this should be "*out of* consideration *for*," since "*in* consideration *of*" means "*in* view *of*" "*on* account *of*" (common in legal jargon). "In consideration *to* others" is also wrong. The American usage "oblivious *to*" (rather than *of* in Britspeak) is probably modelled on "indifferent *to*," though the distinction between "oblivious *of*" and "indifferent *to*" is surely worth retaining.

One of most common misuses these days is to say "bored *of*" rather than "bored *with*." Could it be that "bored *of*" is subconsciously modelled on a phrase (similar in sound and meaning) like "tired *of*"? Or that the strange-sounding "*in* jeopardy *of*" (not found in the *OED*) is based on the more familiar "*in* danger *of*"? Or that "comment *about*" (instead of *on*) is patterned on "talk *about*"? Or "centre *around*" (instead of *on*) stems from "revolve *around*"? As Webb wrote as far back as 1925: "A not infrequent source of error is the fact that sometimes words related to each other in form and meaning are followed by different prepositions" (Webb 82). The examples he gives are "consequent *upon*, but subsequent *to*," "equal *to*, but equally *with*," "contrast (noun) *to*, but contrast (verb) *with*," and "full *of*, but filled *with*."

The temptation to add a redundant *on* to the verb "infringe" can possibly be attributed to the crossover from "impinge *on*" and/ or "encroach *on*." In a sign which reads "you are prohibited *to* smoke in the playground" the preposition *to* (it should of course be "*from* smoking") has been lifted from the expression "it is forbidden *to* do" something (as, conversely, the incorrect "forbidden *from*" has been lifted from the correct "prohibited *from*"). Crossover is also at work in the phrase "innate *to*" as in "conscience is said to be innate *to* human beings." Here "innate *to*" should be "innate *in*," the *to* possibly borrowed from the cognate "intrinsic *to*."

Noting that *for* is "the common preposition most rarely misused," Blamires offers an instance of crossover or what he terms "constructional transfer": "Local Tory and Labour leaders share a fierce pride *for* their city." He comments: "Because we speak of affection, fondness or love *for* a city, the writer wrongly transfers this usage to the word 'pride' (2000, 164)." It should be "pride *in*" not "pride *for*." He gives a further example, citing "a father who has an obsession *for* sport." You can say that a person has a love *for* sport, but the preposition which governs "obsession" is not *for* but *with*. Again, in "we were proud and thrilled *for* Canada's gold medal" *by* should replace *for* (and, incidentally, *of* should follow "proud").

"My parents never paid any interest *to* me." There appears to be a double mix-up here, the expressed grievance blending "pay attention *to*" and "show interest *in*." You don't "take umbrage *with*" someone's racist remarks, you "take umbrage *at*" them (here the crossover appears to be with "take issue *with*" an alien viewpoint).

People add a redundant *on* to the verb "continue" because they transpose it from a verb of similar meaning, like "carry *on*." They say and write "yearn *after*" (instead of "yearn *for*") because at the back of their minds they hear the *"after* in "hanker *after*." "In respect *of*" gets entangled with *"with* respect *to*" to produce the ungrammatical *"in* respect *of*." The conflation of "ten years hence" and *"in* ten years' time" produces the ungainly hybrid *"in* ten years hence." A TV newscaster's mind juggles with two competing phrases, "give a wide berth *to*" and "keep away *from*," and his tongue responds by saying the highly unidiomatic "keep a wide berth *from*." A football commentator will say that "the weather is likely to *play* a factor" (rather than *"be* a factor" or *"play* a role"), and point out that "home advantage will *play* into a team's favour" (perhaps an echo of "play into someone's hands") rather than *"be* in a team's favour." A defender is described as "cutting the ball *down*," as if it were a tree, instead of "cutting the ball *off*."

To veer away from prepositions for a moment, it's worth noting new words get invented by this act of transposition: "roisterous" is a hybrid of "roistering" and "boisterous," and "heart-wrenching" a mismatch of "heart-rending" and "gut-wrenching" (Jenkins 68–69). Likewise, "disenheartened" is the result of "disheartened" and "disenchanted" overlapping or being unwittingly superimposed.

I say "unwittingly" because this kind of error seems to be made without the speaker being aware of what is going on. Getting wires crossed is most likely to occur when someone is under stress (speaking in public, for example, or being interviewed on television): sentences get themselves started and then lose a sense of where they are going. There is a momentary loss of direction and control. All speakers have a right to change their minds about what to say and how to say it, but when they are caught in two minds in the middle of a sentence they are heading for deep trouble. The politician who wanted to say that his opponent had "strong leanings *towards* communism" decided that "connections" might be better than "leanings" so out popped "strong connections *towards* communism." The commentator at a tennis match wanted to say that a young player's parents were "proudly looking *on*" but got sidetracked into saying "proudly watching *on*." Defending a co-worker who had just been fired a woman said: "She was a loyal employee *to* the company." But it's "loyal *to*," "employee *of*." A way round this problem might be to rearrange the word order, i.e., "she was an employee loyal *to* the company." Due allowances can and should be made when mistakes of this kind occur, particularly in people's unrehearsed speech.

Mishearings account for a few mistakes. "By and large" gets spoken and written as "by *in* large (just as "would have" gets spoken and written as "would *of*," "out of" as outta," and the parliamentary sign of approval of "Hear, hear!" gets transcribed as the doggy "Here, here!").

As E. B. White has acknowledged, "English usage is sometimes more than mere taste, judgment, and education—sometimes it's sheer luck, like getting across a street." But rather than trust to luck, some speakers—uncertain about which preposition to use and not prepared to resolve their uncertainty through careful thinking—will play it safe, settling for a vague prepositional phrase like *in terms of*. What follows is an alphabetical list of prepositions, some of them problematic, giving examples of use and misuse. It does not attempt to provide the whole range of meanings, sometimes wide, of the prepositions cited. For such information a good dictionary or grammar-book should be consulted. Should more comprehensive coverage be desired see the works by Fernald, Fowler, Heaton, Hill, Lindstromberg, Prieur and Wood (all listed in the Selected Bibliography).

A—Historically a form of the preposition *on*, "a-" is a grammatical particle commonly found at the beginning of verbs ending in "–ing", e.g., "a-bleeding," "a-coming," "a-going," a-hunting," "a-sleeping," "a-weeping," "a-wooing" (all these examples to be found in Shakespeare). Without any dictionary meaning in itself, the hyphenated "a-" frequently affects the meaning of the following verb by stressing the repetitive nature of an action, the length of time it takes to complete it, or merely the ongoing process itself (as in Bob Dylan's song "The Times They Are A-Changin'"). Unhyphenated, "a-" can also mean *on* (as in "afoot"), *in* (as in "nowadays"), and "in a specified state" (as in "aflutter").

ABOARD—In the United States you will be accorded a welcome whenever you say "thank you," and you will also be welcomed *aboard* a bus or a train. That's because *aboard* is used there about any form of public transport, whereas in Britain it is usually limited to ships or planes.

ABOUT—Prepositional phrases generally synonymous with about include "concerning," "in regard to," "regarding" and "with regard to."

There is a tendency, in informal English, to use *about* in place of *of*, as in these examples cited by Bollinger: "We're more aware *about* it," "a little more conscious *about* that," "keeping us abreast *about*," "downright disdainful *about*," "wary *about*," "proud *about*" (1988, 238). These uses, brought about by an impressive process known to linguists as "reiconization," are, according to Bollinger, "on the growing edge" of the language. Even though these examples "illustrate the latest stage in a development that has been going on during the entire Modern English period, and has accelerated since the turn of the century," I believe that their total respectability is still round the corner.

When used of place, *about* and *around* are often interchangeable: "Where have you been?" "Oh, *around* and *about*." But a distinction can be drawn: "It would seem to be that *around* keeps closer to the suggestion of surrounding, encircling movement, while *about* more readily applies to distributed activity: to travel *around* the earth is to encircle it; to travel *about* the earth is to go in various directions here and there over it" (Fernald 19–20).

The "abstract" *about* in a phrase like "this isn't *about* you" may be "a great rebuke" but "it's better to avoid it in very formal English" (Brians 2).

Notice the distinction between knowing *about* Genghis Khan (knowing something *about* him) and knowing *of* him (having heard *of* him).

When used (like "around") to mean "approximately," as in "I'll see you about seven o'clock," "about" is an adverb.

The difference between *about* as a preposition and "about" as an adverb is illustrated in the following exchange between an interviewer and Tom Stoppard: "What is *Rosencrantz and Guildenstern Are Dead* about?" "It's about to make me very rich." Or Roger Garland's response to the question "what is *Uncle Vanya* about?" "I would say it is *about* as much as I can take."

ABOVE—Do not use "the words quoted *above*," "the *above* words" or even just "the *above*." Do use it to rhyme with "love" since there is, as legions of poets have discovered, not much choice—only three other perfect rhymes are available ("dove," "glove" and "shove").

ABSENT—Common in American English, *absent* (as a preposition, not an adjective) means *without*: "*Absent* the necessary controls, the proposed system will fail."

AFTER—Charmingly, the Irish use this preposition to express a recent action, whether completed or not. In cases of completed actions this use corresponds to the standard English "just have": "He was *after* his dinner," "there's a cat *after* chasing a dog up the street," "they're *after* traveling to England for ten years or more."

In the US you are often named *for* a relative, in Britain *after* a relative. Gerard Hoffnung: "I was named Gerard *after* my father, and Hoffnung *after* [longish pause] Gerard."

AGAINST—A classic question illustrates this preposition's literal/ metaphorical, concrete/abstract distinction: "If I said you had a nice figure would you hold it *against* me?" (The distinction holds for "hold" as well as for *against*.)

Against appears in the ninth Commandment: "Thou shalt not bear false witness *against* thy neighbour." Christopher Hitchens, in his book *Arguably*, describes it as the "fulcrum" in the sentence: "If you are quite sure of somebody's innocence and you shade the truth a little in the witness-box, you are no doubt technically guilty of perjury and may be privately troubled. But if you consciously lie in order to indict someone who is *not* guilty, you have done something irretrievably foul" (418–19).

ALONG—The English, particularly, are guilty of perpetrating "*along* the same vein," a crossover or "bastard child" of "*in* the same vein" and "*along* the same lines."

ALONGSIDE—*Alongside* and *alongside of* are equally acceptable, though the latter is sometimes frowned upon by the fastidious.

AMID(ST)—*Amid* is far more common than *amidst*. It's been suggested that *amid* can be used for a sense of being surrounded by something vague, like "*amid* the confusion" or "*amid* the group of students," and also for two events happening simultaneously, e.g., "he scored the winning goal *amid* cries of jubilation." Otherwise reserve these two "rather flowery" words "for talking to the local poetry society" (Howard 20). For further observations and examples see Burchfield 48.

AMONG(ST)—"*Among* clearly presupposes a number of surrounding but separate entities, 'among those countless hungry children'; whereas *amid* denotes a position in the middle of something larger but of a piece and not divisible, for example, 'amid all that bustle.' This is an example of what I would call verbal sibling rivalry: pairs of almost but not really twin words getting into each other's hair" (Simon 14). "*Among* seems to purport a general positioning, *amongst* more a sense of physical positioning" (Levin 25). But Americans stay away from *amongst* (as well as from *amidst* and *whilst*) on the grounds that the "st" ending is quaint, archaic, and pretentious (Garner 37) or that it "makes you sound like a character out of P. G. Wodehouse" (Yagoda 169).

For further observations and examples see Burchfield 49.

ANENT—This preposition, one meaning of which is *about* in the sense of *concerning* or *in reference to*, is to be avoided even in the legal parlance where it is most often found lurking (especially in Scotland). "In general English," writes Burchfield (53), "it is used to mean 'with respect to', but it often carries an air of affectation or of faint jocularity. It is also frequently used, with a tinge of pomposity, in letters to the editor." William Safire says he burns all mail beginning with this word; however, it's still thriving in Scottish dialect, in Vladimir Nabokov's novel *Lolita*, in John Updike's fiction and, for good measure, in the correspondence of Louis MacNeice. Both W. H. Auden and Ogden Nash have used it in their verse.

The *OED* labels the thirteen other meanings of *anent* as either obsolete or archaic, and I, for one, have no objection to *anent* (in the sense of *concerning*) meeting the same fate fairly soon. This is not a view shared by all: in November 2010, I found the word as the (hidden) solution to a cryptic crossword clue: "Concerning *an* *ent*ertainment in part."

AROUND—A preposition which tends to be used far too loosely these days, either in the sense of "concerning," "*on the subject of*," or "having as a focal point" or, even more loosely, "*in the general area of*." The CBC's Peter Mansbridge once referred to "dire predictions *around* the Canadian economy" and one of his colleagues talked about "Canadian laws *around* prostitution." Americans in particular are fond of talking or speculating about problems *around* something (software, orphans, Brussels, kidney disease, sludge, even the environment—"around the environment" sounds freakishly redundant). Such problems do get *around*, but shouldn't take it. We experience problems *with* or *regarding* something.

Julian Barnes has been quoted as saying that novelists don't write *about* their themes but rather *around* them. This seems to me a legitimate use of *around*.

Not so in "I've been *around* wolves all my life." Better (though hardly easy) for the speaker to encircle wolves than for them to encircle him.

"If you are going to be *around* water, learn to swim." If you find yourself physically *around* water you would not need to swim.

Where *around* is definitely spatial (problems "*around* the house," "*around* the garden," "*around* the world") the preposition seems quite in order.

The *OED* notes that *around*, rare before 1600, is found in neither Shakespeare nor the Authorised Version of 1611. The famous hymn "Abide with Me" uses it in the more usual sense of *about*: "Change and decay in all *around* I see." Citing this, Amis counsels: "Stick to *round* and *about* unless *around* strikes you as preferable" (17–18). Would it be preferable to say "a father should never smoke *around* his son"?

AT—"Prepositions are not to be trifled with. The collision of two 747s in 1997, killing 583 people, resulted from a misunderstanding over the preposition *at*. "*At* take-off" was understood by the air controller to mean that the plane was waiting at the take-off point, not that it was actually taking off." Prieur and Speyer, *The Writer's Guide to Prepositions.*

"During the Gulf War, we were frequently told of missiles that were 'launched at' Israel or Saudi Arabia. What was meant was that they were aimed at these targets. They were, of course, launched *at* (or *in* or *from*) some site in Iraq" (Blackburn 73).

"The house was listed *at* (not *for*) $600," but "The house was sold *for* (not *at*) $550."

"The victory on D-Day came *at* (not *with*) a heavy toll."

There is a story of somebody offering to meet a man "*at* your convenience," only to be informed "Oh, but I don't have a regular public lavatory" (cited in Howard 35).

Some authorities, even the most lenient, object to *at* as in the question "where are you *at*?" on the grounds that the sense is covered by "where," making *at* redundant: "It's not only a tautology, it's also a barbarism. Which is to say, it's not English. There we are" (Jenkins 159). However, we might well say to someone reading a book, "where are you *at*?" in the sense of "how far have you got?" But anyone caught saying "I know where it's *at*" (meaning the speaker professes understanding of a situation) risks "being labeled as a quaint old baby boomer" (Brians 248).

Delete *at* from the expression "*at* the end *of* the day." You might care to dispense with *of* as well, and, while you are at it, "the end" and "the day."

Although unrefined, the expression "*at* it" is a fine example of English idiom at its most characteristic: everyone knows, from a given context, what it means. For example: "Mum says that's why the young are at it all the time. You know, *carpe diem*. Gather ye rosebuds" (Martin Amis, *The Pregnant Widow*). The term "*at* it" can be traced as far back as 1611, and "it" on its own (sometimes capitalized to mean simply "sex appeal") has been used (in addition to Amis) by such diverse writers as Joyce, Wolfe, Wells and Mitford. However, no one seems to know how "it" came to mean what "it" does mean.

At can play mischievous tricks: "I can still enjoy sex *at* 80—I live *at* 79 so it's no great distance."

ATHWART—I used to think that the charming word *athwart*, having been largely superseded by *across*, would not be often encountered these days (outside the fiction of John Updike). That was until I read Geoffrey Nunberg's *The Way We Talk Now* (2001): "All of a sudden *athwart's* gotten popular again. You can't throw a rock without hitting a sentence like 'Modern Yugoslavia sat *athwart* the fault lines of European history" or "He sets himself *athwart* the tide of conventional wisdom" (21). These usages, he says, have ruined *athwart,* one of his "favourite words" since he first delighted in the line from *Romeo and Juliet* about the queen of the fairies galloping "athwart men's noses as they lie asleep."

They clearly haven't ruined it for Tony Judt ("opinions cut *athwart* those of the majority," *Ill Fares the Land*), for Martin Amis ("not right, not left—but aslant, *athwart,*" *The Pregnant Widow*) nor for David Foster Wallace ("centrally located *athwart* both one-way main drags," "The View from Mrs. Thompson's").

The *OED* notes that *athwart* "is still in everyday use in Scotland as *athort.*"

BEFORE—Be careful with *before*. A reporter once wrote that "the bomb was defused before it exploded." Citing this, Blackburn observes that we won't waste time "wondering how it came to pass that the bomb exploded despite having been defused. We know it did not explode.... Suppose, though, that he had said something like 'the bank robber was arrested before he made his getaway'. That's the same construction, and, in this case, we would have to assume that the robber had been arrested and then escaped, because that is what the writer said" (41)

Before can come first in a sentence but in some cases, as in this sign in a Japanese restaurant, should be placed later in the word order: "Before your cooked right eyes."

Prepositions which are both spatial and temporal (like *around, before* etc.) lend themselves to punning, as in this piece of comic dialogue: "Judge: 'Have you ever been up *before* me?' Defendant: 'I don't know—what time do you get up?'" (cited in Rees 145). Mark Twain pulled the same trick when he designed a poster advertising an upcoming speech: "Mark Twain has given lectures *before* all the crowned heads of Europe," and then, in much smaller type, "thought of giving lectures."

Avoid using *ahead of* instead of *before*.

In the statement "on the eve *before* the wedding" *before* is redundant. Say "*of* the wedding."

BELOW—At first sight *below* and *under* "appear to be synonyms, but in a wide range of contexts one or the other is to be preferred. *Below* tends to be regarded as an antonym of *above*, and *under* as an antonym of *over*. *Below the bridge* means with it higher up the stream; *under the bridge*, with it overhead" (Burchfield 103). Burchfield (103) gives (as an illustration of catachresis) a phrase from Dylan Thomas's poem "Fern Hill": "once *below* a time" (*below* substituting for the familiar storybook *upon*).

A golfer who is *under* par is almost certainly not *below* par. For useful distinctions between *below*, *beneath*, *down*, *under* and *underneath* see Fernald 67–68.

Although you can refer, adjectivally, to "the above illustration" you cannot say "the below illustration." It must be "the illustration *below*."

BEHIND—Choose simple (*behind*) instead of compound (*in back of*).

BESIDE(S)—*Beside* and *besides* are often confused. *Beside* (a preposition) means "*next to*," "*by the side of*," or, more generally, "*outside of*" (as in "*beside* the mark, "*beside* the point," or "*beside* himself"). *Besides* (a conjunction) means "other than" or "in addition to" (as in "*besides* being a chartered accountant, John is a keen lion-tamer").

BETWEEN—Some useful and detailed advice on the use of *between* will be found in Burchfield 105–9.

"There is a widespread belief that *between* should be used only with two things, and that *among* must be used with three of more. This belief is not supported by examinations of English usage in the past or today. Nevertheless, you might be wise to follow this rule, since doing so will annoy nobody. So, I recommend writing *relations between Britain and France* but *relations among Britain, France and Germany*" (Trask 46).

The distinction between *between* in its abstract and concrete senses is well caught in one of Woody Allen's many comments on a human preoccupation other than grammar: "Sex *between* a man and a woman can be wonderful—provided you get *between* the right man and the right woman."

Between in "the winner *between* Arsenal and Chelsea will meet Tottenham in the final" should be *of* (substituting perhaps "Arsenal *versus* Chelsea), unless you write "the winner *of* the match *between*…." Similarly, *between* in "the joint exercise *between* the army and the police" should be "*on the part of*" or simply *of* (or *by*).

When *The Economist* speaks of "the mistrust *between* the US and Russia" one feels that the preposition is being used awkwardly. The phrase should be recast, possibly making use of "mutual mistrust" or "mistrust of each other."

In "*between* you and I" it isn't the preposition that is wrong. Say "*between* you and me." And it's "*between* him and me," not "*between* he and me."

Try to avoid using *between* to mean "approximately" as in "*between* ten and twelve thousand attended the soccer game." And certainly not "*between* ten *to* twelve thousand…."

A football commentator confessed to being "*between* two minds" about a referee's controversial decision. The appropriate idiom for "wavering" or "undecided" is "*in* two minds."

A commonly misused phrase is "falling *between* the cracks." A person, or preferably a thing, falls *through* the cracks or *into* them.

Spot the error in this ad for a toothbrush: "It cleans deep *between* each tooth."

BETWIXT—Survives in some dialects in Britain and the US but in standard English is found only in the alliterative phrase "*betwixt* and *between*," i.e., "in a middle position," "neither one thing nor another."

BEYOND—A newspaper editor once pointed out "the usefulness of *beyond* when one is stuck for a headline for a lifestyle article": "A piece about trends in Japanese food—'Beyond Sushi'; about backyard games—'Beyond Badminton'; about choosing annual plants—'Beyond Geraniums.' The formula is endlessly adaptable, and endlessly adapted it has been" (Yagoda 169).

BUT—As a preposition *but* means "except," "apart from," "other than," "save": "The word 'penultimate' means 'last *but* one'."

BY—This is a word with many meanings. Lord Alfred Douglas belongs to a select group of people who have been shocked to read their own obituary. In 1921 he bought a newspaper carrying the headline "Sudden Death of Lord Alfred Douglas—Found Dead in Bed by a Maid." Did the maid do the finding, or was she herself found with him at the time? A headline reads: "Escaped inmate found on farm *by* prison" (the prison must have beaten the police to it). Greenbaum (103) cites "an empty aspirin bottle was found *by* the deceased." This, he says, "sounds as though the dead person found the bottle rather than, as was presumably meant, that the bottle was found *beside* him." The art section of my local newspaper ran the headline, "the world of ballet has been blessed *by* many fine composers," suggesting that composers, en masse, have been usurping a priestly prerogative. *By*, of course, should have been *with*. The broad distinction is that *by* denotes the agent, or essential agent, of an action, and *with* the instrument of an action. Compare "he was struck by the sun" with "the sun struck *with* its rays," "the tree was shaken *by* the wind" with "the wind shook the tree *with* its strong hands," "the city was destroyed *by* fire" with "he destroyed the city *with* fire" (examples cited by Fernald 189). In practice, *by* and *with* are used less strictly, but "where *with* or *at* can reasonably be used instead of *by*, they should be" (Greenbaum 103).

You can say that Bach is "*by* far" your favourite composer or that he is "far and away" your favourite composer but not, by combining these two phrases, "*by* far and away."

By can indicate a deadline or the end of a specific period of time: "I have to hand in my essay *by* Friday (i.e., it could be *on* Friday or *before* Friday) or "the new conference centre will be completed *by* the year 2015" (i.e., it could be *in* 2015 or *before* 2015).

In "two football matches were postponed *by* unplayable pitches" *by* should be "because *of.*"

Notice the difference in meaning between "the parade passed him *by*" and "the parade passed *by* him." In the first case he must have felt "hard done *by*" (not "hard done *to*").

It's "*by* the same token" not "*on* the same token," and it's "*by* accident" not "*on* accident."

CHEZ—Borrowed from the French, this handy preposition has two meanings. The first (the most familiar because of its use in names of restaurants like "Chez Michel") is "at the home (or place, office, shop) of." The second non-literal meaning corresponds to prepositions like *among, for, in the manner or work, of, with.* For about two centuries after its first recorded use in English (1740) it was followed mainly by a personal pronoun in French (*moi, elle, nous*).

CUM—This preposition, meaning *with* in Latin, likes to nestle between two nouns, and is liable to stump Americans not acquainted with British place-names. Trask (85) advises against its use, but if you do use it, he says, spell it correctly: "I was recently dumbfounded to see someone described, in a book written by an academic, as "the philosopher-come-academic." Calling it "a valuable link word," Philip Gooden, in his book *Faux Pas*, also notes that it is "quite frequently misspelled—as in the erroneous 'actor-come-director'": "This is a mistake, and a fairly stupid one at that, since a moment's thought will indicate that 'come' makes no sense in this context. What or who is coming? Where are they going?" (48).

DESPITE—"Dictionaries define *despite* as *in spite of*, so there isn't a whisker between them. If anything, *despite* is a more literary word" (Howard 120). As Howard says, *despite of* is a vulgarism.

DOWN—Try and make sense of the following headline: "Sharp nails *down* another Canadian women's title."

DURING—This preposition can only be used with reference to time: "You can say 'I felt tired *during* the afternoon', and you might even say 'I felt tired *during* the long country walk', but you cannot say 'I felt tired *during* the steep hills and the bad weather'" (Blamires 1994, 151).

ERE—"I mention this dead and unlamented word only to note that its ghost is sometimes raised by jocular chaps and affect phrases like 'ere long' and 'ere now.' I have two messages for such chaps: one is unprintable, the other goes, If you must write this shred of battered facetiousness, for Christ's sake get it right. The word is *ere*, not *e're*" (Amis 60).

EXCEPT—Don't write "*except if*"—write "unless."

EXCEPTING—"All the members of the committee were present, not *excepting* the chairman." In this double negative construction, "not *excepting*" produces the positive meaning of "including." As Howard notes, "*with the exception of* has twice as many syllables as *except for*, so why use it? (156).

FOR—The innocuous-looking *for* is increasingly supplanting more idiomatic prepositions, especially *of* and *to*. A newspaper headline reads: "Fear of adults has devastating effects *for* (*on*) kids" and a weatherman predicts "a likelihood *for* (*of*) more thunderstorms." A sports commentator remarks that "giving the ball away is a characteristic *for* (*of*) Mexican soccer teams." Other examples: "she had a great dislike *for* (*of*) noisy extroverts," "he was generous in his praise *for* (*of*) the novel," "he showed no appreciation *for* (*of*) my work." The list goes depressingly on: "He was playing *for* (*to*) the camera," "the occasion *for* (*of*) the Pope's visit," "the major obstacle *for* (*to*) her happiness," "nothing can surpass my devotion *for* (*to*) ballet," "politician seeks an end *for* (*to*) the dispute," "he caused laughter *for* (*because of*) his accent." It should be "in favour *of*," not "in favour *for*." And who can fail to notice with what regularity, these days, worthy people are congratulated (sometimes mispronounced "congradge-julated") *for* (instead of *on*) some achievement or other?

Users of computers, according to Auberon Waugh, "have a blind loyalty, not to say infatuation, *for* them which brooks no criticism." As dear Auberon ought to know, it is "loyalty *to*" and "infatuation *with*."

Non-native speakers plump for *for* when in a linguistic jam: "We have confidence *for* (should be *in*) him," "the gangster is known *for* (*to*) the police," "she was nervous *for* (*about*) the race."

If you say "characteristic *for*," "typical *for*" or "symbolic *for*" you are not exactly making an egregious error, but you are likely to be much younger than those who prefer "characteristic *of*," "typical *of*" or "symbolic *of*." Being longer in the tooth than most, I prefer the traditional *of*. So, not "risk *for* cancer" but "risk *of* cancer," not "chance *for* success" but "chance *of* success."

In "the cross is a symbol *for* Christians *of* the redemption of Christ" the distinct difference between *for* and *of* is well illustrated.

In Scotland *for* is sometimes used in the sense of "want" or "desire," e.g., "Are you *for* a walk?"

Unless being an American gives you license, do not write "I'd like *for* you to cook tonight," "I want *for* her to answer," "she said *for* me to open it," "I'll tell you *for* why" and "I didn't intend *for* her to hear." Rephrase in each case (Greenbaum 287).

An informal usage (almost entirely confined to North America) is "the reason *for* why." The sentence "not sleeping enough is the reason John is always so tired" does not require "*for* why" (or even the conjunction "that") before the word "reason."

"For sure*"* is also informal, as is the phrase beloved of advertising copywriters, *"for* free." *"For* fair" (meaning "completely, altogether") and *"for* real" (meaning "seriously") are found in American slang. *"For* starters" is found in Alan Bennett's list of current dislikes (together with "Brits" and "sorted").

Note the difference between "he is all business" and "he is all *for* business."

"It's a free kick in dangerous territory *for* Chelsea" creates doubt as to whether the free kick was awarded *to* or *against* Chelsea. And a headline in the *Guardian Weekly*, "China could pressure Rangoon to offer clemency *for* Suu Kyi," suggests that clemency was offered in exchange *for* Suu Kyi: *"for"* should be replaced by *"to."*

To avoid redundancy it's *"for* security reasons" not *"due to"* or "owing *to."*

Finally, join the multitudes who still embrace "en route *to"* and shun the relative minority which perpetrates "en route *for."*

FRO—Meaning *from*, this preposition came into Middle English via Old Norse. Variant spellings include *fra* and, especially in Scotland, *frae*. Nowadays it is rarely found outside the idiomatic expression "to and fro" ("back and forth').

FROM—A husband who said he was reluctant to part *from* his ailing wife would have meant something quite different, possibly Hitchcockian, had he said he was reluctant to part *with* her.

Write "he lived and worked in Australia *from* 1924 to 1939," not *"from* 1924–1939."

Don't forget to place *from* after the –ing forms of debar, discourage, hinder, preclude, prevent, prohibit. The sportscaster who said that the Montreal Canadiens "denied the Toronto Maple Leafs *from* scoring" should have used "prevented" instead of "denied."

The sentence "the sculptor learnt to carve *from* his uncle" could use a little rewording.

"I stopped him *from* driving his car," not the ungrammatical and ambiguous "I stopped him *to* drive his car." The sentence "Russia's reputation for hard drinking is an aberration *from* the 20th century" is not ungrammatical, but *from* is ambiguous.

"There aren't many choices to pick *from.*" What's wrong here is not the placing of *from* at the end, but the sin of redundancy committed by the last three words. Just say "there aren't many choices."

"He rescued the crying child, who didn't suffer any negative consequences *from* his ordeal." The problem here is that, indeed, "suffer" takes *from,* but "consequence" (the immediate antecedent of *from*) takes *of.* Suggested rewording: "He rescued the crying child, whose ordeal didn't entail any negative consequences."

From is, strictly speaking, redundant before "hence" and "whence," although Shakespeare uses it frequently in both cases. Hence (in the sense of "away *with*") "*from* hence" and "*from* whence" (see Burchfield 316, 357, 842).

Occasionally *from* can cause mischief: "He passed away *from* cancer" leaves in doubt whether he managed to escape it or succumbed to it, and "dying *from* a cup of coffee" would be a prime candidate for a tabloid headline.

IN—*In* can be ambiguous: the headline "Police use rifles *in* gang killings" raises a problem: did the police kill any member(s) of the gang, or use them, possibly lethally, on gang members who had attacked other gang members? And consider a phone call from your physician's receptionist asking to you change an appointment because he is "*in* surgery" that day. Do you suppose that your physician will be *on* the operating table, or *next to* it?

Trouble can also ensue if care is not taken to position a prepositional phrase correctly in a sentence: "One morning," reported Groucho Marx, "I shot an elephant *in* my pajamas. How he got *in* my pajamas I'll never know."

"Andy Murray gained a berth *in* (not *into*) the finals."

"Don't waste your time *in* school." The ambiguity here stems from the double meaning of *in*: "while attending school" and "by attending school."

"*In* my opinion," not *after* or *according to* my opinion. "*After* my opinion" is apt to be used by speakers of German ("meiner Meinung nach").

In the lyrics to "Live and Let Die" Paul McCartney refers to "this ever-changing world *in* which we live *in*." Critics often zoom in on this final *in* as being redundant. "But if you listen closely, you'll hear instead a quite correct "this ever-changing world in which we're livin'." Americans have a hard time hearing the soft British *R* in 'we're'" (Brians 181).

"*On* form" is beginning to challenge "*in* form." But "*in* route" should never be allowed to challenge "en route."

INSIDE OF—*Inside of* is informal: "Something *inside of* me went pit-a-pat." It is less unacceptable when meaning "less than a stated period of time": "You must be back home *inside of* a week."

INTO—There is a difference of meaning, often ignored in spoken English but not difficult to figure out, between "the boy ran *in* the house" (*in* being static) and "the boy ran *into* the house" (*into* being directional) or between "immigrants *in* Canada" and "immigrants *into* Canada." "Influx" should be written with *into* (not, as it often is, with *in*: "In 1956 there was an influx *of* refugees *from* Hungary *into* Canada." There is a clear, and in the second case more painful, distinction between "Humphrey walked *in* the door" and "Humphrey walked *into* the door." However, in colloquial English, *in* (or *on*) can be used to indicate motion rather than simple position: "He plunged *in* the water," "she fell *on* the floor."

Tennyson invited his Maud to come *into* the garden, not *in* it, a totally different meaning.

Often we see "*into*" when "*in to*" is "probably meant or should have been written, as in, say, 'Then we went *into* where the others were'" (Amis 112) or "the glowing sun was beginning its imminent plunge *into* the horizon" (Coffmann 220, adding "ouch!") In the contrary case of "the book came *in to* my possession last week" (example, tut-tut, from the *London Review of Books*) *in to* should be written as one word, *into*.

"Trains," writes Hugo Williams, "no longer arrive *at* the tautological 'station stop' or 'London St Pancras', but 'into' them, perhaps to encourage the illusion that 'we're keeping Britain moving'.

How long before we are arriving 'into' places ourselves, making little chuffing noises?"

Many grammarians are not into *into*. Trask (160) is violently opposed to this popular, colloquial equivalent of "keen *on*," arguing that it "has no place in formal writing. "Too informal for serious writing," echoes Greenbaum (383). Amis shows his rare liberal side: "The use of *into* as shorthand for 'actively interested in,' as in, say, 'He's interested in Georgian silver plate,' seems handy and harmless to me, though it is admittedly trendy, or was" (Amis 112).

It still is: note the excessively informal title of a movie released in 2009: "He's Just Not That Into You."

IN TERMS OF—In 1993 this complex preposition was described by the Oxford philosopher Michael Dummett as representing "the lowest point so far in the present degradation of the English language" (cited in Burchfield 406). As Samuel Levin has observed, this compound phrase seems to be on everyone's lips: "Whenever a connection needs to be made between two grammatical units—of whatever sort—*in terms of* is invoked. It has become a veritable connective-of-all-trades" (106). He offers a few examples recently heard: "Casey was not clear *in terms of* his role at the office" (*in terms of* should be *about* or *concerning*), "I can't answer *in terms of* what the judge decided" (should be *concerning*), "her reaction is typical *in terms of* women who have been harassed" (should be *of*), "oil prices are going up probably *in terms of* the winter season" (should be *because*). Levin theorizes that the attraction of *in terms of* resides in its being a kind of neutral "counter" providing no clear grammatical or logical linkage between the units being connected. Jacqueline Rose provides us with a spectacularly ungainly example: "[Marilyn Monroe] is not the one whom I find it most useful to think of in terms of being ill." Peter Mansbridge runs a close second with "*in terms of* Canada" (*in terms of* ungainliness, that is).

For some interesting indications of how this preposition came into being, and for more examples of its use, see the article in Burchfield (406–7). For some "awkward uses" and "recommended alternatives" see Brians, 121.

Also giving examples of the "ubiquitous" use of what he calls this "all-purpose" preposition, J. M. Coetzee makes an intriguing if debatable point: "The merging of the old repertoire of prepositions into a single one suggests that an as yet unarticulated decision has been made by an influential body of English speakers, that the degree of specificity demanded by approved English usage is unnecessary for the strict purposes of communication, and that therefore a degree of simplification is in order." *Diary of a Bad Year* 145 (see also 143, 144).

Yet one is entitled to wince at cumbersome constructions such as this: "Chelsea's sixth-place finish was a tragedy *in terms of* the Premiership."

LIKE—As a preposition (meaning "in the same manner as" or "having the same characteristics as") it used to be hard to imagine *like* being used otherwise than correctly: "Students resent being treated *like* children," "his motorcycle is rather *like* mine," "a novel *like War and Peace* takes an eternity to read." Now I can imagine it, having come across a question posted on the Internet: "What are similar sites like Wikipedia?"

One of the choruses in Handel's great oratorio *Messiah* begins, chirpily: "All we like sheep," a phrase which gets repeated before it continues, after a pause, with "are gone astray." What, for a confused moment, we mistakenly took for a verb turns out to be a preposition. Similar puzzlement arises during pledge breaks on American public television: corporate donors and sponsors are thanked for their contributions, as are individual subscribers, in the latter case by means of a message taking up the whole screen: "VIEWERS LIKE YOU."

To digress further, *like* can also function as a noun, a conjunction, an adverb, an adjective and—especially in the mouths of younger people—an interjection (often inserted as a stalling device, a way of expressing hesitation, or a mindless filler, in the same irritating way French speakers use "tu vois" or German ones "genau."). It often carries the meaning of "approximately" or "let's say."

Originating in California in the 1960s or 1970s and now spreading, in the words of John Singler, "like a global brushfire," the adverbial "like quotative" (as linguists term it) is used instead of "say" or "said" to introduce some form of quotation whether it be verbatim, paraphrased or summarized: "He was, like, totally awesome," "I was like, 'Totally awesome!'" The quotation can also represent an interior monologue or stream of consciousness, or even, on occasion, a non-verbal attitude or emotion. This tiresomely ubiquitous "like quotative" (additionally used to hint that the material quoted may be less than completely accurate) has come to replace what might be termed the older and, to my mind, equally tiresome "go quotative" (e.g., "And I'm going, 'You can't really mean that?'"). It's been suggested that, in time, the modifier *all* (as in "I was *all* like, 'Totally awesome'") may supplant *like* altogether.

Perhaps the overuse of *like* began with the hippie generation. Amis (126) relates the story of the hippie who cried "like help" when he was near drowning.

In May 2011 Agence France-Presse reported that an Israeli couple, taking their inspiration from Facebook, named their newborn daughter "Like." So, during her entire existence she is condemned, when she overhears conversations around her, to wonder whether she is being addressed or, worse, talked about behind her back.

For further takes on *like* see Brians (139), Burchfield (458–60), Hitchens (736–38), Yagoda (55–56) and "A Likely Story" (in O'Conner 57–59).

OF—"However innocent it may appear, the word *of* is, in anything other than small doses, among the surest indications of flabby writing" (Garner 464). Garner cites a 1992 *New York Times* article entitled "All About Of": "Clearly, *of* is now something more than a mere preposition. It's a virus." Garner revises a verbose sentence containing five *of*s, omitting them all and, in the process, reducing 56 words to 38. He also points out that *of* is guilty of playing truant (as in "a couple dozen") and also intruding unidiomatically, as in "not that big *of* a deal," not too smart *of* a student, "somewhat *of* an abstract idea." This usage, says Jenkins, is "relatively recent, oral American idiom, rare in print except in reported speech." "May it remain rare in print," he concludes, "and if people stop speaking that way, that will be fine, too" (22). Yagoda (170–71) speculates that a phrase like "not that big *of* a deal" could be echoing phrases like "a prince *of* a fellow" or "not that much *of* a problem" which are "grammatically unimpeachable because *prince* is a noun and *much* used that way is a pronoun." "Big," he points out, is an adjective, and doesn't require an *of*.

As Garner says, avoid too many *ofs* in one sentence. Praising John O'Hara's novel *Rage to Live* Clifton Fadiman fails to avoid: "I know *of* no finer presentation in our recent fiction *of* the culture *of* the rich Americans *of* our medium-sized towns." Even the ultra-fastidious Henry James can parade a procession of *ofs* when he reports a character hoping for "some chance *of* feeling the brush *of* the wing *of* the stray spirit *of* youth" (*The Ambassadors*). A useful corrective to the overuse of *of* is Herbert Lust's 2012 novel *Violence and Defiance* which banishes this preposition altogether on the grounds that it is too abstract.

Like *for*, *of* is a much-misused preposition. Examples (recommended preposition in parenthesis): "Canada's commitment *of* (*to*) reducing carbon dioxide emissions," "he has a bookish side *of* (*to*) him," "we are sympathetic *of* (*to*) those who have suffered from Hepatitis B," "he played opposite *of* (*to*) the center-back," "he proposals are lacking *of* (*in*) substance."

"The Port Authority is not responsible for loss or damage *to* your vehicle." Should be "…for loss *of* or damage *to* your vehicle."

In November 2009 a book entitled *The Oxford Handbook of Samuel Taylor Coleridge* was reviewed in the *TLS*. The reviewer found the title odd, since it "suggests a handbook that one belonged to Coleridge, not a book about him," adding, "*A Handbook to Coleridge* would make more sense."

Like many other prepositions, *of* can sometimes lead to ambiguity. "'They have a right to speak out,' said Jones *of* the protesters." Was Mr. Jones actually one of the protesters, or simply speaking about them? Recently a newspaper reported that, at Easter celebrations in Hungary, there is a peasant ceremony known as the "watering *of* the girls." This suggests that it is the girls who are being watered as we might water plants in the garden. But, as other words in the caption, as well as the accompanying photograph, make clear, it is village girls who are throwing buckets of water at their local men-folk.

The minister who asked his flock to "pray for all those who are sick *of* our church" might have meant exactly what he said, but it is more likely that *of* should have been *in,* though even *in* could also lead to ambiguity. Ambiguity could be eliminated if the sentence were recast with the word order changed: "Pray for those *of* our church who are sick."

A political party is reported as being "on the brink *of* history." Does *of* mean "*of* making history" or "*of* becoming history"? "A mother *of* 19" was reported to have made speech during an anti-Putin rally in Red Square in December, 2011. One wonders how she managed to find the time.

Is the title of the TV documentary "The Many Lovers *of* Jane Austen's Novels" free of ambiguity?

My paternal grandmother (1872–1964) was fond of using the expression "*of* an evening." Did she mean "*on* most evenings" or "*at* some point *in* the evening(s)"?

Among illiterates, *of* is bidding fair to replace "have" in such sentences as "I would (or could, or should) *of* kicked him." "However willing," in the words of the Oxford English Corpus, "we may be to convert *have* to *of* in spoken English, the Corpus shows that the habit has not, thankfully, spread into written English." However, in *The Great Gatsby* Scott Fitzgerald several times puts *of* instead of *have* in direct speech to indicate the sub-standard speech of certain characters (e.g., Rosy's "if we'd *of* raised the blinds we'd *of* seen daylight").

While *of* takes over from "have," it itself is prone to be taken over, or elided, by "a" in such phrases as "a cuppa tea," "drinka pinta milka day," "Housa Commons" and "Banka Canada" (both frequent on CBC TV news), "get outta here" and "prepositions cause lotsa problems."

There is a difference between "a picture *of* Peter" and "a picture *of* Peter's." "The jocular 'what is she a doing *of*?' is allowable only as a facetious imitation of Cockney grammar" (Greenbaum 492).

"I'm better *of* not knowing." You'd be better *off* using *off*.

"It has been argued that an expression such as "that long nose *of* his" is allowable only if he has several noses. But it clearly means 'the nose which is his,' and is a well-established construction that only pedants would criticize" (Greenbaum 492). A similar point is made by Burchfield in his long note on *of* (541–44).

OFF—"Used in the sense 'from the hands, charge, or possession of', *off* ... is construed especially with *take, buy, borrow, hire* and the like. But there is no doubt that, despite the antiquity (mid-16c. onward) of the construction, it is now regarded as not quite standard. One no longer buys a car *off* a stated garage or person but *from* a garage or person" (Burchfield 544).

"In restaurants, *off* can be ambiguous: 'the fish is *off*' may put you *off* the fish, or may simply be short for '*off* the menu'" (Howard 291). Here *off* is being used in three ways: as an adjective ("the fish is *off*"), as an adverbial particle ("put you *off*") and as a preposition "*off* the menu."

Still on food: I thought that "dine *off*" (as in "dine *off* steak tartare") had long been superseded by "dine *on*" until I found an advertisement for losing weight which read "dine *off* the pounds."

In Malaysian English "have an off-day " does not mean "have a bad day" but "have a day off."

A newspaper ad reads: "Save up to 50% off." No, please make a choice: either "save up to 50%" or "up to 50% off."

Royals betray their blue blood by pronouncing *off* as "orf".

OFF OF—"Considered a barbarism" (Jenkins 59). And with good reason: why say "the ball bounced *off of* the wall" or "he borrowed money *off of* me"? *off* is all that is really needed to express a clear meaning and thereby avoid a stuttering cacophony of *f*s. The fact that a famous shipwrecked mariner uses this locution, which the *OED* traces back to the 1400s and which dictionaries usually designate as "non-standard," in Defoe's novel ("I had indeed gotten two pair of shoes now, which I took *off of* the feet of two drowned men," chap. 14), and that a character in Shakespeare, Saunder Simpcox, says that he "fell *off of* a tree" (2 Henry VI 2.1.96) cannot justify this usage: Crusoe was uneducated, and Simpcox was both uneducated and an impostor.

However, ever since Mark Twain used it in *Huckleberry Finn* ("I'd borrow two or three dollars *off of* the judge") *off of* has been conspicuous in American speech, though not in educated American writing. However, I have found one use of it, from the mouth of a (thankfully) fictional university professor, in John Updike's *Roger's Version* and another, less excusably, in the same novelist's *Bech: A Book* ("*off of* war-darkened Broadway") Some American writers, seeking to replicate colloquial speech, will resort to conflation, e.g., "offa" (as in Jeffrey Eugenides' "get yo' hands *offa* them, motherfucking pigs!" or in the Rolling Stones' "hey, you, get offa my cloud"), "affa" or, as in Faulkner and O'Neill, "offen." It's hard to determine whether Philip Roth is deliberately flouting standard usage when Alexander Portnoy describes his father's genitals in this way: "They hung down off of, they were connected on to, they could not be taken away from, *him!*"

It seems that *of* and *off* have always given trouble: when the phrase "chip *off* the old block" first appeared in the sixteenth century it was "chip *of* the old block." Uniting them could reflect this uncertainty. Although a phrase like "there appears to be a levelling *off of* the flood waters" just manages to pass muster, it might be best to follow this simple advice: "Lay off *off of* and stick to *off.*"

ON—"Evidence is accumulating that *on* is beginning to invade some of the traditional territory of some other prepositions," especially in newspaper headlines (Burchfield 549). The citations show it has replaced *about, for* and the prepositional phrase "as a result of." *On*'s "colonizing ambitions" have also led to it supplanting *against, at, beside, in, of, to* and *with* (Humphrys 119). We used to say "*at* (or *over*) the weekend": now "*on* the weekend" or "*on* weekends" is heard more and more. We also say, following American idiom, that we will phone someone *on* a number rather than *at* one. The phrase "*on* the invitation *of*" is bidding fair to challenge "*at* the invitation *of.*"

"Few besides New Yorkers speak of standing *on* line. Follow the usage of the rest of the English-speaking world: *in* line." Citing this excellent advice, Jenkins adds: "The *on* version may be spreading, but *in* is still the unassailable choice" (85).

Don't write "early *on*," just "early." Even though Alan Bennett entitled one his plays *Forty Years On*, you do not need to follow his example (prefer "forty years later"). After all, it was Alan Bennett who made this admission: "I made copious notes *on* the manuscripts I studied." One can only hope the librarian wasn't looking.

"We learned from the African-American community *on* how to be vocal"—omit the *on*.

"He explored the Alps *on* foot" (not, Peter Mansbridge among other culprits have, "*by* foot"). It's also "*on* Shanks's pony" and "*on* horseback."

In Shaw's play *Misalliance* a character asks: "Anybody *on for* a game of tennis?" I suppose *on* here means something like "ready" and/or "willing." Possibly colloquial.

In the commercial for a sandwich that comes with "a sauce you pour on yourself," a phrasal verb ("pour on" has become entangled with the combination of "pour" (verb), "on" (preposition), "yourself" (predicate)," creating the comic ambiguity. One wonders to what degree the advertising copywriters are deliberately mangling the language as an attention-getting device (as in the eye-catching slogan of my childhood: "Drinka pinta milka day)." In Blackburn's view, "most TV advertising is an affront to human dignity," and he hopes that "there is a special place in hell for the people in the advertising industry who have crassly perverted our language in the pursuit of profit with no concern for the damage they wreak on our main means of understanding each other" (55).

Back to *on*. Lewis Carroll once set his readers this riddle: "How is a raven like a writing desk?" The point, obviously, is that there is no resemblance at all. But one smart Alec came up with a clever solution: "Poe wrote *on* both." The ambiguity of *on* is also illustrated in this quip from Roy Brown: "I admit the most recent fight with my wife was my fault. She said: 'What's *on* the TV?' and I said: 'Dust.'"

The person who wrote "she left the hotel *on* her cell-phone" has a strange idea of modern transport.

Finally, the headline "Bishops Agree Sex Abuse Rules" could have spared the bishops much embarrassment had *on* been strategically inserted.

ONTO—"This form, rather dated now, will strike many readers as a would-be neat or smart or up-to-date version of *on to*, as of *into* were a neat etc. version of *in to*, which it is not. I have no great personal objection to *onto*, though I have found by experience that no one (not no-one) persistently using *onto* writes anything much worth reading" (Amis 143). Trask disagrees: he thinks that *onto* in the sentence "she tossed her books *onto* the table" is acceptable because the books actually end up on the table, adding: "Observe the difference between the following two examples: 'We drove *on* to the beach' means 'We continued driving until we had reached the beach' (though we didn't necessarily take the car right onto the sand), but 'We drove *onto* the beach' means 'We moved the car so that its wheels where sitting *on* the beach'" (205). In the first sentence "drove *on*" is a phrasal verb (*on* being an adverb), in the second *on* is a preposition.

The following sentence is cited, and generously excused as a probable typo, in an amusing review of mistakes in travel brochures: "We cross the Firth of Forth on the modern suspension bridge into the kingdom of Fife and *onto* St. Andrews" (Coffmann 150, her italics). She continues: "When I last checked, *onto* meant 'on top of.' The writer surely meant that the group traveled *on to* St Andrews" (150, her italics).

"*Onto*" in "a show *onto* itself" should of course be "*unto*."

OUT—In Britain it is becoming increasingly common to omit the particle *out* in the phrasal verb "sort *out*" (just as *in* is frequently omitted in the phrasal verb "come *in*" when responding to a knock on the door).

OUT OF—"*Out of* a job," "two *out of* three," and "*out of* charity" are all perfectly acceptable phrases. But "he slipped *out of* the side door" suggests that it was the door itself, not the doorway or room, he was emerging from (Bernstein 345). Suggestion: "he slipped *out* the side door," or "he slipped *out by* the side door."

I prefer to say I am *out of* doors (or simply "outdoors"), rather than I go *out of* doors. How else would one leave? How come doors were is such short supply?

Americans let the cat *out* the bag, the Brits let it *out of* the bag.

Please, not *outa* or *outta*.

OUTSIDE—In keeping with their tendency to string prepositions together, Americans are much fonder than the British of adding *of* to *outside* to form, with no difference in meaning, the compound *outside of*. Groucho Marx: "Outside of a dog, a book is man's best friend. Inside of a dog, it's too dark to read."

As for the expression "*outside* the box," don't even think it.

OUTWITH—A common term in Scottish legal parlance. It means *outside* or *without*.

OVER—Like *about, for* and *in terms of, over* is one of those prepositions used far too loosely. North Americans are more likely than Britons to employ *over* in a loose sense of "on the subject of" or in place of a more specific preposition. "They will be surely punished *over* this incident," "I am getting very frustrated *over* this issue" (the first *over* should be *for*, and the second should be *by*). In the sentences "the pool was closed *over* safety concerns" and "she resigned *over* a bitter dispute with her boss," *over* should be replaced by a compound term such as "because *of*." The prevalence of "happy *over*" is not something to be happy *about*.

Nor is, with its bunching of nouns, "Rachel Carson's aims *over* pesticide use reduction." Write "aims *to* reduce pesticide use" or "aims *at / for* reducing...."

"Most Americans blamed Bush *over* Obama for the state of the 2012 economy." Instead of *over* write "not," "rather than" or "instead *of*."

Over is quite acceptable as the equivalent of "more than": "They have been married for *over* fifty years," "a room at the hotel costs *over* 200 dollars." However, "I don't think I would say that I flew *over over* five countries on my vacation," and "it would be a bit much to say that the party was *over* over two hours ago" (Blackburn 66).

"No need to walk home in this awful rain—I can easily run *over* you in my car." "I'd prefer you to use the phrasal verb and run me *over*."

Citing "the policeman struck him *over* the head," Ambrose Bierce commented: "If the blow was *over* the head it did not hit him" (49). A similar ambiguity attends the phrase "near miss": does this mean "a miss that was *nearly* a hit" or "a miss that was *actually* a hit"?

OWING TO—This compound was not fully developed until the nineteenth century: "The growing tendency to substitute *due to*, under American influence, is one of the most contentious issues of current grammatical propriety" (A. C. Partridge 100).

PAST—Over the last ten years the English have fallen into the habit, when referring to time, of saying "half eight" (8:30) instead of "half *past* eight." If this habit, which Burchfield (348) considers an imitation of Scottish and Irish usage, catches on in North America, the Toronto rock band "Half Past Four" will have to rename itself in order to be even more "innovative" and "progressive" than it claims to be. Incidentally, "half eight" might be confusing for native speakers of German for whom "halb acht" means 7:30.

You can say "run that *past* me again" or "*by* me again" (in either case it means "I was *past* caring" or "sorry, I wasn't listening"). Learners of English might be flummoxed by the idiom here, as they also might be by "I wouldn't put anything *past* him."

PER—A favourite with bureaucrats, as in "five days *per* week." "The English 'five days a week' is much more natural. Similarly, 'miles an hour' is the natural phrasing, despite the standard abbreviation MPH. Does anybody, in conversation, ever say 'miles *per* hour'?" (Jenkins 116).

"Using 'per' to mean 'according to' … is rather old-fashioned business jargon and is not welcome in other contexts" (Brians 172).

For more on *per* see Burchfield 583–84.

PLUS—As a preposition *plus* can mean "with the addition of" ("two *plus* two is four"), "together with" ("you will receive $1000 *plus* interest"), and "above zero" ("in Phoenix it often gets to *plus* 40 degrees in summer").

"Its presence should not affect the question of whether a following verb should be singular or plural, which depends on the plurality of the first item mentioned: 'his earnings plus his pension come (plural) to $100; his pension plus his earnings comes (singular) to $100'" (Greenbaum 545).

Incidentally, except in very informal English, *plus* does not mean "and." That would make it a conjunction, which it isn't. Nor should it be used to mean "and moreover" or "additional and welcome" (Greenbaum 545).

Plus it is very irritating to find talented writers, David Foster Wallace for instance, consistently beginning sentences with this word.

PRIOR TO—"Stilted" (Bierce 53), "formal and perhaps rather pretentious" (Greenbaum 564), "this ghastly thing" (Trask 229). Agreed: what's wrong with the crisply non-Latinate *before*? John Bremner, a copywriter and a legendary teacher at the University of Kansas: "If you don't use posterior to, why use prior to? Would you say 'Posterior to the game, we had a few drinks? So why say, 'Prior to the game, we had a few drinks?'" (cited in Jenkins 123).

SURROUNDING—There is some doubt whether this word (present participle of the verb "to surround" (as in "the fields surrounding the house") or an adjective (as in "the surrounding countryside") should also be considered as a preposition. The venerable *OED* rules against it. You will, however, come across such usages as these: "Our reporters have information *surrounding* the flu epidemic" (substitute *about* or *on*), "the debate *surrounding* the Abominable Snowman" (*about, on* or *over*), "old pagan beliefs *surrounding* Christmas" (*about*). A legitimate use might be "circumstances *surrounding* the outbreak of flu," where the prefix "circum" (=around) could be thought to justify *surrounding* used as a preposition.

THAN—In the phrase "Einstein is more intelligent than I" *than* functions as a conjunction linking two clauses ("Einstein is more intelligent" and "I [am]"). Here "I" is a subject personal pronoun. In the phrase "Einstein is more intelligent *than* me" *than* functions as a preposition and is followed by a personal pronoun in the objective case. Both phrases are correct, yet the second (although similar uses are found in all the great writers) has long been regarded as anathema by purists. However, "my husband loves cricket more *than* I" and "my husband loves cricket more *than* me" mean two very different things.

THROUGH—A CBC reporter said that "the government is trying to rush through legislation" to end a postal workers' strike. Citing this, Blackburn comments: "I believe that the government was trying to rush it through, not rush through it" (72). His well-taken point reminds us that, like its companion word "throughout," *through* can be an adverb (as in "the sunlight streamed through") or a preposition "the sunlight streamed *through* the window").

The American use of *through* to mean "up to and including" should be encouraged, but perhaps not its meaning of "fired" or "jilted": "British telephone operators still say, when making a connection, 'You're through,' although it sometimes gives Americans a nasty turn" (Howard 389).

"*Thru*, a variant spelling of *through*, should be shunned. Oddly, it appears in parts of the Internal Revenue Code" (Garner 654). An earlier formation, *thro'*, was thought by Samuel Johnson to be eminently shunnable: "Contracted by barbarians from *through*," he snorted.

TILL—Amis asserts that this word "is a genuine English preposition and conjunction with its roots in Old English and Old Norse and is not a daringly informal shortening of stuffy old upper-class *until*" (229). Amis reminds us that *till* is not spelt *'til*.

Or, for that matter, *til* or *'till*. For further commentary see O'Conner 185–86.

TO—In most cases do not omit after "write." Fowler points out that we can say "I will write you a report" but not "I will write you": "It may be said that *I write you* is good old English. So is *he was a-doing of it; I guess* is good Chaucerian. But in neither case can the appeal to a dead usage—dead in polite society or in England—justify what is a modern vulgarism" (1938, 174). "Vulgarism" it may or may not be, but Fowler would find it alive and well throughout America.

The use of *to* in "I will try *to* do my best" is standard practice, but "I will try *and* do my best" is not the "colloquialism" and "vulgarity" many sticklers accuse it of being.: "We often find 'and' between two related verbs. It makes absolutely no sense to criticize a remark like 'try and see him' when it's acceptable to say 'come and see him' or 'go and see him' or 'stop and see him' (O'Conner 56). O'Conner adds that the "and" construction (already in use in the early 1600s) "didn't seem to bother Thackeray, Dickens, Melville, Twain, George Eliot, and many others" (57).

In the US especially *to* is ousting the more standard *of*: "she was the secret girlfriend *to* her boss," "she is the mother *to* his son." An ad for the new ILX Acura begins: "Introducing the newest member *to* Acura." Wasn't the car already a member of the Acura stable?

To can be omitted after "dare," "help" and "need" when they are followed by an infinitive verb. It should be omitted in a phrase used by a Tour de France commentator, "the Italian rider is closing the gap *to* the leader," and replaced with *on*.

Should a book be dedicated *to* somebody or *for* somebody? It's been suggested that *for* is *for* the living, and *to* is *to* the dead.

As my penultimate point, the practice of dropping the *to* from "second-to-last" (with or without hyphens) is, regrettably, becoming more common. "Second-last" is second-best.

To is not omitted in the slogan "good *to* the last drop," used in advertising coffee as far back as the early twentieth century: "President Theodore Roosevelt was visiting Joel Cheek, perfector of the Maxwell House blend. After the president had had a cup, he said of it that it was 'Good ... *to* the last drop.' It has been used as a slogan ever since, despite those who have inquired what was wrong with the last drop. Professors of English have been called in to consider the problem and ruled that *to* can be inclusive and not just mean 'up to but not including'" (Rees 89).

NB: We mustn't turn a blind eye *on* prepositional errors, but *to* them.

TOWARD(S)—Is there a difference between *toward* and *towards*? Not according to the indefatigable American Sherwin Cody (of "Do You Make These Mistakes in English?" fame). For Cody it was simply a matter of euphony—choose the one you think sounds better. Nowadays very few people make any distinction between *toward* and *towards*, though Americans prefer to exclude the "s," the British to preserve it. A case can be made, however, to reserve or preserve *toward* after a noun as part of a prepositional phrase (e.g., "the poet turned his gaze *toward* Bethlehem"), and *towards* as part of an adverbial phrase ("slouching *towards* Bethlehem to be born").

Upper-class Britons will often shorten this two-syllable word to the monosyllabic "twards." *Towards* can take it on the chin: prepositions are used to being abbreviated.

The *Globe and Mail* reported that the Chinese Communist Party was "taking a tough line *toward* its critics." The idiomatic preposition required here is *on* (even *against* is better than *toward*).

The normally punctilious Auberon Waugh describes his Somerset neighbours as law-abiding "probably because of the affection and respect we feel *towards* our police force." *Towards* should be *for*.

Many people are not bothered by "thoughtless *towards*" but I'm not one of them. I don't know why: after all, I'm not bothered by "inconsiderate *towards*."

To my knowledge no one has yet used "untoward" in the sense of "in the opposite direction" but that moment cannot be far off.

UNDER—"It used to be widely held by purists that to say *under* the circumstances' must be wrong because what is around us cannot be over us. '*In* the circumstances' was the only correct expression. This argument is characterized by Fowler as puerile. Its major premise is not true ('a threatening sky is a circumstance no less than a threatening bulldog') and even if it were true it would be irrelevant, because, as cannot be too often repeated, English idiom has a contempt for logic. There is good authority for '*under* the circumstances,' and if some of us prefer '*in* the circumstances' (as I do), that is a matter of taste, not of rule" (Gowers 164–65).

During winter you might read or hear that "the city was blanketed *under* a foot of snow." At first sight nothing seems wrong with this, but what the sentence actually implies is that the layer of snow was *on top of* whatever was doing the blanketing. Revised sentence: "The city was blanketed *in* (or *by* or *with*) a foot of snow."

Like all prepositions, *under* is usually unstressed. But, again like all prepositions, it can carry a stress if it's deemed desirable or necessary to convey meaning. A possible example can be found in Woody Allen's "I Had a Rough Marriage": "It was partially my fault that we got divorced .... I tended to place my wife *under* a pedestal."

British English has the charming "*under* the weather" or "one degree *under*" ("mildly ill") and also "*under* the doctor" ("undergoing medical treatment or surveillance"). A 1976 British sex comedy, in which a Harley Street physician takes advantage of his female patients, was entitled *Under the Doctor*.

UNDERNEATH—"From earliest times in competition with *below*, *beneath*, and *under*, this word is tending to be restricted to its literal sense, 'directly beneath or covered by'" (Burchfield 806). Burchfield cites Fowler's examples, "*underneath* the bed" and "*under* the stimulus of competition."

UNTIL—While *till* is still the usual locution, the more formal *until* is perhaps preferable at the start of a sentence, especially when the clause or phrase precedes the main sentence. Compare "*Until* I die, I will love you," and "I will love you *till* I die."

Until does not need to be prefaced by *up*.

The Irish have an endearing use: "Come *until* I show you something."

UNTO—I include this preposition not because it is used incorrectly but because I would like to see it restored to its honourable place in the language rather than being summarily dismissed as "archaic." It's a matter of deep regret, as well as of wide-eyed amazement, that the versatile *unto* has almost entirely disappeared from the language, slipping away into virtual obsolescence. Yet such is its semantic richness that the *OED* provides no fewer than twenty-nine major definitions (to which are appended several additional subsidiary entries). Given that, how on earth are we managing to do without it? After all, Shakespeare recognized its utility, employing it, in various nuances of meaning, nearly five hundred times.

Devotees of contraction, enemies of the redundant, we moderns now tend to make do with *to* rather than *unto* as found in such Biblical phrases as "like *unto* us," "say *unto* you," "render *unto* Caesar," "*unto* us a child is born" (or drop *unto* altogether, "like *unto* Him" becoming "like Him"). However, it's some consolation that *unto* still clings stubbornly to life in the familiar phrase "law *unto* oneself," first recorded in the Authorized Version of 1611.

UP—Besides being a preposition, *up* can function as an adjective, an adverb or a verb. In the sentence "I have watched my granddaughter grow *up* (and *up* and *up*)" the first *up* is an adverbial particle ("grow *up*" being a phrasal verb), the second and third *ups* are prepositions.

UP TO—Because of the sense of vague optimism these two words emanate, Amis sees the use of *up to*, as in "the plan will create up to fifty new jobs," as an example of political "dishonesty" since nothing specific has actually been promised (159). Another example might be "*up to* 50% off." *Up to* is never spelt as one word.

Notice the hyphenization difference between "the dictionary is *up to* date" and "it is an *up-to-*date dictionary."

UPON—*On* is far more frequently used than the more formal *upon*. Which of these one chooses may depend on such factors as tone, euphony, pace and rhythm. Some set idioms and established phrases require one or the other: "*on* the dot," "*on* your marks." "*upon* my word," "row *upon* row of soldiers." "*Upon* is a formal word, often unnecessary in place of *on*.... *Upon* is inferior when a shorter, simpler and more direct word will suffice" (Garner 671). Some authorities, including Garner, recommend using *upon* when the meaning is "on the occasion of" (or did, once *upon* a time).

When, around 1840, Coleridge employed the word "unreliable" (the first recorded use) to describe the behaviour of Alcibiades, he was criticized on the grounds that we do not "rely something" but "rely *upon* something": he should therefore have used "unrelyuponable." Cited by Davies, 110. By the same token we do not say "dependuponable," but simply "dependable."

UPSIDE—Can mean *against* or *on* in informal American usage: "The old lady hit the burglar hard *upside* his head."

VIA—Deriving from the Latin word for a road, this preposition should strictly be used for journeys: "We are flying to Hawaii *via* Vancouver." Yet more and more it is coming to signify *by means of* as in "I found out about it *via* the Internet" or *by way of* or *through* as in "my wife and I obtained a loan *via* our local bank.*"*

WITH—In *The Queen's English* Harry Blamires devotes ten pages to the misuse of this preposition which he calls "now the most overworked word in the language" (1994, 137). Mistakes, he notes, are particularly likely to occur when *with* is the first word in the sentence: for example, in "With the clock striking three he strode down the road… " *with* should be replaced by "As [the clock was striking three]," and in "With tourists set to become the biggest industry in the world…" *with* should cede to "Now that [tourists are set]." I found two examples from a January 2009 edition of the *Sunday Telegraph*: "With female drinking rates rising…" and "With the nation in an economic downturn…".

In a later book, Blamires reiterates that misuse of *with* "has run riot in contemporary journalism. Journalists, it seems, are prepared to force the preposition to do numerous jobs for which it is unfitted" (Blamires 2000, 168). He again gives examples to show that in some sentences *with* should be replaced by *and, but, since* or *because*, and in others by a rephrasing to clarify a specific temporal or causal connection.

The following quotation illustrates both the overuse of *with* and the ambiguity that can sometimes bedevil its use: "We Liberals find ourselves competing *with* two other parties *with* simplistic messages." Reword: "We Liberals find ourselves competing *with* (or *against*) two other parties who offer simplistic messages."

From a sports report: "Michael Jordan did not play *with* a dislocated shoulder." This suggests, unintentionally, that the shoulder had healed before the game, enabling Michael to take part (*with* should be *because of*).

A columnist worried that her new washing machine was too complex for her and she would have to beat her undies with a rock to get them clean: a concerned reader recommended she beat her undies *on* a rock since doing so *with* a rock would severely shorten their lifespan.

In the following sentence, not enough care seems to have been taken to avoid ambiguity: "She cleaned the house *with* her mother."

Yet on occasion *with* is indispensable. A sentence like "women men want to have a good time" would make more sense were *with* tacked on to the end.

With is certainly a slippery infiltrator into sentences where it does not belong (recommended prepositions in parentheses): "I am getting closer *with* (*to*) Jesus every year," "he credits his longevity *with* (*to*) a healthy life-style," "the path *with* (*of*) least resistance," "Australia is incredibly immersed *with* (*in*) good cyclists," "the apartment did not conform *with* (*to*) established safety standards," "the show culminated *with* (*in*) a brilliant fireworks display," "the thief was suddenly confronted *with* (*by*) a policeman" (*with* suggests that both of them were up to no good).

Sometimes the distinction between *with* meaning "*by means of*" and *with* meaning "possessing" is not always maintained, as in this headline: "Enraged cow injures man *with* axe." "*By means of*" would be better than *with* in the headline "parents seek closure *with* Canada visit" except that it is too cumbersome.

"Getting tough on crime is an obsession *with* the government." I don't know about you, but I have never had an obsession with the government. The line should use *of*, not *with*. "Chez" would also fit the bill did it not seem so pretentious.

Note that "fight *with*" can mean both "fight *against*" and fight *alongside*." A TV recruiting commercial in my country urges me to "fight *with* the Canadian Forces." As the dying Thoreau said when asked whether he had made his peace with God, "I am not aware we had ever quarrelled." In this case, too, there would be the danger of being seriously outnumbered.

"The use of *with* for 'employed by' suggests a job in at least middle management. The person who says *I'm with ICI* is not in its typing pool" (Greenbaum 777).

"*With* it," like "*at* it," is a typical English idiom. "*With* it was popular slang in the 1960s for knowing what is going on, being in the swing and up to date. If you are still using it, you are certainly not *with it*" (Howard 411). Nor are you "*with* it" if you abbreviate *with* to "w/" (even though David Foster Wallace is fond of doing so).

If you're calling a meeting to order you do not, Blackburn (59) reminds us, "pound a gavel": "You pound *with* a gavel, although I suppose you *could* pound a gavel, perhaps with another gavel, if you happened to have two handy."

Signing off in her interview with Jimmy Carter before he became President, Barbara Walters also opted, twice, for an inappropriate *with*: "Be wise *with* us, Governor, be good *with* us." Where did these *withs* come from? John Simon had an answer: "The sort of novel where the adorably virginal heroine, finally yielding to her defloration-bent lover, jumps into bed in her slip, pulls the covers up to her chin and whispers, 'Be kind to me, darling. Be gentle with me'" (Simon 97).

WITHIN—"*Within* a month" not "*inside of* a month." "*Within* a month" means "at any time in the next four weeks," "*in* a month" means "at the end of four weeks."

WITHOUT—There is a famous hymn beginning "There is a green hill far away, / *Without* a city wall." Why, I wondered as a naïve chorister many years ago, would a green hill have a city wall? I notice that in some modern hymnbooks *without* has been dumbed down to *outside*. The double meaning (abstract + concrete) of this preposition is exemplified by its second use in the maxim "Marriage *without* love leads to love *without* marriage." Setters of cryptic crosswords find this double meaning useful. Clue: "Mockery of an attempt *without* a garment (8)." Solution: "TRAVESTY" (TR + A + VEST + Y).

In *Pygmalion* Shaw gives the Cockney pronunciation of *without* as "athaht." Would not "wivarht" be more accurate?

Please avoid *w/o* in formal writing.

Quiz #4.

In the following sentences, is the preposition correct or incorrect (misused, misplaced, redundant or missing)?

1. This device will guard your house *against* burglars.

2. Although on a diet, she is not averse *from* a little chocolate from time to time.

3. Megalomaniacs are dominated *with* one idea.

4. The plane departed New York *at* 9:00 a.m.

5. The monkey managed to board a plane bound *to* London.

6. He was warned *on* the danger of going too close to the cliff edge.

~

Answers: 1. *against* is correct,
2. averse *to*, 3. dominated *by*,
4. departed *from*, 5. bound *for*,
6. warned *of*.

CHAPTER 8

WHICH PREPOSITION?

Bear in mind that many a prepositional phrase (word plus preposition) can be troublesome: many words will take a specific preposition depending on the meaning of the word itself. Take the word "concerned." If it means "worried" or "anxious" the idiomatic preposition is *about, at, for* or *over*. If it means "involved" or "involving" the preposition becomes *with* or *in*. If it means "occupied" the preposition is *with*. And compare the following uses of prepositions following "impressed": "They were most impressed (i.e., filled with admiration for) *by* him," "The blast was impressed (i.e., indented) *into* the concrete wall," "The young men were impressed (i.e., forced to serve in) *into* the Navy," "If you don't impress (i.e., convince) it *on* (or *upon*) her now, you never will," "I was impressed (i.e., struck by) *with* her performance" (Prieur 115). The adjective "mad" will take a different preposition depending on whether it means "infatuated," "foolish," "enthusiastic," "angry" or "frantic."

The same applies to the different senses of a common word like "good." For example, "he is good (skilled) *at* carpentry," "that will be good (useful) *for* something," "he was very good (helpful) *to* me," "that is very good (kind) *of* you," "she's good (able to handle) *with* children." Sometimes, however the preposition remains the same even though the meaning of the word preceding it is different. Compare the following instances: "the razor is charged (loaded) *with* electricity," "they've been charged (given the responsibility) *with* the job," "he was charged (accused *of*) *with* the crime." Context and stress-pattern can determine the difference between "beer is good (healthy) *for* you" on one hand, and "good *for* you" (well-done!) on the other; someone who thinks your clothes are or look "good *on* you" means something different from an Australian saying the same three words.

A nodding acquaintance with Greek and Latin prepositions can be of some help. Latin prepositions like "ab" (*from*), "ad" (*to*), "cum" or "con" (*with*), "de" (*from*), "ex" or "e" (*from* or *out of*), as well as the Greek preposition "sym" (*with*), have become absorbed into English as prefixes and tend to attract equivalent English prepositions: "absent *from*," "adhere *to*," "communicate *with*," "different *from*," "exempt *from*," "sympathize *with*." But, as has been pointed out, the exceptions are many: "For example, *impute* takes *to*, *prepare* takes *for*, and *recoil* takes *from*" (Garner 520).

It would be very convenient if *every* word followed by a preposition took the same preposition each time. Unfortunately this is not the case: the choice of preposition often depends on the specific word or combination of words (or their absence) preceding or following the preposition. Whether one says "*in* my experience" or "*from* my experience" will often depend on the words immediately preceding and/or following the phrase. A person can be short *of* breath (or money), short *on* talent, short *with* a misbehaving child; a jacket can be short *in* the sleeves, "etc." is short *for* "etcetera." You may have a fear *of* flying, but fear *to* fly. You fall a victim *to* Cupid's wiles, but are a victim *of* them. You *show* respect *to* someone, but you *have* respect *for* him or her. We take advantage *of* a person, but we give a person an advantage *over* us. We write "have mercy *on*," but write "show mercy *to* or *toward(s.)*" Similarly, one has or feels compassion *for* the sick, but one has or takes compassion *on* them, or offers compassion *to* them. And just compare "I learnt to suffer *in* silence" with "I suffered *for* my beliefs."

Even a minor change, like a switch from a definite to an indefinite article, can cause a corresponding switch in the subsequent preposition: "she is *the* slave *of* her passions" as opposed to "she is *a* slave *to* her passions," or "*the* knack *of* lip-reading" as opposed to "*a* knack *for* lip-reading." A change from active to passive voice will determine whether a preposition is used or not: "Children evacuated the war zone," "children were evacuated *from* the war zone."

In the following uses of "satisfaction" each of the accompanying prepositions is idiomatically used: "I find great satisfaction *in* outdoor activities," "John experienced the satisfaction *of* gaining a degree," "our aim is to give satisfaction *to* all our customers." The choice also depends on the combination of words after the preposition, as in these examples with "similarity": "there is a similarity *between* the two newspapers," "the critic discussed the similarity *of* Bach *to* Handel," "Peter bears a striking similarity *to* his brother." In the following instances the preposition is clearly determined by the entire prepositional phrase (which I have italicized) following the verb: "give me an answer *by next Tuesday,* " "the marksman aimed *with great precision,*" "the house was furnished *in contemporary fashion,*" "give *with grace and generosity,*" "it happens *around the world.*"

The word or phrase that follows the preposition may in fact dictate the preposition to be employed. One can therefore distinguish between "drunk *on* whisky," where the preposition is linked to and governs the word "drunk," and "drunk *on* Sunday," where the identical preposition is part of the phrase "on Sunday". Compare "drunk *with* success" and "drunk *with* friends."

Can you spot the identical error in "an analysis and opinion *on* the issues" and "a knowledge and passion *for* cricket"? Yes, you're right: *of* should follow both "analysis" and "knowledge." In "many of us are sensitive and aware *of* climate change" the preposition *to* should follow "sensitive" ("sensitive *of*" is unidiomatic).

From the stylistic point of view it's advisable to avoid strings of interdependent prepositional phrases, like those found in the following sentence: "The ambassador took the opportunity *for* a lecture *on* the necessity *for* improvement of relations *between* the Soviet Union and the United States" (Greenbaum 134). His suggested revision reads: "The ambassador took the opportunity *to* lecture *on* why it was necessary to improve relations *between* the Soviet Union and the United States" (this version also eliminates too many abstract nouns). Revision is also called for if the prepositions happen to be identical: "I have read *of* the achieve-ments *of* the Irish *of* the southern regions *of* New England." Change to: "I have read *about* the achievements *of* the Irish *in* the southern regions *of* New England" (Greenbaum 134). Sometimes in a series of phrases a preposition will be needlessly repeated: "The driver was issued a ticket *for* running a red light, *for* speeding, *for* honking his horn and *for* driving with due care and attention." The first *for* will carry over its meaning: eliminate the last three *fors*.

By providing more detailed explanations and illustrations the following list clarifies some of the more complex or controversial collocations in Part I of Chapter 11.

ACCOMPANIED—In a general sense both *by* and *with* mean "together *with*" but *by* denotes "in the company of" ("King Lear was accompanied *by* his three daughters") whereas *with* points to "being alongside" ("the barbecued ribs were accompanied *with* potatoes and haricots verts").

ACCUSED (v.)—I much prefer "accused *of*" to "accused *for*" (though "accused *for*" was once acceptable), but, according to Bollinger, "*for* does a better job of conveying 'cause'" (1988, 240). Bollinger cites "Northrop has been accused *for* cheating the government."

Avoid "he was accused *in* the murder."

ACQUIESCE—Some authorities (e.g., Benson) sanction both *in* and *to*. However, *in* is the time-honoured preposition and is more generally favoured even nowadays, outnumbering *to* by a ratio of roughly six to one. That a headline-writer in the *Guardian Weekly* (in October, 2010) opted for "acquiesce *to*" (a usage possibly mod-elled on "accede *to*") slightly disturbed my sense of the fitness of things, did "acquiesce *with*" from the pen of a *TLS* reviewer. The *OED* classifies *to* (along with *under* and *with*) as obsolete. Charles Darwin is possibly alone in using "acquiesce *on*."

ADEQUATE—"The water system was adequate *for* the community," "he proved adequate *to* the task."

ADORATION—As in the case of LOVE (see below) we are torn between two prepositions, *for* and *of*. We can say either that a father was "lost in adoration *for* his children" or that he was "lost in adoration" *of* them. However, we do not see paintings entitled "The Adoration *for* the Magi."

ADVANTAGE (n.)—"We recognize the advantage *of* this economic policy." "A university degree is *of* advantage *to* many people." "Being taller, I have an advantage *over* him in basketball." "We all hate to be taken advantage *of*."

ADVOCATE (n. v.)—Is it an "advocate *for*" or an "advocate *of*"? Current usage offers no clear guide. One can be an advocate *for* animals, fatty foods, prisoners, highway safety, higher education, human rights, and assisted suicide; one can be an advocate *of* children, moral reform, gun control, intelligent design, fighting in ice-hockey, freedom, and nuclear disarmament. All hope, alas, must be abandoned for keeping some useful distinctions, such as reserving "advocate *for*" to mean "a campaigner, an intercessor, or someone who pleads or intervenes actively on behalf of a person or cause" (by analogy with a court of law or with the phrase "play the devil's advocate") and "advocate *of*" to mean "a defender or supporter of a person or cause who does not assume a significantly active role." I can be an "advocate *of*" women's rights without doing anything (shame on me) to further them: "advocate *for*" would be misleadingly generous in this case.

No preposition is required after "advocate" when it is used as a verb to mean "recommend," as in "we all advocate higher pay *for* nurses."

AFFINITY—If "affinity" implies a mutual attraction, sympathy or liking then it will take *between* or *with*; if the relationship or understanding is one-sided then it is followed by *for* (e.g., "an affinity *for* art").

Ronald Reagan, *The Wall Street Journal* noted, "ushered in an affinity for dark blue Brooks Brothers suits." Warning: "affinity" should not be used as a synonym for "preference."

AFRAID—You can be afraid *of* big dogs or a stock market crash, but afraid *for* your health or safety. People "afraid *of* life" are those who, for what ever reason (shyness, say, or hypersensitivity), cannot cope with life's burdens and challenges; people "afraid *for* their lives" are those who fear their lives might be taken away.

It's been remarked that "as parents age they change from being afraid *for* their children to being afraid *of* them."

AIM (n. v.)—"Aim" can mean point or direct an object (weapon, camera) or "intend to achieve." But, as a verb, is it aim *at* or aim *for*? Very often "aim *at*" is found in the expression "take aim *at*": "The new policy takes direct aim *at* school bullies." Here *for* would not be possible. Nor would it be possible in "the demonstrator aimed a shoe *at* George Bush," unless of course Bush could be imagined inciting him to throw the shoe at someone else. *For* is used when *at* would not be idiomatic: "We are aiming *for* a Thursday departure date," "car manufacturers are aiming *for* improved fuel efficiency." Note also the infinitive usage ("my husband aims *to* achieve solvency by 2050") and the phrase "with the aim *of*…"

ALLOCATE—"Funds were allocated *to* the students *for* a new sports complex."

ALTERNATIVE (n.)—"He was given the alternative *of* paying the fine or going to prison." But which is it, "alternative *for*" or "alternative *to*"? Certainly *to* is far more common: "Counting wild birds at Christmas-time is an attractive alternative *to* shooting them for fun." Or: "Hiring an account to calculate your tax is an alternative *to* doing it yourself." But when *for* has the sense of "for the purpose of" it can be used in constructions where *to* would be odd: "An alternative *for* calculating your tax is to hire an accountant" (there is no alternative to paying your tax—you are legally bound to pay it). Note the difference between "an alternative *for* young girls" (i.e., playing football rather than rounders) and "an alternative *to* young girls" (i.e., possibly young boys or even older women).

Sentences could be constructed referring (with different meanings) to an alternative "*for* clean energy," "*of* clean energy" and "*to* clean energy."

AMENDS—"He wanted to make amends *to* his girlfriend *for* damaging her car," "he made amends *by* paying for the necessary repairs."

AMUSED (adj. v.)—"My mother was amused *at* (or *by*) my father's jokes; it amused me *to* hear her giggles." "My grandmother used to amuse us *by* telling ghost stories; she also amused us *with* card games."

ANCESTOR—For "ancestor" and related nouns like "forebear," "forerunner," "harbinger," "precursor" and "predecessor" the recommended preposition is *of* (even though *of* is being challenged by *to* and, in the case of "precursor," *to* is nowadays more often found).

ANTICIPATION—"Keen anticipation *for* the Olympic Summer Games," "she felt great anticipation *for* her upcoming wedding." *For* does seem very intrusive and awkward. Why not: "The Olympic Summer Games greeted *with* keen anticipation" and "she looked forward eagerly *to* her upcoming wedding"?

It's "*in* anticipation *of*," not "*in* anticipation *for*."

APATHY—This word gives no end of trouble. We feel or show apathy *towards* (a sport or sportsman, for example, not *against*, *for*, *on*, *to* or *regarding* it or him). When the baseball player Alex Rodriguez, of the New York Yankees, finally notched his 600th home run in August 2010 the *Globe and Mail* carried a headline for which it should be ashamed: "Apathy abounds *for* A-Rod's triumph." A recast version would read "A-Rod's triumph meets *with* apathy" (as do, it must sadly be acknowledged, most grammar books like this one).

APPEAL (n. v.)—Both meanings of "appeal" as a verb ("to request a decision be reversed" and "to be attractive" as in "football appeals *to* millions") take *to*, but ambiguity is enhanced by this usage. As Blackburn (246) puts it, "Is someone who is appealing to the Supreme Court more likely to win that someone who is not?" As a noun in the sense of "attraction" one can use "appeal" with different prepositions: "the popular appeal *of* football," "football has an appeal *to* millions" (*to* is preferable to *for* here), and "football exercises an appeal *on* millions."

Whether as verb or noun when "appeal" means "call" it takes *for*: we appeal *for* information or aid, we make an appeal *for* donations or peace.

We are free to appeal *to* authority, emotion, someone's finer instincts and the umpire. We can also appeal *against* a verdict or a sentence (in the US, however, the preposition is often dropped).

APPRECIATION—"They showed their appreciation *for* his help." "They gave him a set of golf clubs *in* appreciation *of* his help." "Besides his interest in golf, he had a keen appreciation *of* music and painting."

APPROVE—There's a difference between "approve *of*" (believe that something, such as a decision, is good or acceptable) and simply "approve" (officially agree to or accept as satisfactory).

ARBITRATE—A judge can arbitrate a dispute, and also arbitrate *in* a dispute, but not arbitrate *on* a dispute (the redundant *on* probably comes from the *on* in "decide *on*"). He may also be called upon to arbitrate *between* contending parties.

ASHAMED—"I was ashamed *about* what had happened," "I was ashamed *of* my disgraceful behaviour."

ASK—"The editor asked me *about* my book" (needing information), "my boyfriend asked *after* my mother" (enquiring *after* her health), "we had a favour to ask *of* them (requiring kind assistance).

ASSIST (v.)—"The young nurse assisted *at* the surgeon's first operation—she also assisted *in* the preparation of the surgeon's report, but is was her brother who assisted *with* the editing of the manuscript" (examples based on Benson 19).

ATTITUDE—A search engine reveals that *towards* (60 million hits) is the most common preposition, as in "we must all try to entertain an optimistic attitude *towards* the future." Lagging far behind are *to* (13 million hits), *toward* (8), *about* (3) and *over* (300,000) and *concerning* (225,000). Although *about* manages to avoid last place, and despite the fact that Benson authorizes it, I think it should be frowned upon. Remain loyal towards *towards*

"Attitude" can also be followed by *of* when it means "consisting *of*" ("attitude *of* gratitude," when it means "on the part *of*" ("the attitude *of* young people") and when it means "arising *from*" ("attitude *of* mind").

ATTRACTED—Whether "attracted" takes *by* or *to* has caused considerable debate. In practice the two prepositions seem to be used almost interchangeably. But consider these examples: "Romeo was attracted *by* Juliet," "Romeo was attracted *to* Juliet."

The use of *by* conveys an initial or immediate response, whereas *to* suggests that Romeo's feelings were based on a more extensive and familiar acquaintance. Compare "the children were attracted *by* the Christmas tree" and "bees are attracted *to* fruit trees." It may be that which preposition we choose depends on the emphasis we wish to give, *by* emphasizing the cause or object of the attraction, *to* emphasizing the person being attracted. For example, we would normally say "I am attracted *by* your offer, not "I am attracted *to* your offer."

ATTRACTION—"Romeo had a strong attraction *to* Juliet" (i.e., Romeo was being attracted), "Romeo had a strong attraction *for* Juliet" (i.e., Juliet was being attracted). Also: "Romeo and Juliet exercised a strong attraction *on* each other." Avoid *towards* as in "I have never been able to feel great emotional attraction *towards* the gipsy life" (Auberon Waugh). *For* will do nicely here.

AVERSION—In 1892 Beatrix Potter confessed to "an unconquerable aversion *to* listening to accounts in the first person of supposed supernatural visitations." The word "aversion" (like the cognate "averse" and "avert") derives from the Latin "aversus" meaning "turned away from" (the past participle of the verb "avertere"). When, as in the Potter citation or in the phrase "aversion therapy," "aversion" means "strong dislike, disinclination or opposition" the most common preposition nowadays is *to* (although Dr. Johnson famously preferred *from* and "historically both constructions … have been used, often by the same writers" (Burchfield 81). But if "aversion" (like "avert") simply means "a turning away of one's eyes or thoughts" then *from* is quite permissible, as in Larkin's line from his poem "Wants": "The costly aversion of the eyes *from* death." *To* is clearly not appropriate in this context.

BANDY (v.)—As a phrasal verb "bandy" can take either *about* or *around* (historically, *about* appears to have the idiomatic edge). It can also take *with*: "I'm not going to waste my time standing here bandying words *with* an idiot like you."

BARGAIN—Takes *with* in its literal meaning: "It was fun bargaining *with* the street vendor." But note the following expressions: "They hadn't bargained *for/on* such bad weather," "we hadn't bargained *on* taking the kids along," "he got more than he bargained *for*."

BASE (n. v.)—"Since acquiring a computer I've made my home a base *of* operations." "We should always base our opinions *on* the facts of the case." "I touch base *with* my brother twice a week."

BASIS—"As I am ignorant of the facts, I have no basis *for* judgment." "Your allegations have no basis *in* fact." "She was given an A on the basis *of* her performance in class discussion."

BEARING (n.)—"Some claim that a poet's life has no bearing *on* his poems" (not, as a *TLS* reviewer wrote, "*for* his poems").

BEHALF— "*On behalf of* is used when a person does something at the behest of someone else, *in behalf of* when a person does something for the benefit of someone (or something) else" (Levin 140). A common error is to confuse "*on behalf of*" with "*on the part of*": "An *effort on behalf of the members* is made for their sake, one *on the part of the members* is made by the members themselves" (Greenbaum 81).

BLAME (n. v.)—You blame someone *for* something, or blame a cause (e.g., arson) *for* an effect (e.g., a fire). You should not talk about blaming a fire *on* someone (or blaming deaths *on* a winter storm, or blaming your troubles *on* your sister, or, like Nat King

Cole, blaming "it" *on* "my youth"). Granted, Kipling wrote (in "If") about people "blaming it *on* you," but you have the right to blame him *for* saying that. In *A Little Learning* Evelyn Waugh wrote "I blame it *on* heredity," a transgression certainly in keeping with his title. We can lay, put or place the blame *on* Waugh, and the blame can fall *on* him.

BLOCKADE—It is "blockade *of* Berlin," "blockade *of* Gaza," not *against* (even though *against* is authorized by Benson, 35) or *on*. Perhaps *against* has come into use by analogy with "bulwark *against*."

BORED—Aren't we all getting bored to death (or at least to tears) by hearing "bored *of*" all the time? Yet in 1967 "bored" was not even listed in Frederick Wood's comprehensive *English Prepositional Idioms.* The expression "bored *of*" (rather than "bored *with*" or "bored *by*") seems therefore to be of fairly recent vintage. As I've already suggested, "bored *of*" may be modelled on the related "tired *of*." Although "bored *with*" appears to be holding its own at the moment, the parody of Tolkien entitled "Bored of the Rings" can be counted on to establish "bored *of*" even more firmly in popular usage.

"Bored *of*" has even been printed as part of a headline in a major national newspaper. On January 8, 2011 (a day that will forever live in infamy) *The Globe and Mail*, reporting on the "drag of being famous," referred to a film director "who's so bored *of* it all." In his English translation (2012) of Flaubert's *Madame Bovary,* Adam Thorpe professed to "use only pre-1857 vocabulary and expressions," but certainly missed the boat by opting to employ "bored *of*." And a regular *TLS* column recently solicited "examples of grammatical malfunction, by people who ought to know better, in publications that pride themselves on seriousness." One submission read: "We all love Maigret, but it seems we are bored *of* reading about his canny crime-busting." This entry was cited from the same column in an earlier issue of the *TLS*.

Clive James takes a charitable view: "If "bored *of*" should succeed in replacing "bored *with*" there will be no real call to object, except from nostalgia: "of" does the job at least as well as "with" and anyway such changes have happened in the spoken language since the beginning" (*Cultural Amnesia* (2008), 384). Can we then soon expect to be bored to death by "bored *of* it"?

BORN—"My love of the outdoors was born *of* holidays with my family." Not "born *out of*" which probably arises from a confusion with "borne *out*" in the sense of "confirmed" or "corroborated." However, "born *out of*" can be used if you are referring to "wedlock."

BREAK (n. v.)—Tired people take "a welcome break *from* work" but the rebellious make "a clean break *with* (not *from*) the past." An indiscreet or undiplomatic remark may precipitate "a break *in* the conversation." You can break either "*from* tradition" or "*with* tradition."

BUILD (v.)—"He built *on* (not *off* or *off of*) his past achievements as a star hockey player."

CARE (v.)—"I don't care *about* (take an interest in) his opinions," "I don't care *about* (worry *about*) him," "I don't care *for* (like) him," "I don't care *for* (look after) him, the nurse does."

CAREFUL—Earlier grammarians condemned "careful *with*" as ungrammatical, but "careful *with*" is slowly supplanting "careful *of*." Who would say "be careful *of* that loaded gun"? Indeed the *OED* describes *of* in a sentence like "be careful *of* the horses" as archaic.

CATCH (v.)—A house "catches fire," the catch being that it does not catch *on* fire. However, "set *on* fire" is good grammar but bad practice: once a house has been set *on* fire at the mischief-making hands of an arsonist, it remains *on* fire until the firefighters extinguish it.

CATER—"Cater *for* or "cater *to*"? "Cater *for*" means to provide for some need, interest or (commonly) a staple like food or water. It can also mean "to take into account," "to make allowances *for*." "Cater *to*," however, has the disapproving or pejorative sense of "to pander *to*": "Reality shows on TV cater *to* the lowest-level tastes of the audience."

In American English "cater *to*" is nearly twice as common as "cater *for*."

CAUSE (n.)—If "cause" means "the basis or reason for an action or response" then use *for*: "There is absolutely no cause *for* alarm"; if "cause" means "the producer of an effect, result or consequence" then use *of*: "Police are investigating the cause *of* death" (but note: "You have no cause *to* complain").

CENTRE (v.)—*On* or *around*? "Database searches suggest that the *on* version is, in fact, preferred by most people, and some commentators prescribe it. It's perfectly logical, and it's unassailable. Whether 'centred *around*' should be banished, though, is another matter. Surely it's possible to have a number of people or things drawn from all points of the compass toward the centre of some location, but leaving space at the centre for whatever is doing the drawing. And how about circular movement around a central point? (Jenkins 27). By this reasoning Jenkins endorses *around* in the following: "The gathering centred *around* the pair of arm-wrestling tables," and "movements of the dance are centred *around* the belly." Greenbaum agrees: "The use of 'centre' with *about*, *round*, or *around* ('Many legends centre *around* him') is now so common as to be virtually established idiom, but still avoided by some careful writers.

Those who dislike the combination 'centre (a)*round*,' but wish to preserve the idea suggested by '(a)round,' may prefer to write 'revolve *around*' (121).

CHANCE (n.)—Whether this word takes *at, for, of* or *on* is largely a matter of idiomatic usage and/or stylistic choice. The first three are virtually interchangeable: "We still have a chance *at* success," "the chances *for* peace in the Middle East are slim," "tigers have a small chance *of* survival in the wild". *On* is limited to certain expressions: "I'll take my chance *on* it," "Honey, I'm free / Take a chance *on* me."

CHANGE (n. v.)—This word takes several prepositions: "change *between* this year and last," "change *for* dinner" (or "*for* the better)," "change *from* riches *to* poverty," "change *in* the weather" (or "*in* colour"), "change *into* ones pajamas" (or "*into* a butterfly"), change *of* pace (or "*of* diet" or "*of* heart"), "change *to* rain" or "*to* the metric system"), "change places *with* a pop star."

CHEAT (v.)—"He cheated *on* his wife; in fact, he cheated *with* his wife's sister."

CHOOSE—In the case of "choose" there are several prepositions to choose from. *From* is one (and is by far the most popular). Others are *among* (choosing *among* three or more alternatives), *between* (choosing *between* two alternatives), *out of, over*. Although apparently respectable, the use of *over* to mean "in preference to" ("it's not easy to choose one detergent *over* another," "if ever I had to choose *over* someone") has always jarred my linguistic sensibilities (it is not, incidentally, authorized by either the *OED* or Benson). *Over* is also used (rather loosely) to mean "regarding" ("China has to choose *over* the yen") and "more than" ("travellers can choose *over* three hundred destinations").

CLEAR—"I hope you are clear *about* (or *on*) your final instructions," "your argument is not at all clear *to* me," "all vehicles must stay clear *of* the main gate," "the location is clear *from* the information we've received to date."

CLOSE (adj.)—Four different prepositions depending on the meaning of "close." 1. "Near or very near": "I live close *to* the sports stadium," "after winning yet another title Federer was close *to* tears," "what she said was very close *to* the truth," "it's so small you can only see it close *up*." 2. "On intimate terms": "Friends close *to* (or, less desirably, *with*) the murdered woman are in a state of shock". 3. "Secretive": "Don Juan was not exactly close *about* his conquests." 4. "Miserly" (somewhat colloquial): "Shylock was very close *with* his ducats."

COLLABORATION—A report in the highly respected *Guardian Weekly* (May 6, 2011) refers to the collaboration of the University of Surrey "*with* the BBC *for* its recent project." No: you collaborate *with* somebody *on* (not *for*) a project.

COMFORTABLE—In the sense of "unstressed" or "not bothered" this adjective takes *with*: "She is comfortable *with* her own sexuality." Avoid the much less common *about* wherever possible.

COMMON (adj.)—"It's quite common *for* planes to be delayed," "acne is common *in* adolescents," "slavery was common *in* ancient Rome," "respect for grammar is common *to* English teachers," "she has nothing in common *with* her husband."

COMPARE—If you are noting the similarity between two things use *to,* as in the opening line of the famous Shakespeare sonnet: "Shall I compare thee *to* a summer's day?" But if you are noting dissimilarity as well as similarity you compare one of them *with* the other. One authority dismisses this "rule" as "having no underlying logic…. Comparing is comparing. It really does not matter which preposition we do it with" (Jenkins 33). "Compared *to*" and "compared *with*" are "indistinguishable in meaning," and when "compare" is "used without an object, *with* is the only choice: 'Our garden can't compare *with* theirs'" (Greenbaum 152).

"Compare *against*" is becoming more common (even Julian Barnes uses it). "Compare" in this newfangled sense has less to do with similarity or dissimilarity than inferiority or superiority, so, "measure *against*" or "stack *up against*." "How does the Lexus compare *against* the BMW?" In other words, "which car is better?"

COMPARISON—"Draw a comparison *between* these two books," "these two books invite comparison *with* one another," "*by* (or *in*) comparison *to* (or *with*) these two books."

COMPASSION—*For* is more idiomatic than *towards* in the following: "We should all have (or feel) compassion *for* sick animals." However, *towards* seems preferable in "we should show compassion *towards* sick animals" (or "be compassionate *towards*" them). Also: "We have a duty to take compassion *on* the poor and homeless." The Bible illustrates this use of *on*: "When he saw the multitudes, he was moved with compassion *on* them" (Matthew 9:36).

COMPLACENT—Standard practice is "complacent *about*." The use of *towards* (authorized, oddly, by Benson) is found far less frequently, and should be discouraged. So should *over* and *with*.

COMPOUNDED—Takes either *of* or *with*. *Of* for the mixing of two (or more) elements: "Little girls are compounded of sugar and spice," *with* for the mixing of one element with another: "When I, perhaps, compounded am *with* clay" (Shakespeare, Sonnet 71).

CONCERNED—"Large corporations are concerned (i.e., "have as their concern or interest") *with* making money." "Large corporations are very concerned (i.e., "worried") *about, at* or *over* not making a profit." "Large corporations are sometimes not concerned *for* (i.e., "keen to obtain or guarantee") the welfare of their employees." "Some large corporations are concerned *in* (i.e., "involved or implicated in") dubious practices."

Write "cause concern *to* me" or "be of concern *to* me," not "*for* me." To be "a concern *for* me" is acceptable.

Headline: "The Bank of Canada expresses concern *for* household debt." *About* or *over* (even *at*) should be used instead of *for*.

CONDOLENCES—"The Prime Minister voiced condolences *for* the victims' families." No, "he offered (extended, expressed) condolences *to* the victims' families." "I send you sincere condolences *for* the death of your wife." No, "I send you sincere condolences *on* the death of your wife."

CONFIDENT—*About* and *of* are pretty well interchangeable: "They are confident *about* (or *of*) a better future." *In* can often be used: "Try and be confident *in* your own abilities." *To* (not authorized by Benson) should definitely be avoided: "I don't feel confident *to* speak in front of an audience," "the team is confident *to* win."

CONFUSED—We can be confused *about, by* or *over* something, but *about* and *over* seem to stress the person being confused, *by* the specific source of the confusion. "He is confused *about* gay marriage," but "the raccoon was confused *by* the car's headlights." "Confused" in the sense of "not properly distinguishing" takes *with*: "He always confused me *with* my brother."

CONGRATULATE—According to the *OED* a now obsolete use of "congratulate" was "to rejoice along *with* another *for* or *on* a thing." In the sense of "felicitate" (cf. the French "féliciter") it formerly took *for* (or even *about* or *in*) but now takes *on* or *upon* (or should, because *for* is creeping back in).

CONGRATULATIONS—You offer congratulations *to* a friend *on* winning the prize (not "*for* winning"). Yet it seems that nowadays *for* is increasingly, especially in North America, invading the space previously occupied by *on*. Many authorities, including Benson, do not (also in the case of "congratulate") sanction *for* as an alternative to *on*. Please avoid pronouncing the word as "congradgulations."

CONNECTED—From a respectable newspaper: "The train has connected London *with* Birmingham." Instead of *with* ("associated") write *to* ("linked"). Alternatively, write "connected London and Birmingham."

CONNECTION—Write "*in* connection *with*" rather than "*in* connection *to*" especially in regard to people.

CONSENSUS—"There is no consensus *among* the experts *on* what to do *about* the problem."

CONSIDERATION—"*In* consideration *of*" and "*out of* consideration *for*" are frequently confused. The first phrase means "*in* view *of*" or "*on* account *of*" or "*in* return (or recompense) *for*." Examples: "We cancelled the trip *in* consideration *of* the bad weather," "she was given the award *in* consideration *of* her outstanding achievements." "Consideration" in the second phrase means, more specifically, "concern," "courtesy," "kindness." Example: "We didn't mention her mother's death *out of* consideration *for* her feelings." When "consideration" means "thought" or "reflection" it takes *to*: "I promise to give serious consideration *to* your request."

CONSIST—If "consist" means "composed *of*" use *of*: "Does not our lives consist *of* the four elements?" (*Twelfth Night* 2.3.10). *From* and *out of* are now obsolete. If it means "equivalent *to*" or "have as its being or essence " use *in*: "*In* her, consists my happiness, and thine" (*Richard III* 4.4.406).

CONSTRAINT—"Feminists are aware of the constraints *of* female sexuality" does not mean the same as "feminists are aware of the constraints *on* female sexuality."

CONSUMED—If "consumed" (in the sense of "eaten up" or "devoured") tends towards the literal then *by* is preferred ("a house consumed *by* fire," "salmon consumed *by* killer whales"). If it tends towards the metaphorical (i.e., in the case of being eaten up by jealousy, spite or passion) then *by* or *with* are equally acceptable. Shakespeare uses "consumed *with* fire" three times (four if we count a line in sonnet 73), but T. S. Eliot writes: "We only live, only suspire, / Consumed *by* either fire or fire" ("Little Gidding," IV). Statistics suggest that *by* is much more frequently used, nowadays, than *with* (curiously, Benson authorizes only the latter).

CONTINUE—"She continued reading," "she continued *by* reading the list of names," "she continued [*on*] *with* her reading," "she continued *to* read," "she continued [*on*] *to* the next village." In "continue *on*" the preposition is used as an intensifier and is therefore optional, whereas, for example, "carry *on*" and "soldier *on*" are phrasal verbs and must always retain the *on* to complete the meaning.

CONTRAST (n. v.)—We contrast one thing *with* another thing: "She contrasted her garden *with* mine." One thing contrasts *with* another: "Her garden contrasts *with* mine." As a noun, "contrast" can be used with *to* or *with*: "The contrast *to* (or *with*) my garden was remarkable" (not "*from* my garden"). "The contrast *between* the two gardens" is also permissible. Quite impermissible is "contrast *against*."

Standard collocations: "*by* contrast *with*" and "*in* contrast *to* (not "*by* contrast *to*").

CONVERGE—Peter Mansbridge on CBC TV: "This week UN delegates are converging *in* New York." No, Peter, it's "*on* New York."

CONVINCED—The *OED* allows only *of*. But ample room can sometimes be found for *about* and *by*. "I am convinced of the truth *of* his arguments," "I am convinced *by* his arguments," "Harriet was convinced *about* ghosts" (i.e., about their existence), "Harriet was convinced *by* ghosts" (i.e., by what they told her, as Hamlet was convinced by the ghost of his father that Claudius was a fratricide).

COUPLE (n.)—The imprecise use of "couple" to mean "a few" is informal, but if you use it in this vague sense don't forget to add *of* as in James Thurber's short story "A Couple of Hamburgers." "A couple hamburgers" is heard all too frequently in McDonald's these days, and even "a coupla hamburgers" (or Simon Gray's "a coupler cats") will not pass muster. But if you can stomach as many as three hamburgers go ahead and say "I'll take a couple more." Even better, "two more."

It is when "couple" is a pronoun that it takes *of*: "I will read a couple *of* stories," but when it's a determiner the *of* is omitted: "I will read a couple more stories." Since "couple" and "more" are already inexact to insist on the *of* here is "a bit precious... a bit like cleaning a muddy pig with a greasy rag" (Brockenbrough, 232).

COURTSHIP—This word presents a stunning example of misuse which, though probably unique, illustrates very well the endemic uncertainty surrounding the use of prepositions. It occurred in a respectable newspaper reporting on "the courtship of Prince

William *with* Kate Middleton." *With*? What, were William and Kate planning, in concert, to set up a ménage à trois before their marriage? *Of* is the only preposition that will decently work here.

COVERED—A surface can be covered *in* or *with* oil, mud, snow, blood. Reserve *by* for the *agent* doing the covering rather than for the *material* doing the covering: "The body was covered *in* a blanket *by* a policeman."

CRAZY—In the sense of "infatuated *with*" you can be crazy *about* or *for* somebody "Crazy for You," the Broadway hit of 1992, is one piece of evidence that *for* is making inroads on the long-established *about*. The phrase "to go crazy" (meaning to go wild or be excited, like to go nuts or bananas) can take *about*, *for*, or *over*.

CREDIT (n. v.)—In many cases either *for* or *with* can be used: "He credited his doctor *for/with* saving his life." But sometimes only one can be used: "The finance minister claimed credit *for* abolishing the tax," "I credit you *with* more intelligence," "Haydn is credited *with* composing 104 symphonies." *To* can also be employed: "He credited his speedy recovery *to* his excellent health." "Andy Murray credits his progress *with* his improved fitness" should be recast as "Andy Murray credits his progress *to* his improved fitness," or "Andy Murray credits his improved fitness *for* his progress."

CRITICISM—As with "critical," avoid *about* if the more usual *of* feels quite appropriate. Sometimes *about* cannot be avoided: "What's critical *about* critical thinking?"

CULPABLE—Sadly, little distinction is made these days between "culpable" signifying "guilty" and "culpable" signifying "blameworthy." In either case there is no authority for this adjective being followed by *for*, *in* or *of* (historically *in* and *of* have been used, but are now tagged as obsolete). So, not "hikers' carelessness culpable *for* forest fires" but (with the advantage of one less syllable) "hikers' carelessness to blame *for* forest fires."

CULPRIT—Like the adjective "culpable," the noun "culprit" can be observed being followed by *for.* "A young boy was the culprit *for* the act of arson." Again, no authority exists for this use of *for* (nor of *of*). It seems that, idiomatically, "culprit" is never followed by any preposition.

CURIOUS—Henry James can write that Isabel Archer was "curious *of*" London but my advice (dare I presume?) is to stick to "curious *about.*" Banish "curious *for*" and "curious *in*" while you are at it.

DATE (v.)—"Experts date the Shakespeare portrait *to* 1623," "the Shakespeare portrait dates *back to* (or *from*) 1623."

DECIDE—You can decide *against* (buying) a car, decide *between* (buying) a boat and a car, and decide *on* (buying) a boat. In the latter case, were you to be crossing the Atlantic by sea at the time, you would be deciding *on* a boat *on* a boat. When, as Noam Chomsky says in his *Aspects of the Theory of Syntax,* "decide on a boat" means "choose (to buy) a boat" we have an example of what he calls "close construction" (what I have been referring to, less technically, as "idiomatic usage"); when "decide on a boat" means "make a decision while on a boat" we have an example of what he calls "loose association," i.e., the use of any number of variable prepositions. It is a major shortcoming of Prieur's *Writer's Guide to Prepositions* not to recognize this important distinction.

DEDICATED—"She dedicated her life *to* science," "the book was dedicated *to* her husband, "they dedicated themselves *to* helping the poor" (Benson 92). *For* (though not in the examples Benson gives) can be used when "dedicated" means "set aside *for*" or "intended *for*": "The additional school funds are dedicated *for* a new science laboratory."

DEFEAT (n.)—A CBC newscaster, reporting on World Cup football, referred to "Italy's defeat *over* Poland." One might ask: were the players airborne? Avoid *over*, taking advantage of other prepositions: "Brighton inflicted a defeat *on* Blackpool," "Brighton rejoiced in their defeat *of* Blackpool," "Blackpool went down to defeat *to* [or *at the hands of*] Brighton," "Blackpool suffered [or "met" or "met with"] defeat *at the hands of* Brighton."

DELIGHTED—"Supporters delighted *in* England's victory," but they "were delighted *at*, *by*, or *with* England's victory." Some grammarians like to distinguish between "delighted *at*" (an event) and "delighted *with*" (a person or object). *In* is to be preferred before a gerund, e.g., "She was delighted *in* seeing her brother again." More usually, "delighted *to* see her brother again."

DENOUEMENT—If you think of this word as meaning "ending" then you will probably choose *to*. The more pedantically-minded, recognizing its French origin (meaning "unknotting"), will probably opt for *of*. Surprisingly, *of* is favoured by a margin of five to one.

DERISION—Very tricky. Do we arouse (draw, excite, provoke) derision (scorn, mockery, ridicule) *about*, *against*, *for*, *of*, *on*, *to* or *towards* (Sarah Palin, Australia, the Oscars, hypnosis)? David Hume wrote about "derision *against* the ignorant multitude" and Jane Austen about "derision *for* disappointed hopes." We can say that some unfortunate was "an object of derision *for* (or *to*) all the bystanders." But, as with "phobia" and "revulsion," the noun "derision" doesn't really seem comfortable with any preposition latching onto it. One happy exception is the phrase "to pour derision *on*."

DIE—Does someone die "*from* cancer" or "*of* cancer"? Benson authorizes both, but there is no doubt that *from* is the upstart here, *of* having long been the standard preposition in reference to disease. The *OED* has the following useful list: "To die *of* a malady, hunger, old age, or the like; *by* violence, the sword, his own hand; *from* a wound, inattention, etc.; *through* neglect; *on* or *upon* the cross, the scaffold, *at* the stake, *in* battle; *for* a cause, object, reason, or purpose; *for* the sake of one; formerly also *with* a disease, the sword etc.; *on* his enemies (i.e., falling dead above them)."

Many older men die *with* prostate cancer rather than *of* it.

From continues to make inroads, even in phrases where *of* would seem more idiomatic, e.g., "die *of* a broken heart," "die *of* natural causes," "die *of* boredom," "die *of* fright."

"Die away," "die back," "die down," "die off" and "die out" are, it bears repeating, all examples of phrasal verbs, i.e., verbs followed by adverbs, not prepositions (for details glance back to chapter 5).

DIFFERENT—As far back as 1864 Henry Alford was complaining that "different *to*" was becoming very common. Taking his cue from a correspondent who noted an analogy with "distant *from*" and "distinct *from*," he suggested that if we substitute "differ" for "different" we recognize that *from* is the only allowable preposition: no one would dream of writing "differ *to*."

"By this argument," counters Fowler, "all words in the same morphological family should be construed with the same prepositions; e.g., we ought to say *according with* (instead of *according to*) because we say *accords with*" (213). Though he notes, and approves of, the prevalence of "different *from*" in British English since 1900, he observes that "different *to*" and "different *than*" (favoured by Americans and by aliens who habitually tell their abductees that "our emotions are different *than* yours") can be useful as a way of avoiding awkward or repetitive constructions. "Different *from*" is "the safest choice for serious writing," but "different *than*" has the advantage that it can introduce a clause: "He wears different clothes on Sunday than he does on weekdays" (Greenbaum 206). "To avoid disapproval," Greenbaum adds, "it would be safer to rephrase this as "different clothes *from* those he wears on weekdays."

Although "different *than*" has been "common in England for centuries and used by such exalted writers as Defoe, Addison, Steele, Dickens, Coleridge, and Thackeray, among others" (Bryson 142), the consensus nowadays seems to be that formal written English requires "different *from*" but "different than" and "different *to*" are acceptable in colloquial speech. See also Burchfield 212–13.

In fact, "different *to*" is becoming increasingly common in Britain. The usage "holds its own despite the condemnation of the snobs and pedants. It can probably be trusted to continue to hold its own, but it might be an advantage if it were allowed to do so in peace" (Davies 113). Davies was writing in the late 1940s.

By the by, I am much distressed by "much different," and "much different than" grates even more. "Much" frequently sets up the expectation of a comparative to follow: "much later," "much more gifted." Despite the example of "much obliged," we would not use "much" with most other words used adjectivally, like "much green" or "much delicious." So what's different about "much different"? I'm happy to report that users prefer "very different" by a margin of ten to one.

So let's unite in squashing attempts by "much different than" to muscle in on "very different *from*."

DIFFICULT—"The questions were too difficult *for* the children," "the castle was difficult *of* access," "the boss was difficult *with* his employees."

DIFFICULTIES—"I had difficulties *with* my teacher *about* (or *over*) the way he assigned grades."

DISAFFECTION—This slippery noun (not listed in Benson) causes great perplexity: the preposition chosen tends to be yoked to an expression regarded as synonymous. So: "disaffection *from*" mimics "alienation *from*," "disaffection *for*" parallels "dislike *for*," "disaffection *to*" echoes "hostility *to*," and "disaffection *with*" imitates "discontent *with*." If push comes to shove I would plump for *with,* especially when the intended sense of "disaffection" is loss of satisfaction with established authority, such as a government, a large corporation or a political leader or even with the general socio-cultural climate as in Eliot's reference (in "Burnt Norton") to London as "a place of disaffection."

Please use *for* and *from* sparingly after "disaffection" and avoid *about* and *to* altogether.

DISAPPOINTED—Students can be bitterly disappointed *about, at, by, in, over* or *with* their poor examination results (*about* and *over,* being the loosest, are not to be encouraged). *In* is preferred when talking about being disappointed *in* a person although *with* is equally acceptable.

DISAPPOINTMENT—Students can experience bitter disappointment *about, at, over* or *with* their poor examination results. These results will be a bitter disappointment *for* or *to* them.

DISAPPROVAL—"His disgraceful behaviour provoked disapproval *from* his family," "his disgraceful behaviour provoked the disapproval *of* his family" (i.e., they disapproved *of* him).

DISCREPANCY—"There is a glaring discrepancy *between* the two reports," "there is a glaring discrepancy *in* the report."

DISGUST (n.)—When this word means "distaste" or "revulsion," it takes *for.* "Many people feel disgust *for* the bombing of innocent civilians." When, more usually, it means moral disapprobation it takes either *at* (disgust *at* something) or *with* (disgust *with* somebody).

DISGUSTED—"*With* is used when the disgust is excited by a person, or by some inanimate thing which is thought of as behaving as a person might: 'I am disgusted *with* you,' 'I am disgusted *with* the weather.' *At* is used of some kind of activity or occurrence: 'I am disgusted *at* your behaving in that way'' (Wood 200). When "disgusted" is used as a participle, it takes *by*: "They are disgusted *by* the bombing of innocent civilians."

DISINTEREST—Should you wish to spark controversy by using this word to mean "apathy" or "lack of interest" (instead of "impartiality") then at least have the grace to link it to *in*, not *for*.

DISPENSE—On a medication packaging I find this note addressed to the pharmacist: "Please dispense with the patient information leaflet." The poor pharmacist must be in a quandary: is he (or she) being asked to provide the leaflet *along with* the medication, or to prevent it falling into the patient's hands by getting rid of it?

DISPLEASED—A teacher can be displeased *at*, *by* or *with* a student's essay (or sullen disposition). *With* is by far the people's choice. The *OED* doesn't mention *by* at all, which is displeasing *to* me, but notes that *against* and *of* are obsolete.

DISSATISFACTION—Benson (104) authorizes *with* but also (far too generously) *about*, *at* and *over*. My advice? Stick to *with*.

DIVIDED (adj.)—Controversy in the States regarding spending led to this front-page headline in the *Guardian Weekly*: "Washington divided *by* cuts." We've all heard of "death *by* a thousand cuts" but in the headline *on* or *over* would have been preferable to *by*.

DONATE—*To* is utilized over twenty times more often than *for*. *To* tends to be used when money (or some other form of help) is given directly to some organization (like the Red Cross); *for* is used when the meaning is "for the sake (or cause) of" as in "donate *for* Japan" (i.e., for victims of the tsunami) and "donate *for* cancer" (i.e., for cancer research).

DOUBT—"The doctor expressed grave doubts *about* the diagnosis," "there is no doubt *of* (or *about*) it—he is going to win," "the evidence casts serious doubt *on* the truth of his testimony."

DREAM (n. v.)—Bollinger (1988, 238) distinguishes between "I wouldn't dream *of* it!" (a phrase "to foreclose an intention") and "I was dreaming *about* you" (when you are the subject of my dream). He notes that "I dream *of* Jeannie" represents the older usage.

"I dreamed *about* (or *of*) you last night" but "I had a dream *about* (not *of*) you last night." In some contexts *of* tends to express hope. Compare the following: "I dreamed *about* my trip to Venice" (a trip taken or planned), "I dreamed *of* a trip to Venice" (a hope or desire).

DRUNK—Followed by *on* or *with*, and less acceptably by *from*. *On* can refer to being drunk both literally and metaphorically ("drunk *on* whisky," "drunk *on* words"), but *with*, unlike *from*, tends towards a metaphorical sense ("drunk *with* success, passion, and power").

ECSTATIC—*About* is the most accepted and acceptable preposition, but *at* and *over* also pass muster and *with* is fast gaining ground (in my view a retrograde step).

EFFECT (n.)—"My speech had no effect *on* the audience," "my speech was *of* no effect," "I spoke *to* no effect."

EITHER—"The use of the preposition *of* is necessary when *two* or a pronoun follows. When a noun follows, the following constructions are used—either student will know the answer; either *of* the students will know the answer" (Benson 115).

EMBARGO—A country will "place (or impose) an embargo *on* certain imports" or "lift (or raise) an embargo *on* (or *from*) certain imports."

EMBARRASSED—"I was embarrassed *at* being asked to give a speech" "I was embarrassed *by* his outrageous conduct". Both these prepositions can be replaced with *over* (but not *of*). "Embarrassed" in the sense of being overwhelmed, as many are by debts, is followed by *with*: "The old lady felt embarrassed *with* all the offers of help."

Don't embarrass yourself by spelling "embarrassed" with only one "r" and/or more than one "b."

ENAMOURED—"The antiquated *enamoured of* [has now been] reshaped on the analogy of *in love with, taken with, fascinated with*: 'Everyone is enamoured *with* big, capital expensive projects'" (Bollinger 1988, 240). But not everyone is enamoured *of* "enamoured *with*," including Greenbaum (242) who finds that "the word is usually jocular, and is better followed by *of* than by *with*." I side with Greenbaum on this one. Of Shakespeare's six uses of "enamoured" three are followed by *of*, three by *on*.

ENCHANTED—"The audience was enchanted *by* her performance" (participial)," "they were enchanted *with* their new house" (adjectival).

ENDURANCE—"I don't have the endurance *for* marathon running, *of* marathon runners, *to* run a marathon." When Julian Barnes writes about "a truly Christian endurance to … daily provocations" he should have used *of*, not *to*.

ENEMY—"Enemy," "the enemy" and "an enemy" all take *of*, but in the case of "an enemy" *to* is possible, says Wood (223), "when the idea of 'enemy' is somewhat weakened, so that it comes to mean

'something that militates against,' or 'someone who is opposed to'."
We all agree, with Sir Toby Belch, that "care's an enemy *to* life"
(*Twelfth Night* 1.3.2). Shakespeare generally preferred "enemy *to*,"
not "enemy *of*."

ENGAGED—Newspaper headline: "Andy Roddick engaged with
gorgeous Brooklyn Decker." He may have been, and with good
reason, but "engaged *to*" is what was meant. "Engaged *to*" means
"having agreed to marry," "engaged *with*" means "having close
contact *with*" as some politicians have with voters and all of us
with problems. "Engaged *in*" means "being involved *in*" such dis-
parate activities as community service or drug-dealing.

ENOUGH—"Enough documentaries" or enough *of* [the] documentaries"? Answer: "The use of the preposition *of* is necessary
when a pronoun follows. When a noun follows, the use of *of*
limits the meaning—we have seen enough documentaries; we
have seen enough of the documentaries that we discussed earlier"
(Benson 118).

ENROL(L)—With "enrol[l]" *in* is most commonly used, and is
preferable to *for* or *on*.

ENTER—"He entered *for* (or *in*) the competition," he entered his
horse *for* (or *in*) the race," "he entered *into* discussions," "he entered
into the spirit of the occasion," "he entered *on* [=began] a challenging career."

ENVIOUS—As with "jealous," *of* gets the nod over *about*
and *towards*.

EQUIVALENT—As adjective: "*War and Peace* is equivalent *in* length *to* three or four standard novels." As noun: "One pint of beer is the equivalent, in alcohol content, *to* two glasses of wine."

ESCAPE (v.)—One escapes *from* danger, *from* prison and *from* a burning house. If the meaning of "escape" is "avoid" or "evade" then the preposition is dropped, e.g., to escape, suspicion, detection, or punishment. Also: "John escaped the fate of his brothers who were forced to go to war." Benson (121) provides this distinction: "to escape *from* the police" means "to escape *from* police custody," whereas "to escape the police" means" to elude the police without being caught."

EXCEPTION—By all means take exception *to* (i.e., resent) an insulting remark about the way you dress, but not *to* the person who made it, and not *with* the remark or the person (the unidiomatic "take exception *with*," like "take umbrage *with*," is probably modelled on the idiomatic "take issue *with*"). Note the phrases "to make an exception *to*" and "with the exception *of*."

EXCITED—*About* is by far the preferred preposition. *At, by* and *over* are acceptable, but the pestilential *for* (as in "the students are excited *for* the new term") is not. But you can be excited *for* the students, i.e., in the sense of empathizing with them or feeling excitement on their behalf.

EXCITEMENT—"I cannot contain my excitement *for* next week's hockey game." Wrong. As with "excited," use *about, at* or *over*.

EXHAUSTED—"Exhausted" (in the sense of "tired") takes either *by* or *from* (avoid *of*). "Exhausted" in the literal sense of "drained" (i.e., "emptied") takes *of*: "The tank has been exhausted *of* oil."

EYE(S)—"We kept an eye *on* the weather," "I turned a blind eye *to* his bad behaviour." Note these idioms: "make eyes *at*," "have an eye *for*," "take one's eyes *off*," "cast an eye *on*," "keep (or have) an eye *out*," "run one's eye *over*," "open one's eye *to*."

FAMILIAR—"Films are familiar *to* people," but "people are familiar *with* films." One thing cannot be familiar *to* another thing: pesticides cannot be "familiar *to*" our gardens," and shouldn't be.

"A news story about a little-known Canadian actress stepping into as role at the Stratford festival said that 'she is familiar to the stage.' That smacks of anthropomorphism. I think it might have been more relevant to let us know if the stage is familiar to her" (Blackburn 237).

FASCINATED—"One is fascinated *by* other people, or fascinated *with* or *by* things; those people or things then have a fascination *for* one" (Greenbaum 271). Neil Armstrong described himself as "someone who was immersed *in*, fascinated *by*, and dedicated *to* flight." Now there's a superb command of prepositions!

FASCINATION—"Do not write "people who have a fascination *for* power politics," which suggests that the people fascinate the politics rather than being fascinated by them" (Greenbaum 271). One can also talk about "the fascination *of* funerals" or "the fascination *in* going to funerals" (but not about having a fascination *in* funerals).

FEEL(INGS)—"He felt *for* (=groped) the keys on the table," "he felt *for* (=commiserated with) me in my loss," "he felt good *about* himself," "he had mixed feelings *about* the trip." To have feelings *about* a person or event indicates either a positive or a negative attitude; to have feelings *for* a person or event indicates a positive one exclusively. My feeling is that it's better to stick to *about* and *for*, avoiding *toward*.

FIRM (adj.)—Compare the following: "As a potential regicide Macbeth was not firm *of* purpose," "Lady Macbeth was firm *in* her determination to become queen," "the drunken Porter was not very firm *on* his feet," "Macbeth tried to be firm *with* those who opposed him."

FOB (see following entry)

FOIST / FOB—"You can foist something unwanted *on* or *upon* a person: 'foist these dirty jobs *on* me.' You can fob a person *off with* something spurious or inferior: 'I won't be fobbed *off with* that excuse.' You can also fob something *off on* a person: 'fobbing *off* inferior goods *on* his customers'; but you cannot properly foist a person *off with* something." (Greenbaum 285). As for *foist off on*, well, that is both "awkward and prolix": "The *OED* quotes Charlotte Bronte as having written *foist off on* but calls the phrase 'rare.' It is fairly rare today. It ought to be rarer" (Garner 297).

FORBID(DEN)—Simon Gray: "I never mind ... not smoking when I'm officially forbidden *from* doing so" (*The Smoking Diaries*, 51). If we are disposed to follow Fowler it should be "*to* do so": "Fowler judged constructions with *from* + *-ing* to be 'unidiomatic' (he believed them to be based on analogical uses of *prevent* or *prohibit*), but the tide seems to be turning in favour of them. While the matter is unresolved, however, it is probably sensible to use alternative constructions or the verb *prohibit* instead" (Burchfield 306).

FORTUNATE—"The human race is fortunate *to* have (or *in* having) antibiotics," not "fortunate *for* antibiotics."

FRIEND—"John is a good friend *to* me" means the same as "John is a good friend *of* mine." Also "I am a friend *of* John." You can say "he is a good friend *to* me" but not "he is a close friend *to* me" (say

[124]

"he was my close friend"). By the way, avoid saying "close personal friend." Do we have impersonal friends?

FRIENDLY—"She is friendly *to(wards)* me" (=she acts in a kind or friendly manner). "She is friendly *with* me" (=she acts as a friend would do). Note also the expression "that was very friendly *of* you."

FRUSTRATED—The *OED* (as so often) offers little help: not much to choose between "frustrated *by*" (participial) and "frustrated *with*" (adjectival). Both *by* and *with* tend to be used in reference to both issues and persons. Less common (and desirable) prepositions (*about*, *at* and *over*) tend to be used in reference to issues alone.

FULL—Normally "full *of*" as in "the chest was full *of* old magazines," but, as Wood notes, "full *with*" is used, especially in conversational English, "when the intention is to stress the idea of 'full' rather than the nature of the contents" (264). His example is: "There is no room for any of my books on that shelf; it is already full *with* yours."

GENEROUS—We should be generous *in* our conduct and attitudes, generous *to* other people, and generous *with* our money. If we are all three, it would be extremely generous *of* us.

GIVE—"The millionaire gave money *for* a new public library," "I'd give anything *for* a cold beer," "a good teacher will give generously *of* his time, and encourage his students to give *of* their best," "I was so lazy that my teachers nearly gave up *on* me," "the ground floor gives *onto* a patio," "she gave the letter *to* me."

GLIMPSE (n.)—"The bystanders caught a glimpse *of* the Queen" (not *at* or *from*). But: "The documentary gave viewers a glimpse *into* the life of the Queen."

GOOD (adj.)—One is often good *with* (skilled *in* managing) children because one is good (kind) *to* them. Healthy food is good (beneficial) *for* children. Some children are good (proficient) *at* getting what they want *from* their parents. Given proper musical training, some children can become quite good *on* the violin.

Also: "it was good (=considerate) *of* you to come," "he is good (=clever) *with* his hands," "my daughter is good (=co-operative) *about* keeping her room tidy."

Hugo Williams has noticed that "good" is replacing "well." When (in response to the question "How are you?") someone remarks "I'm good, thanks," as if referring to something more than mere health, he always says "Good *at* what?" When the waiter asks if a patron wants more to eat or drink, a common response is "No, thank you, I'm good" or "I'm fine." My admittedly ultra-proper grandmother taught each of us grandchildren to say, in response to similar questions, "No, thank you, I have had an excellent sufficiency." Times have changed.

For more than two centuries, Ben Yagoda writes, grammarians have been disputing the shades of meaning among "I feel good," "I feel well," "I feel bad" and "I feel badly." "The matter has not yet been resolved and does not look to be soon" (48).

GOOD LUCK—In Waugh's novel *A Handful of Dust* (1934) a character says to another "good luck *to* the excavations." Standard practice nowadays is to deploy *to* when wishing luck *to* a person, *on* (or *with*) when wishing it *on* an enterprise. Looking for examples on a search engine, I was startled when I came across "Good luck *on* your autopsy," a phrase which required a moment or two to puzzle out.

GRADUATE (v.)—"Graduated Harvard," or any other university, "is a common error; the phrase needs *from*. Technically, it's the institution that does the graduating—moving the student up a grade— and some traditionalists still hold out for 'was graduated *from*'. The 'was' is uncommon these days, but the *from* is not optional if we don't want to look illiterate" (Jenkins 65).

GRIEVE—"I grieve *at* (or *over*) your loss," "I grieve *for* (or *over*) the skiers killed in the avalanche." The use of *about* is fairly common but is to be frowned upon specially when it displaces the more idiomatic over: "What the eye does not see the heart does not grieve about" (Auberon Waugh). Proverbs should not be interfered with in this inept way.

HAND (n.)—"*To* hand" and "*at* hand" mean "available," "near," "within reach." On the other hand, "*on* hand" means "ready for use." "The idiomatic phrase *at hand* 'close by; about to happen' is sometimes expanded by the insertion of *close*, perhaps under the influence of *at close quarters*: thus *at close hand*. But *close at hand* is more idiomatic" (Burchfield 349).

HAND (v.)—A jury hands *up* a verdict to a judge, a judge hands a ruling *down*.

HAPPY—"George was happy *about* (or *at*) his daughter's rapid recovery," "George was happy *for* her," "George was happy *with* what the doctors had achieved."

HARK—"Hark *at*" is an informal British expression used to deride a just spoken comment as foolish, proud, hypocritical or inconsistent. "Hark *back to*" means to "revert *to*" or "evoke." "Hark *to*" means "listen *to*." Gospel writers, says Sam Harris, "insist that Mary conceived as a virgin (Greek *parthenos*, harking to the Greek rendering of Isaiah 7:14)" (*The End of Faith*). We certainly need a *back* before *to* here.

HATE / HATRED—You can show hate (or hatred) *for* or *towards* your enemies not *against* (in either case). You can have hatred (but not hate) *of* your enemies. But be careful: the phrase "hatred *of* your enemies" can mean your hatred *of* them or their hatred *of* you. After "hate" Shakespeare tacks on *of* (especially in the phrase "*in* hate *of*"), *unto* or *upon*—very rarely *for* (now the standard idiomatic usage).

HAVOC—Bad weather can play, raise or wreak havoc *with* the pitch, but it doesn't play, raise or wreak havoc *for* the players.

HEAR—"When can I expect to hear *from* you?" No problem there. But can a distinction be drawn between "hear *about*" and "hear *of*"? I think *about* is used when a person is being given some knowledge of a fact, *of* when simply being told of the existence of a fact. Compare "I heard *about* his death" (i.e., the circumstances surrounding his death) and "I heard *of* his death" (i.e., the fact that he died). Or note this exchange: "Have you ever heard *of* Victor Hugo?" "No." "Then why not come to the lecture tonight and hear *about* him."

In the case of polite refusals, *of* is preferable: "Can I repay you?" "No, of course not, I won't hear *of* it."

HELL-BENT—"Rafael Nadal was hell-bent *on* (not *for*) winning another title at Wimbledon. He was hell-bent *on* (or *for*) further success." Apparently the phrase "hell-bent *for* leather" dates from 1926: an American coinage, it conflates "hell-bent" and "hell-for-leather" and means "recklessly fast."

HOPE—Headline: "Canada's rowers have high hopes *for* bringing back boatloads of Olympic medals" (prefer *of* here). "She has high hopes *for* Jim" means "she has great expectations that Jim will prosper, succeed or benefit"; "she has high hopes *of* Jim" means "she has great expectations that she will prosper, succeed or benefit because of Jim." Note also: "Many Londoners put their hope *on* Arsenal winning the Premiership," "people buy lottery tickets in the hope *of* winning the jackpot."

A newspaper report about a medical breakthrough carried this headline: "A great hope *on* lung cancer." "Hope *on*" here is totally unidiomatic. A better wording would have been: "High hopes *for* new lung cancer treatment."

HOPELESS—"Sometimes I feel hopeless *about* my future." "I am absolutely hopeless *at* math." "My dreams appear hopeless *of* attainment." "I am hopeless *with* small children."

HYSTERIA—A Canadian journalist notes, as widespread, "the hysteria *for* the Harry Potter books." The use of *for* here is lazy and makeshift. *About* would be much better than *for* (and certainly preferable to *concerning*). In any case I opt for "hysteria caused (or aroused) *by....*"

IDENTICAL—"Identical *to*," though frowned on by the persnickety (including Frederick Wood), is much more common than "identical *with*," and can be used without loss of social prestige. If you really insist on using what Garner (348) calls "a cant phrase," you must say "identify *with*," not "identify *to*."

IMPACT (v.)—As a verb "impact" is more common in American than in British English. But Americans should avoid, for example, saying "road construction is impacting public safety" and say, even if it makes the sentence fifty per cent longer, "road construction is impacting *on*" (or, better "having an impact *on*") public safety."

IMPORTANT—Either *for* or *to* can be used, but compare the following: "It is important *for* us to eat well" and "your call is important *to* us."

IMPRESSED—Consider the following: "They were most impressed (i.e., filled with admiration for) *by* him," "The blast was impressed (i.e., indented) *into* the concrete wall," "The young men were impressed (i.e., forced to serve in) *into* the Navy," "If you don't impress (i.e., convince) it *on* (or *upon*) her now, you never will," "I was impressed (i.e., struck by) *with* her performance" (Prieur 115).

INCULCATE—"He tried to inculcate *in* his students a respect for others" (NOT "he tried to inculcate his students *in* a respect for others"). Also: "He tried to inculcate his students *with* a respect for others." This less standard use of *with* (roundly condemned by Fowler) "probably arises by analogy with *to indoctrinate* (a person) *with*, which is the better construction of the two" (Burchfield 390).

INDEPENDENT—Although Benson (who gives no examples) authorizes both *from* and *of*, *from* is about seven times more common (and sounds, at least to my ears, much more idiomatic). However, it has been argued that *from* should be used when we mean "not ruled by another country," and *of* when we mean "separate, unaffected by." So: "Ukraine is independent *from* Russia, "children should learn to become independent *of* their parents."

INFUSE(D)—*Into* or *with*, rarely *by*. Active voice: "Dickens infused a sense of humour *into* his novels." Passive voice: "Dickens's novels are infused *with* a sense of humour." Terry Eagleton, who should know better, once praised a book by saying it was "infused in its every phrase *by* a passionate humanism." Yes, "infused *by*" is admissible, but perhaps only when *by* is limited to the sense of "*by means of*."

INJURY—"The harsh tackle inflicted a serious injury *on* the footballer," "the harsh tackle resulted in a serious injury *to* (not *for*) the footballer."

INSTIL[L]—"You can inspire men with hope, or hope in men; but you can only instil it into them, not them with it" (Fowler 277). Quoting this with approval, Burchfield (401) adds: "He was right. In such circumstances the word to use is *imbue* or *infuse*."

INTENTION—"I intend *to* go" and "it's my intention *to* go," but "I have the intention *of* going (not *to* go).

INTEREST—"Few people have a keen interest *in* maggots." Say or write "in the best interest *of* the community," not "*for* the community."

INTERESTED—Christopher Hitchens writes about a sect of early Jews who "had become bored *by* 'the law,' offended *by* circumcision, interested *by* Greek literature...."(*God is not Great*, 2007). At the risk of disturbing the stylistic parallelism the third *by* should probably be *in*. Attempts have been made to distinguish between the two prepositions. The best (despite the suspect grammar) I've come across I found on the Internet: "You wouldn't say 'I'm interested *by* pop music.' It would have to be 'I'm interested *in* pop music.' It's something you have chosen to like. But you could perhaps say 'I'm interested *by* heavy metal, it amazes me how they can shout so much and call it music. To be honest, I'm more interested *in* drum and bass.'" Along these lines "interested *in*" can be taken to express an extended engagement, "interested *by*" to be impressed, piqued or curious (perhaps or normally by a recent event).

An author can be interested *in* avalanches but also be interesting *on* them should he write on the subject.

INVOLVED—From a letter to the *Globe and Mail*: "The federal government has a moral responsibility to be directly involved *with* health care delivery." My intuition is that *with* should be *in*. Whatever the meanings of "involved" (entangled, implicated, occupied, engrossed, embroiled) the *OED* opts for *in*, often tagging *into* and *with* as obsolete. As the *OED* also notes, a recent development has seen *with* reserved for a person: to be "involved *with* a person" means to have an emotional and/or sexual relationship. So: "The wife found out that her husband was involved *with* another woman," but "the husband found out that his wife had been involved *in* prostitution." The two prepositions here are clearly not interchangeable. For more on "involved" (and "involve") see Burchfield 412–13.

JUSTIFICATION—"There is no justification *for* her outrageous behaviour," but "there is nothing to be said in justification *of* her outrageous behaviour."

LACK (n. v.)—"It was lack *of* money that prevented me from attending university, but my friend John didn't lack *for* money so he was able to go."

LAUGH (n. v.)—The ambivalent "laugh" is tricky. Whether noun or verb, "laugh" usually takes *about* or *at*. However, the *OED* oddly makes no mention of "laugh *about*." It notes that *of*, *on* and *upon* are obsolete, and *over*, *up* and *to* "rarely" used. Yet *on* and *over* are nowadays often used with "laugh" as a noun, and less often as a verb.

About and *at* are sometimes difficult to distinguish—what's the significant difference, I wonder, between "nothing to laugh *about*" and "nothing to laugh *at*"? There are cases where *about* seems rather out of place: "We laughed *at* (found funny or amusing) his joke," "we laughed *at* (didn't take seriously) his proposal," "we laughed *at* (ridiculed, scorned) him." And there are also cases where *at* seems wrong and *about* right: "We laughed *about* our misadventures," "the inhabitants of New Orleans laughed *about* the hurricane." The nuances here are difficult to capture, but *at* may signal a relationship which is more specific, direct and immediate than the relationship signalled by the more generalized *about*. Perhaps this is an issue people can laugh over over [*sic*] coffee.

One can of course "laugh *out of* court" (but not by "laughing *up* one's sleeve").

LEASE—The British tend to opt for "lease *of* life," Americans for "lease *on* life."

LESSON—A *Globe and Mail* headline reads: "Seven Lessons *for* Raising Successful Kids." The preposition *for*, after "lesson," is usually applied to the object for which the lesson is intended: "a lesson *for* children, *for* beginners, *for* professionals." The headline could, and perhaps should, have read "Seven lessons *for* parents *in* raising successful kids."

By far the most common preposition after "lesson" is *in*: "a lesson *in* first principles," "a lesson *in* good manners," "a lesson *in* English" (though this latter example could be construed as ambiguous). But *on* is also found (though much less frequently): "He took lessons *on* the art of investing but preferred his lessons *on* golf." It would appear that *in* and *on* are virtually interchangeable, the choice between them largely a matter of personal preference and feeling for idiom. However "a lesson *in* forgiveness" suggests that "lesson" means "example" or "model" to be followed, whereas "a lesson *on* forgiveness" suggests that the lesson means "instruction" consisting of a definition or description of forgiveness as a moral category.

LINGER—Here in Canada TV meteorologists habitually predict, for example, "a cold front lingering *into* Manitoba." No, my good friends: it can only linger *in* Manitoba (assuming it is already there). If you wish to denote movement you must use, not "linger" (which implies stasis) but verbs like "creep," "spread" or "extend" (all of which can be followed by *into*).

Many of us, to prolong the enjoyment of the weather forecast, like to linger *over* a cup of coffee, a meal or a book.

LOVE (n.)—"Love *of*" (food, money, music, gardening, football, the girl next door) is still more common than, and seems idiomatically preferable to, "love *for*" these objects (*for* sneaking in on the analogy of "fondness or affection *for*." "For the love *of* God" (or "*of* Mike") leaves it unclear whether the love is going *towards* or *from* God (or Mike). Sometimes the context, as with the phrase "the love *of* his children," will clarify which way the love is moving. In Prokofiev's opera *The Love for Three Oranges* the Russian preposition translated by "*for*" is "k" which means "*towards*." So *for* is a less ambiguous translation than *of* would be in this case.

Soldiers sacrifice themselves *for* (or *out of*) love of their country.

LUST (n. v.)—As a noun "lust" can take either *after* or *for* (*for* being more common as in the title of the 1956 film on Van Gogh, *Lust for Life*. As a verb most people use *after* probably basing this usage on Biblical precedent: "Whosoever looketh on a woman to lust after her hath committed adultery with her already in his heart" (Matthew 5.:28).

MADE *Of*—in "the spoon is made *of* (or *out of*) silver" denotes composition, *from* in "steel is made *from* iron ore" denotes the source of a physical transformation. As for *with*, Benson (204) illustrates nicely: "A stew can be made *with* vegetables" (i.e., vegetables are not the only ingredient used); "a stew can be made *of* (or *out of*) vegetables" (i.e., vegetables are the only ingredient).

MARKED—"The match was marked *by* the large number of fouls committed," "Julius Caesar was marked *for* death," "the voter marked his ballot *with* a cross."

MARRIAGE—Neither the *OED* nor Benson gives any guidance regarding the use of *of* or *between*. Shakespeare spoke of "the marriage *of* true minds" (Sonnet 116) and Blake of "the marriage *of* heaven and hell." Although *of* (the traditional usage) is far more extensively used, *between* is found in such phrases as marriage "*between* man and woman," "*between* close relatives," "*between* people of different races or religions." So why might "the royal marriage *of* Prince Andrew and Kate Middleton" be regarded as preferable to "the royal marriage *between* Prince Andrew and Kate Middleton"? I think that it's a matter of emphasis: *of* places the stress on the marriage itself, *between* on the differences, real or supposed, of the two being conjoined. When the differences are thus accentuated, there's often a sense that the marriage (literal or metaphorical) is somehow illegal, inappropriate or unacceptable.

MARTYR (n.)—Takes (variously but not always interchangeably) *for*, *of* or *to*. You can be a martyr *for* (or *of* or *to*) love, freedom, truth, Jesus, human rights. But in P. G. Wodehouse's novel *Carry On, Jeeves,* Jeeves tells Bertie Wooster of an aunt who was "a martyr *to* swollen limbs." Substituting "*for* swollen limbs" or "*to* swollen limbs" would not achieve the same idiomatic result. Similarly, *to* seems the only possible preposition in the phrase "a martyr *to* migraine." Madame Curie can be called "a martyr *to* science" perhaps because her suffering was voluntary, whereas Giordano Bruno was "a martyr *of* science" because he was burnt at the stake very much, one presumes, against his will. All three prepositions seem to carry two meanings: "*at* the hands *of*" (implying victimization) and "*for* the sake *of*" (implying some form of self-sacrifice). The Catholic Church has produced martyrs who were victims of the Spanish Inquisition as well as martyrs who have suffered or died upholding their faith. Turning a conveniently blind eye to so-called heretics the Catholic Church itself only distinguishes between "a martyr *of* the faith" and "a martyr *of* charity."

MEET (v.)—Unlike Americans, Britons might wish to avoid saying "he will meet *with* John" yet still permit him to "meet *with* success or resistance" when he does so. However, John Wells of Cambridge University Library points to lines in "Walsingham" (a poem attributed to Sir Walter Raleigh): "Met you not with my true love / By the way as you came?" Such usage suggests that the American "meet *with*" may go back to Elizabethan English.

"I met her *at* lunch" implies an accidental meeting probably with other people present, "I met her *for* lunch" implies something planned and even, suggestively, an intimate rendezvous.

The phrase "meet *with* one's approval" doesn't meet with every-one's approval.

MERCY—Let's take criminals: we can find ourselves *at* their mercy, have mercy *on* them, show mercy *to(wards)* them.

MODEL—Better to say that "we model ourselves *on* those we admire" than (*pace* Benson, 215) "*after* those we admire."

MONEY—In refusing, truthfully or not, a request for money you might find yourself saying "sorry, I don't have any money *on* me" ("*with* me" is also in widespread use). It's alleged that "*about* me" is common in Britain, but I have not been able to verify this nor heard it spoken there even once (not getting, as it were, about much). The French say "je m'excuse, je n'ai plus d'argent sur moi," the Italians "scusi, non ho soldi con me."

MONOPOLY—In many cases *of* is preferable to *on* or *over*.

MUSE (v.)—The *OED* authorizes *about* (as in "he mused *about* the problem"). It also allows *of, on, over* and *upon* (but regards *in* as obsolete). Benson sanctions *on, over* and *upon,* but not *about.* In popular usage the rough order of preference is *over* (Thomas Hardy uses "muse over" in *Jude the Obscure*), *on, about, upon, of.* My feeling is that not a single one of these prepositions fails to sound awkward when used with "muse." Perhaps we should avoid linking "muse" with any preposition, reserving it for such locutions as this: "He seemed to be facing a big problem, he mused." Or get rid of "muse" altogether, as affected and precious.

NAME (n. v.)—"We named our son *after* my brother Jack" (British), "we named our son *for* my brother Jack" (American). Instead of "*by* the name *of* Jack" an "informal shortening" ("name *of* Jack") is "now emerging in the best circles" (see Burchfield 511).

NATIVE (adj.)—"The arbutus tree is native *to* British Columbia."

NATIVE (n.)—"He is a native *of* British Columbia."

NERVOUS—American usage: "She is nervous *around* strangers." British usage: "She he is nervous *of* strangers." Students might also be "nervous *about*" seeing their exam results.

OBLIVIOUS—*Of* or *to*? "Oblivious *to*" (perhaps modelled on "indifferent *to*") is threatening to usurp the traditional "oblivious *of*." British authorities (e.g., Greenbaum 489) tend to favour *of*, American ones prefer *to*. Both are condoned by the American Benson (226); however, Trask (an Englishman) concedes "you may use either, but, if you choose *to*, be prepared for objections" (200).

"Oblivious" means (as in its Latin root) "forgetful" as in "he was oblivious *of* his past failures". But nowadays it is more commonly used to mean "unmindful," "unaware," "unconcerned," "indifferent to," "uninterested." The *OED* calls this "now the usual sense" (and accepts both *of* and *to*). It remains difficult to determine which sense is intended regardless of which preposition is used.

Another ambiguity arises: you can unmindful of something because you are unconsciously not aware, or you can be unmindful because you are deliberately ignoring something, disregarding it, not paying attention, turning a blind eye: "The difference

is the substantial one between *not noticing* and *taking no notice of*"
(Amis 139).

Most people are not bothered by this array of ambiguities.
Not Amis's son, Martin, who describes "oblivious" as "unusable
through ambiguity," a class of words which, he notes, includes
"infamous," "brutalize," "decimate," "crescendo," "dilemma," "alibi,"
"avid," "optimistic," and "refute" among many others. He would,
presumably, be quite happy for "oblivious" be consigned and even
restricted to another of its meanings, i.e., ("attended by, or associated with, or in a state of oblivion") as in Shakespeare's "some
sweet oblivious antidote" (*Macbeth* 5.3.43).

OBSESSED—The millions of people who say they are "obsessed
with baseball" (rather than the insignificant thousands who say
"obsessed *about*" or "obsessed *by*") are to be warmly congratulated
on their feeling for language.

OFFENCE—For instance, "I took offence *at* her unkind remark."
The *OED* gives no advice on the preposition to be used, but I
had always assumed that such authorities as Benson were right
in plumping for *at*. Now I find many respectable writers saying
"took offence *from*," which sounds very strange to my ear. "Took
offence *to*" (increasingly seen in print and perhaps patterned on
"took exception *to*") is also to be avoided. You can *give* offence *to*
people, but not *take* offence *to* them. Sometimes you hear politicians saying things which are an offence *against* common decency.

OPPOSITE—Can take *of, from* or *to*: "*Of* is preferable when *opposite* compares two nouns: 'Mary's attitude is the *opposite of* John's';
'her attitude is the *opposite of* mine.' *To* or *from* is required when
opposite compares two directions or positions: 'they left in the
opposite direction *to* (or *from*) the one were taking'; 'our house is
on the *opposite* side of the road *to* (or *from*) theirs'" (Howard 295).
"Her attitude is *opposite* mine" and "her attitude is *opposite to* mine"

e omitted) are also possible.

("the" being omitted) are also possible. In these cases *of* is omitted, the word "opposite" changing from a noun to a preposition.

In the phrase "the opposite purpose *for* which it was intended" insert *from* or *to* after "purpose": "Too much elision is undesirable" (Burchfield 554).

OPTIMISM—*About* as in "I feel optimism *about* the future" is more idiomatic (and more common) than either *at* or *over*. The use of *toward* is to be discouraged.

OPTIMISTIC—*About* as in "I am optimistic *about* the future" is more idiomatic (and more common) than either *at* or *over*. The use of *toward* is to be discouraged.

OVERJOYED—Hard to arbitrate between being overjoyed *at*, *by* or *with* the birth of your first child. I'd plump for *at*, but *by* sounds only slightly less acceptable. Despite its growing popularity, I'd stay clear of *with*. Buck the trend.

PAINTING—An art-lover can have a painting *by* Van Gogh, a painting *of* Van Gogh and, had he been a contemporary, a painting *from* Van Gogh. All three could be the same painting.

PASSIONATE—Used in the sense of "enthusiastic" the adjective "passionate" goes best, idiomatically speaking, with *about* not *for* (though the two seem equally favoured nowadays). Until the middle of the eighteenth century *for* was used when "passionate" possessed the sense (now almost obsolete) of "angry" or "enraged." *In I Like It Here* Kingsley Amis playfully resurrects the archaic meaning: "His wife ... was frequently described as passionate without it being revealed what she was passionate about or at."

PERTURBED—*About, at, by* and *over* are all permissible, but *by* is by far the most common usage, and by far the most preferable.

PESSIMISM—*About* as in "I feel pessimism *about* the future" is more idiomatic (and more common) than either *at* or *over*. The use of *toward* is to be discouraged.

PESSIMISTIC—*About* as in "I am pessimistic *about* the future" is more idiomatic (and more common) than either *at* or *over*. The use of *toward* is to be discouraged.

PHOBIA—Coleridge confessed he had "a perfect phobia *of* inns and coffee-houses." *Of* (perhaps on the model of "fear *of*") continues to be the most popular preposition for "phobia," but confusion reigns: *about, against, for, over,* and *towards* jostle for supremacy (a character in John Updike's novel *Villages* confesses to a phobia "about" spiders). None sounds right, not excepting Coleridge's *of.* Advice? Try to avoid using any of these six prepositions, possibly by avoiding having or mentioning phobias of any kind.

   The BBI Dictionary of English Word Combinations (241) gives only *about. About* seems right for "phobic": "A sufferer from arachnophobia is phobic *about* spiders." ("Spider phobia" is a quite common term, but equally brief equivalents of, say, "agoraphobia," "homophobia" and "xenophobia" are not so handily available.)

PLACE (n.)—"I couldn't find any place *for* me at the table," "the state has no place *in* the bedrooms of the nation," "Père Lachaise Cemetery is the final resting place *of* (not *for*) Oscar Wilde, Edith Piaf and Jim Morrison."

PLEASED—Voters can be pleased *about, at, by,* or *with* the results of an election (*with* is by far the most commonly used). But in some constructions only one preposition is allowable: "She *was* pleased *at* finding her watch," "she pleased him *by* finding his watch." "Were you pleased *with* me?" and "were you pleased *by* me?" have radically different meanings.

PLEASURE (n.)—"May I have the pleasure *of* your company?" "Yes, of course, for I always take pleasure *in* yours." By all means write "I had the pleasure *of* attending the dinner" or "I had pleasure *in* attending the dinner," but eschew "pleasure *to* attend."

"Attending your wedding was a great pleasure *for* me," "it gave me great pleasure *to* attend your wedding."

POPULAR—"Rock music is popular *with* young people." *With* is five times as popular as the alternative *among* (yet "popularity *among*," oddly, is five times more popular than "popularity *with*)."

PORE (v.)—CBC's TV anchorman Peter Mansbridge once introduced a TV reporter by noting that she had been "poring *through* the numbers" in an economic report. Sorry, Peter, but rain can pour *through* the studio roof (as you might notice) but readers pore *over* documents, maps, written records etc.

POSSIBILITY—"Visiting you on Christmas Day is certainly a possibility *for* me as I don't think there's a possibility *of* snow."

PRAISE—"He had praise *for* his son," "he spoke a few words in praise *of* his son," "he lavished praise *on* his son," "he gave praise *to* his son."

PREFERABLE—"Football is preferable *to* (not *over*) cricket." Most authorities, including the *OED* and Benson, frown on the use of *over* instead of *to* in this and the following examples.

PREFER(ENCE)—"I prefer football *to* cricket" (avoid saying "*over* cricket"), "I prefer *to* watch football," "I watch football in preference *to* (not *over*) cricket," "I have a preference *for* football." Schoolchildren might have a preference *for* outdoor sports whereas physical education instructors might give preference *to* them, that is, in preference *to* (not *for*) indoor sports.

PRIDE (n.v.)—"I take great pride *in* my work," "I pride myself *on* my work." Avoid *about, for* and *toward* in either case.

PRIORITY—Not "with the priority *on* …" but "with priority given *to* …."

PRIVILEGE (n.v.)—"It's a privilege *to* be his friend," but "I have the privilege *of* being his friend" (not "*to* be his friend"). In the passive of the verb, "I was privileged *to* be his friend." You can privilege one thing *over* another, but you cannot spell "privilege" as "privelege."

PROBLEM—"Car drivers have a problem *with* skateboarders," "skateboarders are a problem *for* car drivers" (not *to*).

PROUD—Parents are entitled to say they are proud *of* their children but not to say proud *about, at* or *for* them. So no kudos to Martin Amis for writing "proud *about* it" in his novel *The Pregnant Widow*. Gordon Brown comes off no better: congratulating the British athletes on their successes at the 2008 Beijing Olympic Games the former Prime Minister is reported to have said: "I think the whole nation is totally delighted and really proud at everything that has been achieved." Delighted *at*, fine, but definitely not proud *at* (at least Mr. Brown avoided the cliché "justly proud").

"I am very proud *with* myself." Had the speaker said "*of* myself" he would have had good reason to be ("proud *with* myself" is probably a crossover from "pleased *with* myself").

Edgar Watson Howe: "Youth is not a thing to be proud of, but rather a thing to be grateful *for*." Mr. Howe may not be celebrated as a major novelist, but, boy, did he know how to use prepositions.

PUNCTUATED—"The chairman's speech was punctuated *by* quotations from Shakespeare," "the chairman punctuated his speech *with* quotations from Shakespeare."

PURGE (v.)—When "purge means "remove" or "get rid of" it takes *from*: "In Soviet Russia dissidents were often purged *from* the Communist party." When it means, more specifically, "cleanse" or "purify" it takes *of*: "The reservoir has been purged *of* accumulated debris."

PURSUIT—My local paper reported on a disturbing shortage of a basic material. The headline ran: "The pursuit *for* plastics." *For*? Surely "*of*." After all, "the pursuit *of* happiness" is a self-evident truth. A better headline would have been "In pursuit *of* plastics."

QUESTION (n.)—"There's no question *about* his liking you" strongly tends toward "he positively likes you," whereas "there's no question *of* his liking you" tends toward the opposite (Bollinger 1988, 239). Greenbaum (583) draws a distinction between "question *of*" and "question *as to*": "*Question of* is correct when question means 'problem' or 'matter' (*It's a question of money*) but question *as to* when it means 'doubt' (*There's some question as to her reliability*)."

REBUKE (n.)—"After the team's third successive loss, the manager administered a scathing rebuke *to* his players."

REBUKE (v.)—"The manager rebuked his players *for* (not *over*) their feeble performances."

RECOGNITION—"He gained worldwide recognition *for* his humanitarian efforts," "he won recognition *from* every quarter of the globe," "in recognition *of* his efforts he was awarded the Nobel Peace Prize."

REDUCED—There is a difference between a Persian carpet "being reduced *by* $500" and it "being reduced *to* $500."

REFLECTION—"The grade you received this term is no reflection *on* (not *of*) your true ability."

REGARD (n.)—"We must have regard *to* the principles of self-government." "He had high regard *for* the poetry of Philip Larkin." When you mean (employing compound prepositions) "*in reference to*" write "*with* (or *in*) *regard to* your last letter" or "*as regards* (or *regarding*) your last letter" (not "*as regards to*" or "*with regards to*").

RELIEF—"The rain brought instant relief *from* the heat," "they found relief *in* looking at their late son's photographs," "the news was a great relief *to* us" (examples from Benson 273).

RELIEVE—"The drunken police officer was relieved *of* his duties" (not *from*).

REPERCUSSIONS—Found more often than in the singular form, "repercussions" takes *from*, or preferably *of*, when the *word* means "*stemming from*" or "as a result *of*," and *for*, or preferably *on*, when it means "affecting" or "having an impact *on*."

REPLACE—"Replace *by*" or "replace *with*"? The usual rule is that *by* indicates the agent and *with* the instrument of an action (see *BY* in Chapter 7). But "replace" and "replaced" present an added problem (apart from the different meanings of this tricky verb), since it is not always certain who or what to regard as the agent. If I say "the Arsenal manager replaced Henry *with* Fabregas," then the agent of the replacing is the manager and the instrument is Fabregas; but it would be also possible to say "*by* Fabregas" since the agent (the manager) has already been specified. However, if I say "Henry was replaced by Fabregas," there is an ambiguity, because here it seems that Fabregas, as agent, is the manager, rather than the player substituted, so it would be better to say "*with* Fabregas" in this instance. Certainly care has to be taken when the names do not reveal who is the agent and who is the instrument. Again in a football context, "Jones replaced Brown" could mean either that Jones decided to take Brown off the pitch or that Jones came on in Brown's stead. In the case of non-human entities it is easier to establish instrumentality, especially in the passive voice: "Her silver filling was replaced *with* composite," "one preposition cannot always easily be replaced *with* another." Still, one reputable dictionary goes with *by*: "Ian's smile was replaced *by* a frown."

REPORT (n.)—"You can conduct an investigation into a matter, like a scandal or a crime, but the result is a report *on* or *of* your findings. You don't make a report *into* anything" (Brians 197).

RESPECT—We can show respect *to* the unfortunate amongst us, thereby having respect *for* them. For "regarding" (or "as regards") say "*in* respect *of*" or "*with* respect *to*."

REVULSION—One can have or express a sense of revulsion *against*, *at*, *from*, *to* or *towards* any instance of genocide, but, as in the case of "phobia," no preposition sounds quite right.

RISK (n.)—Some "risk" analysis is in order. As a noun "risk" can take *from*, *in*, *of* or *to* (not *for*, although *for* is becoming quite common in American English). Examples: "There are risks *in* travel, skydiving, climbing high mountains," "at risk *from* starvation, smoking, climate change" "at the risk *of* upsetting the apple-cart" "at a serious risk *to* her health, safety, children," "the escaped criminal was a risk *to* the whole community." *In* seems to be used in the case of some form of activity, and *to* when the stress is on what is specifically put at risk. The precise distinction between *from* and *of* is harder to measure. "Risk *from*" has come into use fairly recently. If you say that "there's a risk *of* obesity" you mean that obesity is the danger which is run; if you say that they "there's a risk *from* obesity" you mean that what constitutes the danger being alluded to is not the obesity itself, which is present already, but its possible consequences (e.g., diabetes). The observation (made in 1982) that "more people are at risk *from* AIDS" than is commonly supposed, suggests that they are in danger of catching the disease, not that they already have it and are facing its nefarious consequences. Perhaps the writer should have used *of* in this context.

ROUGH—"King Lear was very rough (i.e., not gentle) *on* his three daughters," "it was very rough (i.e., difficult) *on* him, the way they treated him," "he was very rough (i.e., abusive, violent) *with* the soldier he found hanging Cordelia," "some critics were very rough (harsh, hypercritical) *on* Shakespeare for giving the play such an unhappy ending."

SAME—"It's the same *for* me" (i.e., "I'm in the same boat"), "it's all the same *to* me" (i.e., it makes no difference to me" or "I can't tell the difference"), "the same *to* you" (i.e., when responding to a greeting, wish, or insult). In "Nadal is in the same half of the draw *with* Murray" "as" is preferable to *with*.

SATIRE—In the seventeenth century it was customary to speak of satires *against* human folly (e.g., Dryden's "A Satire Against

Sedition," Rochester's "A Satire Against Reason and Mankind"). Nowadays it is much more usual to say "satires *of*" or "satires *on*."

SATURATE(D)—Prefer, as most people do, *with* to *by*: "Because of the heavy rain the football pitch was saturated *with* water." But: "To preserve meat you can saturate it *in* brine."

SCRUPLE (n. v.)—"He has killed once, he won't have any scruples *about* killing (not *to* kill) again," or "he won't scruple *to* kill again."

SENSITIVE—Benson authorizes both *about* and *to*, but "sensitive" can signify, among other related meanings, "self-conscious" and "distressed." Compare "he is very sensitive *about* the acne on his face" and "he is very sensitive *to* criticism *about* the acne on his face."

SERVANT—The title of Robert Frost's poem "A Servant to Servants" is ambiguous. Frost is referring to a servant addressing other servants, not to a servant serving other servants, i.e., a servant *of* other servants. In the "dramatis personae" of Shakespeare's plays we find "servant *to*" not "servant *of*," just as we find *to* indicating other relationships (mother, son, daughter, wife, friend). However, *of* tends to get deployed when, as in "a son *of*," an article ("a," an" or "the") precedes.

SHAME—"The lies he told brought shame *on* (or *to* or *upon*) his family," "he didn't feel shame *at* (not *for*) telling them."

SHARE—"Peter shares the same dentist *with* John" is not felicitous English. Alternatives: "Peter and John share the same dentist," "Peter has the same dentist as John."

SIEGE—"The Christians laid siege *to* Grenada" (not, pace Bettany Hughes, "Grenada was laid *to* siege"). *Of* and *under*: "When the Christians conducted a siege *of* Grenada" "the city was "*under* siege."

SIGN (n.)—helpful headline in a newspaper medical column: "The warning signs *for* frostbite." Shouldn't it be, more idiomatically, "the warning signs *of* frostbite" along the lines of "the signs *of* Alzheimer's disease," "the sign *of* the cross," "a sign *of* the times"? Granted, there is ample space allocated to *for*: "Aquarius is the zodiac sign *for* someone born on February 16," "higher employment numbers are a good sign *for* the economy," "Canada puts out the welcome sign *for* immigrants" (in the last two cases *of* would not be possible).

SIGN (v.)—In informal American English the phrasal verb "sign off" is sometimes followed by the preposition *on* to mean "approve formally and definitively" (as in "the President has signed off *on* the report"). According to Samuel Levin the expression apparently originated in Washington, DC. It puzzles him: "Since *sign off* means 'to cease broadcasting (or transmitting),' it is not clear how *sign off on* is to be taken as 'agree to' or 'join in on'." "There is," he continues, "a certain perverseness about the expression; it is semantically unsuited for the role it is being asked to play. Like other such arbitrary usages, however, it is currently fashionable and thus will probably have to be put up with for a while" (Levin 175). Levin published his book in 1998.

SOAK(ED)—"The football pitch was soaked *by* the heavy downpour," "allow the chicken to marinate *in* the broth overnight," "the floodwater soaked *into* the carpets," "the blood soaked *through* the bandages," "without a waterproof coat, I got soaked *to* the skin," "boxers must learn to soak *up* punishment." On the Costa del Sol you can soak *up* the sun (as well as the lively Spanish atmosphere).

SOURCE (n.)—I think most educated English speakers would lean towards saying "a source *of* information (or inspiration, pride, danger, irritation, what have you) than "a source *for*" such things. But that persistent interloper *for* seems to be making inroads, here as elsewhere, on traditional idiomatic usage. However, no objection can be lodged against *for* in the following example: "The *OED* is a wonderful source *for* historians of the English language."

SPEAK—Is it speak *on* or speak *about* a subject? Generally *on* is the more formal of the two. "He spoke *on* whales" implies a formal lecture or speech, whereas "he spoke *about* whales" indicates a topic that came up in casual conversation. And what of "speak *of*"? Perhaps "he spoke *of* whales" implies that he mentioned them in passing. For "speak *to* or *with*" see TALK below.

The ever-watchful Mr. Levin objects strongly to the use of "speak *to*" as in "speak *to* the problem of the homeless" or "speak *to* the sad condition of our national railways." To his ears "it conveys a subtextual sense of self-congratulation, an intimation that those who so speak regard themselves as linguistically au courant," turning up their noses at the usual alternatives such as "address," "discuss," "raise," "speak about" and so on (Levin 178).

SPEND—According to the *OED* you can spend money *for*, *in*, *on*, or *upon* new clothes. *About* it tags as obsolete. *In* is used much less than heretofore, except in expressions like "I spend much of my spare time *in* gardening" (and even here the *in* can usually be omitted). How to choose, then, between *for* (seemingly an American preference) and *on* (seemingly a British one)? Benson authorizes both, but I give the nod to *on* (or *upon*). Ponder this headline: "Navy spends $516 million *for* rockets." Surely principles of clear usage require the use of the preposition *on*, not *for*, in such a sentence: *for* here could imply the absurd notion of "on behalf of." Again, there is a difference between "what did you spend that money *for*?" and "what did you spend that money *on*?"

"Spend *for*" is possibly modelled on "pay *for*."

START—"They made a start *at* cleaning the house," "they got off to a bad start *on* their marriage," "the start *of* the race" (not *to*).

SWEAR—Rarely is a mistake made in the case of this verb, but it's instructive to observe the different meanings of the six prepositions which can follow it: "He swore *at* me when I trod on his toe," "I swear *by* Almighty God that I will tell the truth, the whole truth and nothing but the truth," "the President was sworn *in* at the inauguration ceremony," "obese people are advised to swear *off* alcohol and chocolate," "witnesses were required to swear *on* the Bible," "I think I've seen her before but I can't swear *to* it," "my friend insisted on swearing me *to* secrecy."

SYMPATHY—"English has two distinctive usages after the word sympathy. We say we have sympathy *with* a friend when we wish to indicate that we share her feelings or convictions in some respect. We say that we have sympathy *for* the friend when we wish to indicate that we have understanding and fellow-feeling for her in her current situation" (Blamires 2000, 164–65).

TALK (v.)—As with "speak" (and "chat") do we "talk *to* a fiend or "talk *with*" one? Some writers use *to* and *with* interchangeably (sometimes in the same sentence or paragraph), but some pundits discern distinctions: "*To you* and *with you* are both prepositional phrases. *To* is a one-directional preposition. It implies that you did most of the talking. *With* implies a joining together, a give and take. *To* is a soliloquy, whereas *with* is a colloquy. Either is correct, but the meanings are different, and *with* is just a bit more couth" (Strumpf 226). To American ears "talk *to*" suggests "a superior's advising or reprimanding" (Garner 640). Note that many a student in England has received a stiff "talking-*to*" from a "school-master."

The omission of *about* in "we are talking millions of dollars here" is colloquial.

TARGET (n. v.)—As noun: "The arms depot was the main target *of* the terrorists" (not *by* or *for*). As verb (in the sense of "single out"): "The ramshackle bridge was targeted *for* extensive repairs."

THEORY—"Theory *of*" seems at least ten times more common that "theory *on*" or "theory *about*." It is customarily used in cases where the theory is known, accepted or scientifically established (Darwin's theory *of* evolution, Einstein's theory *of* relativity), and in mathematics (theory *of* numbers, equations, functions, probabilities, etc.). However, there seems little objection to be lodged, for example, against "a new theory *about* (or *on*) evolution.

THINK—"Think *about*" if we mean "ponder," "think *of*" if we mean "bring to mind." Bollinger (1988, 240) contrasts "I'm thinking *of* leaving" (i.e., planning to leave) with "I'm thinking *about* leaving" (i.e., considering leaving). Compare "I don't think much *about* him" and "I don't think much *of* him." We can also "think something *over*," i.e., reflect at length upon it (but here *over* is an adverb).

"Think *to*" has several meanings. We can also think *to* (in the sense of "ahead") the future as well as think *to* (in the sense of "back") the good old days. "Think *to*," i.e., "remember *to*," as in "she didn't think *to* invite me," is possibly colloquial. "Think *to*" can mean "expect" ("I never thought *to* see him again"), and "not occur" (" I never thought *to* ask him to the party"). "Think *to*" i.e., "think *of*," is increasingly common in England, and is rightly regarded by Hugo Williams as "wayward."

"Think *on*," also in the sense of "think *of*," is biblical ("think *on* these things"), dialectical (especially Scottish) and literary: the ghost of Richard's wife, Lady Anne, tells her husband on the eve of the battle of Bosworth Field to "think *on* me" (*Richard III* 5.1.277). Cleopatra uses the same phrase (*Antony and Cleopatra* 1.4.17) as does David Crystal in the title of his book *'Think on My Words': Exploring Shakespeare's Language* (2008).

As in all matters, think *for* yourself. Whatever you can think *up*.

THRILLED—"She was thrilled *at* the thought of visiting Venice" (here *at* seems appropriate to express some immaterial idea or prospect). "She was thrilled *with* her new dress" (here *with* expresses some material object of delight, and *by* could easily be substituted). Also: "She thrilled *to* Bach's organ music."

TIRED—If you're "tired *from*" physical activity then you feel exhausted enough to need rest and sleep; if you're "tired *of*" physical activity then you are bored or impatient with it. You should not say that you are "tired *by*" physical activity, though you might be tired *by* supper time. In Sonnets 27, 50 and 66 Shakespeare wrote "tired *with*," not "tired *from*."

TOLL—"There was a huge death toll *from* the earthquake." "The toll *of* cats *on* millions of birds is horrendous."

TOUGH (adj.)—"Tough" has several overlapping meanings: 1. arduous, difficult, challenging, 2. painful, distressing, unjust, and 3. strict, harsh, severe. Some examples: "It was tough *for* him to get into university." "The government has vowed to get tough *on* crime." "The mother's premature death was tough *on* her very young daughters." "The US has decided to get tough *with* Iran." (Less common than *for* or *on*, *with* is generally applied to people, countries or some other form of agency.)

TRUE (adj.)—When "true" means "faithful," "loyal," "constant," "consistent (or in keeping) with" then it is "true *to*" (life, nature, habit, principle, form, type): as Polonius advised his son, "*to* thine own self be true." "It's true *for* me" means "I believe it to be true" (but the independently-minded Irish say "true *for* you" to mean they agree that what someone else has just said is true!). "It's true *of* me" means "it's true in my case." In the latter instance avoid using *for* or *with* (perhaps *with* is mistakenly employed on the model of "the same *with* me").

UMBRAGE—It is "take umbrage *at*" (i.e., be annoyed or offended) not "take umbrage *with*" (which is probably modelled on "take issue *with*" i.e., contest or dissent *from*).

UNDERSTANDING (adj. n.)—As an adjective "understanding," in the sense of "tolerant," can take *of* or *about*: "My wife is very understanding *of* my weaknesses," and "my wife is very understanding *about* them." As a noun it can mean "agreement" (usually tacit) as in "we have an understanding *with* our trading partners *about* what steps we have to take," or it can mean "comprehension" or "harmony" as in "he shows a good understanding *of* the issues" or as in "understanding *between* different races is always to be welcomed."

VARIANCE—"Your position is at variance *with* the facts" (not "*from* the facts").

VENERATION—"Muslims have great veneration *for* Mohammed," "Islam deplores the veneration *of* images."

VICTIM—We fall victim *to* Cupid's wiles, but are victims *of* them.

VIEW (n.)—Compare "he joined the team *with* a view to having more success," and "he took an impartial view *of* (not *to*) the situation."

WAIT (v.)—In informal English, Americans sometimes say "wait *on*" in the sense of "wait *for*." The British prefer to reserve "wait *on*" to describe one person serving another, as a waiter serves in a restaurant, or as a parent will serve a child, often with exasperated resentment: "I'm just about fed up with waiting *on* you hand and foot."

WATCH (v.)—You can watch *for* a bus or watch *over* your flocks by night, but you cannot watch *on* anything. So you cannot be caught watching *on* (should be "looking *on*"—you are an "onlooker" not an "onwatcher.") You can put your watch (n.) *on* a runner, but you cannot "watch (v.) *on*" a race—"watch" will do just fine.

WINNOW—Best to use "winnow" ("to extract the valuable from the worthless, as the grain is separated from the chaff") without the intensifier *out* tacked on. "Winnow *down*" is not admissible: it seems to model itself on the similar-sounding "whittle *down*."

WONDER (v.)—"Wonder" takes *about* if the sense is "reflect or speculate curiously," e.g., "she had reason to wonder *about* her husband's mental health." If the sense is "admire, marvel, be amazed or surprised" it takes *at* (or, less commonly, *over*): "every visitor wonders *at* the awe-inspiring vista of the Grand Canyon." In its gradual escape from inflections the English language often took time to settle on one preposition: it experimented with "wonder *of*," "wonder *on*" and "wonder *upon*" long before "wonder *at*" finally established itself.

Quiz #5.

In the following sentences, is the preposition correct or incorrect (misused, misplaced, redundant or missing)?

1. The subtitle of *With Malice Aforethought* is "A Study of the Crime and Punishment for Homicide."

2. There appears to be a general indifference *to* classical music.

3. The Queen is confined to the Palace: she is suffering *with* a severe chill.

4. The new computer has similar features *to* those of its predecessor.

5. "Human beings have no trouble falling short *from* perfection."

6. Guy Fawkes Day culminates *with* a fireworks display.

∾

Answers: 1. Crime *of* and, 2. *to* is correct, 3. suffering *from*, 4. features similar *to*, 5. short *of*, 6. culminates *in*.

CHAPTER 9

A DIP INTO SHAKESPEARE

There is a scholarly consensus that Shakespeare contributed about 1,800 words (and phrases) to the English language. Most of his lexical innovations were nouns (e.g., *addiction, assassination, bedroom, discontent, investment, luggage, moonbeam, pedant, radiance, watchdog, zany*) and verbs (e.g., *arouse, besmirch, donate, grovel, impede, negotiate, submerge, undervalue, widen*) and adjectives (e.g., *abstemious, bloodstained, deafening, equivocal, fashionable, jaded, lonely, obscene, sanctimonious, unreal*). A few adverbs also figure as products of his inventiveness (e.g., *abjectly, tightly, unaware, vastly*). But he did not add one single preposition to the fifty or so which already existed in his

"The *OED* cites more than 33,000 passages from Shakespeare to illustrate the sense of English words. About 1,900 of its main entries have first citations from Shakespeare. Although these figures are certain to over-estimate the impact of Shakespeare on the language there is no doubt that his vocabulary of about 29,000 words left English greater in all ways than it was before."

—Colin Burrow, review of Frank Kermode, *Shakespeare's Language* time. As we have seen, they had been in existence for centuries. He made use of all of them, with a few exceptions (though some of these he employs as other parts of speech): *alongside, across, amid(st), around, atop, inside,* and *outside.* He never uses *onto,* a word first recorded in 1715.

In fact, as is the case with the English language in general, prepositions (together with articles, pronouns and conjunctions) are the most frequently used parts of speech. Of the first sixteen most frequently used words in Shakespeare five are prepositions: after *the* (in first place), *and* (second place), and *I* (third place) they are *to* (fifth), *of* (sixth), *in* (tenth), *for* (fourteenth) and *with* (sixteenth). Not a single noun, adjective or adverb appears in the first forty of Shakespeare's most frequently employed words, and only four verbs (*be, have, do, are,* as well as *will* if we realize it also gets counted as a noun).

Because language in Shakespeare's time was still in a state of flux, authors were more or less at liberty to opt for any preposition they fancied: for example, the verb *repent* could be followed by *at, for, in, of* or *over.* The very meanings of prepositions differed: "In fact it is a characteristic of the various prepositions at an earlier period of the language that they all had a much wider range of meanings than we are accustomed to today. There were in the Elizabethan period fewer prepositions in any case, so each had to serve a wider function; as we have increased the number of prepositions by employing phrases and present participles in this role, so we have been able to restrict the range of meaning that each one has" (Blake 1983, 111).

> Although Shakespeare did not invent any new prepositions, he did employ them in phrases which he appears to have been the first to use: "*against* the grain," "*at* one fell swoop," "*beyond* my depth," "*by* the book," "*for* goodness' sake," "*in* a word," "pride *of* place," "fubbed *off*," "laid *on with* a trowel," "*to* the manner born," "wear my heart *upon* my sleeve," "hoist *with* his own petard."

Since meanings were so variable there was no sense of fixed or "proper" usage: no rule could be broken, no idiom transgressed, because there were no formal or formalized standards to be violated. Shakespeare had the good fortune to live at a time well before stern, fuddy-duddy grammarians had imposed their unbending notions of absolute correctness on the language.

On the English language, that is. Grammarians there were, but they were interested in the morphology and syntax only of the ancient languages of Greek and Latin, languages which Shakespeare had drummed into him (not, according to Ben Jonson, entirely successfully) while attending his Stratford-upon-Avon grammar school. Two passages in his plays may well express a lingering resentment at the labours he was compelled to undergo. One is the scene (4.1) in *The Merry Wives of Windsor* in which Sir Hugh Evans, the Welsh parson, tests a hapless boy, William Page, on his knowledge of Latin grammar, especially on the declension of nouns— William's knowledge turns out not to be impressively extensive. The other passage is a speech by the leader of a popular uprising, Jack Cade, after he has just arrested a member of the aristocracy and threatens to have him beheaded for manifold crimes and misdemeanours, levelling the following charge: "Thou hast most traitorously corrupted the youth of the realm in erecting a grammar school.... It will be proved to thy face that thou hast men about thee that talk of a noun and a verb, and such abominable words as no Christian can endure to hear" (2 Henry VI 4.7.33–35, 39–42).

Many of the prepositions Shakespeare employed have the same meaning (or meanings) as they do today (*above, along, below, beyond, concerning, despite, during, except, excepting, inside, round, till, underneath, until*), and therefore do not pose any problems of understanding. But many of his common prepositions have meanings not in currency nowadays: examples are *against, at, by, for, of, out, to* and *with* (each of which can be assigned eight different obsolete or current meanings or more). It is regrettable that many editions of Shakespeare texts make little or no attempt to gloss these deceptively simple words satisfactorily. For readers to be informed that *to* frequently means "compared *to*" can assist enormously in the task of understanding: "Prepositions are important words which can modify the sense of a clause and so need to be interpreted correctly" (Blake 1983, 113). This is especially true of prepositions now regarded as archaic or obsolete: *again* (in the sense of *against*), *betwixt, crosse* (*across*), *maugre* (*in spite of*), *sans* (*without*), *sith* (*since*) and *withal* (emphatic form of *with* when occurring at the end of a sentence).

As if the prepositions he inherited were not short enough, Shakespeare complicates matters by contracting them even further. So *of* becomes *a* (as in *time a day*), *from* becomes *fro* (now obsolete though we still use in the idiom *to and fro*), *in* becomes *i* or *'i* (especially before *the*), *before* becomes *'fore* and *over* becomes *o'er* or even *ore*. Perhaps because they were both commonly abbreviated to *'o,* the prepositions *on* and *of* were frequently confused. Shakespeare sometimes felt the need to dispense with prepositions entirely: *for* is omitted before *me* in "fear me not," and *during* is omitted before "which" in the line "which time she chanted snatches of old lauds" (*Hamlet* 1.3.51, 4.7.149).

The definitions listed in David and Ben Crystal's *Shakespeare's Words* provides, in parentheses, the modern preposition wherever it differs from the one Shakespeare uses.

What follows is a brief sampling of prepositions, especially confusing or ambiguous ones, occurring in Shakespeare's plays. For a fuller account of their use see Abbott, *A Shakespearian Grammar* (1966), 93–139, and Blake, *A Grammar of Shakespeare's Language* (2002), 177–200.

A- —Historically, as already noted, a form of the preposition *on*, "a–" is a grammatical particle commonly found, especially in nursery rhymes and folk lyrics, at the beginning of verbs ending in "–ing." Shakespeare uses this prefix copiously, e.g., "a-bleeding," "a-coming," "a-going," a-hunting," "a-sleeping," "a-weeping," "a-wooing" and many more (Shakespeare also uses "a–" as a prefix substituting for prepositions other than *on*, e.g., *at*, *in*, and *to*.) Without any dictionary meaning in itself, the hyphenated "a–" frequently affects the meaning of the following verb by stressing the repetitive nature of an action, the length of time it takes to complete it, or merely the ongoing process itself (as in Bob Dylan's song "The Times They Are A-Changin'"). Unhyphenated, "a" can also mean *on* (as in "afoot"), *in* (as in "nowadays'), and "*in* a specified state (as in "aflutter").

ABOUT—When Hamlet, addressing himself, says "*about* my brains" (2.2.599) he is not using a preposition meaning "in reference to." Using *about* as an adverb, he is telling his brains to get cracking on a scheme to trap uncle Claudius into revealing he was the murderer of Hamlet's father. Unaware of what we know today about the dangers of obesity, Julius Caesar observed: "Let me have men *about* me that are fat" (1.2.102). He means *around*. He wants *round* men *around*.

ABOVE—The use of *above* to mean "more than" has long been frowned upon. But Shakespeare uses it in this sense: "I heard thee speak me a speech once, but it was never acted, or if it was, not *above* once" (*Hamlet* 2.2.441–42).

AFTER—Hamlet advises Polonius to "use every man *after* his desert" (2.2.536–37). Nothing to do with dinner: *after* here means *according to*, as in the modern expressions "*after* his own heart" and "*after* a fashion."

ASLANT—This uncommon preposition means "*across* at an angle." Shakespeare uses it only once: "There is a willow grows *aslant* a brook" (*Hamlet* 4.7.166) is the first line of Gertrude's report on Ophelia's death by drowning. Despite the obvious difficulty in drowning, especially *aslant*, in anything as shallow as a brook, one theory proposes that Gertrude deliberately pushed Ophelia into the water and is trying to deflect suspicion by presenting the death in as picturesque a light as possible.

AT—Shakespeare will write *at* rather than *in* a large city, "*at* her hands" rather than "*from* her hands," "*at* full" rather than "*in* full," "took exceptions *at*" as well as "took exceptions *to*." *At* can also mean *under* and "at the value of," and is placed after such verbs as "envy" and "chide" where nowadays we would not use a preposition at all. The journalist who misquoted Macbeth's "*at* one fell swoop" (4.3.219) as "*in* one foul stroke" succeeded in getting three of the four words wrong: quite an accomplishment. Possibly led astray by the reference to "pretty chickens" in the previous line, the writer who perpetrated "*at* one fowl swoop" did, let's be charitable, manage to get three words right.

"*In* one fell swoop" remains a common misquotation, even in the work of celebrated writers (e.g., Martin Amis in his 1989 novel *London Fields*).

BEHIND—Many a smut-loving schoolboy has smirked and sniggered at Macbeth's "the greatest is *behind*" (1.3.117). But the word has nothing to do with posteriors: in this and similar contexts it means "still to come." Intriguingly, it can also mean the very opposite, "in the past," as in the last line of Sonnet 50: "My grief lies onward and my joy *behind*." So *behind*, at least in Shakespeare's use, belongs to that small class of words, known as contronyms, which manage to have contradictory meanings. Examples are "chuffed," "cleave," "let," "ravish," "wind up," "sanguine," "fast" and "blunt." *Behind* is, apparently, the only preposition belonging to that elite group.

BESIDE—When Macbeth says "we have met *with* foes / That strike *beside* us" (5.7.28–29) he means "miss us *with* their blows," not "fight *on* our side."

BY—The ambiguity of prepositions, in this case *by* signifying *near* (its original meaning) as well as *by means of*, sometimes misleads students into writing such sentences as "Romeo's last wish was to be laid *by* Juliet." It is also exploited by Shakespeare himself for deliberate comic effect, as in the opening scene of *Twelfth Night*, Act 3:

> **Viola** Save thee, friend, and thy music. Dost thou live by the tabor?

Clown No, sir, I live by the church.

Viola Art thou a churchman?

Clown No such matter, sir. I do live by the church; for I do live at my house, and my house doth stand by the church.

Viola So thou mayst say, the king lies by a beggar, if a beggar dwell near him; or, the church stands by thy tabor, if thy tabor stand by the church.

DESPITE—Shakespeare employs the five prepositional phrases *despite, despite of, in despite of, in spite of* and *spite of* almost interchangeably, showing no far-sighted awareness that only two of these (*despite* and *in spite of*) would be regarded as standard English today—even these two, perhaps in part because of his shilly-shallying, often get hopelessly confused.

IN—*In* (like *for*) has a wide range of meanings. *In* can mean *about, at, because of, by, during, into, of, on, while* and *within*. For example, when Macbeth reflects that "our fears *in* Banquo stick deep" (3.1.49) we would prefer to substitute *about* or *of*. Shakespeare sometimes falls into redundancy with this preposition: "*in* what enormity is Martius poor *in*" (*Coriolanus* 2.1.16–17) and "the scene / *Wherein* we play *in*" (*As You Like It* 2.7.137–38). Lynne Truss calls Hamlet's line "I am too much i' the sun" (1.2.65) an example of an apostrophe indicating a missing letter (in this case "n"). This is, she states, "a clear case of a writer employing a new-fangled punctuation mark entirely for the sake of it, and condemning countless generations of serious long-haired actors to adopt a knowing expression and say i'—as if this actually added anything to the meaning" (38). Perhaps the apostrophe was the printer's, not Shakespeare's.

IN/INTO—Like his contemporaries Shakespeare often confused *in* (position) with *into* (motion towards).

MAUGRE—Derived from old French (modern version "malgré") this now archaic word is used three times by Shakespeare. It means "in spite of."

OF—Shakespeare uses *of* in many cases where we would use a different preposition: "I wonder *of* (*at*) their being here together," "not be seen to wink *of* (*during*) all the day," "it was well done *of* (*by*) you," "I have no mind *of* (*for*) feasting tonight.

ON—This small preposition is casually introduced by Iago to exacerbate Othello's incipient jealousy even further. Iago insinuates, at the very moment he denies exact knowledge, that he has heard Cassio boasting of his conquest of Desdemona. Othello is desperate, insisting on finding out what Cassio actually said:

> **Othello** What? What?
>
> **Iago** Lie—
>
> **Othello** With her?
>
> **Iago** With her, on her; what you will.
>
> **Othello** Lie with her? Lie on her? We say lie on her when they belie her.—Lie with her! Zounds, that's fulsome.... It is not words that shakes me thus (4.1.33–38, 42–43).

Othello is mistaken: it is indeed mere "words" which have made him so distraught, precipitating the trance into which he is about to fall. It's possible that his first "*with* her" puts the stress on "her" but Iago deliberately shifts the emphasis to *with*, then to the much more explicitly suggestive *on* (= *on* top of) and finally, by means of the throwaway phrase "what you will," to any sexual position likely to find a niche in Othello's inflamed imagination.

While on *on*, one of the most quoted lines in Shakespeare is Prospero's "we are such stuff / As dreams are made *on*" (*The Tempest* 4.1.156–57). The line is misquoted more often than not: Humphrey Bogart misquoted it in his famous last line in the 1941 film *The Maltese Falcon,* and it continues to be mangled in media advertisements. Perhaps Shakespeare's *on* seems awkward if not plain wrong. When Philip Larkin alluded to the line in his poem "Toads," he took commendable care to quote it correctly, but he needn't have bothered: a critic thought that Larkin had written *on* only to obtain a rhyme for a previous word, "pension." That Shakespeare could write "what stuff 'tis made *of*" (*The Merchant of Venice* 1.1.4) confirms the widespread suspicion that he did not care a fig for consistency. To absolve him, it could be argued that *on* means "based or founded *on*," whereas *of* means "consisting *of* a certain substance or material."

OPPOSITE—As a noun *opposite* means "antagonist," as an adjective it means "antagonistic." There is one case where it might conceivably be parsed as a preposition: "the office *opposite to* Saint Peter" (*Othello* 4.2.90).

SANS—Like *maugre* this equally odd and archaic word is derived, unaltered, from old French. It means *without*. It occurs sixteen times in Shakespeare, four of these in one line alone, the final line of Jaques' "Seven Ages of Man" celebrated speech in *As You Like It* (2.7.138–65): "The last scene of all that ends this strange eventful history, / Is second childishness and mere oblivion, / *Sans* teeth, *sans* eyes, *sans* taste, *sans* everything" ("mere" = utter, complete, total). According to Trask, it is "now merely a joke word. Don't use it" (p. 251).

SAVE—This rather archaic or stilted word is, like *sans*, derived from French (*sauf*). *Save* and the preposition *but* (both in the sense of "except") differ from all other prepositions in that they are sometimes followed by the nominative case ("I," say, rather than "me"). In *Julius Caesar* Brutus addresses the crowd after the assassination of the emperor: "I do entreat you, not a man depart, / *Save* I alone, till Antony have spoke" (3.2.61–62). Elsewhere Shakespeare is just as happy writing the accusative ("*save* thee") as the nominative ("*save* thou").

TILL—Shakespeare uses *till* nearly seven hundred times, and *until* only eighty. Perhaps he found the monosyllabic *till* more versatile metrically than the iambic *until*.

TOUCHING—A preposition used by Shakespeare in the sense of *concerning* or *in regard to*, as in "*touching* that point" (*Measure for Measure* 1.1.83). But the suggestive connotations of touch and touching sometimes provide Shakespeare with an opportunity for light-hearted bawdy that he found irresistible. "*Touching* our person, seek we no revenge" (*Henry V* 2.2.174) is one possible example, and another might be Ophelia's "something *touching* the Lord Hamlet" (1.3.89). What that something was Ophelia may have had fairly direct knowledge of. As John Barrymore, that most virile of Hamlets, said when asked whether Hamlet and Ophelia were lovers: "In my company, invariably."

UNTO—As already noted, Shakespeare used *unto* in different senses, nearly five hundred times. But *unto* has long fallen out of fashion: Henry V opens his rousing speech at the gates of Harfleur with the famous line "Once more *unto* the breach, dear friends, once more" (3.1.1), but so unfamiliar have we become with this archaic-sounding word that we often substitute *into*.

WITH—When Antigonus is described as having been "torn to pieces *with* a bear" (*The Winter's Tale* 5.2.65) it does not mean that the bear suffered the same terrible fate as he did: *with* here means *by*. And note that Shakespeare wrote "hoist *with* his own petard" (*Hamlet* 3.4.208), that is, "raised or blown up *with* his own explosive device" not, as popularly misquoted and misunderstood, "hoist (or hoisted) *by* (or *on* or *up*) his own petard," that is "entangled in his own net, or, like a hangman, in his own rope." Even though he may not have intended the phrase to be cited verbatim, Tom Stoppard, in *Rosencrantz and Guildenstern are Dead*, has the Player say "Traitors hoist *by* their own petard."

The preposition *with* in Macbeth's "I have supped full *with* horrors" (5.5.13) is often replaced by *of* or *on*" (see the 2009 album by the pop group Romance of Young Tigers or p. 141 of Martin Amis's 1989 novel *London Fields*).

In *Titus Andronicus* 3.1.234 there is an unintentionally amusing stage direction: "Enter a Messenger *with* two heads and a hand."

WITHOUT—This preposition has long had the meaning *outside*, but it can still pose problems for the unwary or uninitiated. Romeo asserts that "there is no world *without* Verona's walls" (3.3.17) not because Verona's walls are globally extensive but because it is in Verona that Juliet resides. York puts this question to Aumerle: "What seal is that that hangs *without* thy bosom?" (*Richard II* 5.2.56). "Seal" is, mercifully, not the mammal but the stamp on a document hanging from Aumerle's neck. In *The Two Gentlemen of Verona* (2.1.), Speed informs Valentine of the "special marks" which make it plain to all observers that he is in love with Sylvia. Incredulous, Valentine responds: "Are all these things perceived *in* me?" Speed replies: "They are all perceived *without* ye," punning on *without* meaning both "*on* your outside" and "not *with*" you. Not satisfied with this degree of wordplay he goes on to use *without* in the sense of "unless."

By the way, Shakespeare uses *outside* mostly as a noun meaning "looks" or "external appearance," as when Viola says ruefully of Olivia: "Fortune forbid my outside have not charmed her" (*Twelfth Night* 2.2.18). I recall the story of a teacher trying in vain to define "leather" to a not-too-bright student. Exasperated, he sought for an illustration and yelled: "Hide, hide—the cow's outside!" Drawing himself up to his full height, the student replied bravely: "I'm not afraid of a cow."

Not puns worthy of Shakespeare, perhaps, but they might have tickled his fancy. Didn't Dr. Johnson observe that a pun, to Shakespeare, was the fatal Cleopatra for which he was prepared to lose the whole world?

~

CHAPTER 10
THE PROSPECTS

What are the prospects that our prepositions can be saved?

In 1864 Henry Alford concluded his *Plea for the Queen's English* with a general statement on the lamentable deterioration of the language. He drew an analogy between the debasing of coinage and the debasing of language, suggesting that there might have been a socio-cultural connection between the two. If Alford is right, we might, by saving our prepositions, be saving much else that is valuable in our culture. In 1925 a writer noted, in sorrow as well as in anger, that "the incorrect use of prepositions is an extraordinarily widespread failing with English writers and speakers, from which even standard authors are not exempt" (Webb 70).

The abuse and misuse of prepositions is part of a much larger linguistic crisis. There is no doubt that the English language is suffering severe strain. Like many before his time Cyril Connolly bewailed: "The English language is like a broad river on whose bank a few patient anglers are sitting, while, higher up, the stream is being polluted by a string of refuse-barges tipping out their muck" (Connolly 121). A generation later George Steiner issued this dire warning: "Unless we can restore to the words in our newspapers, laws, and political acts some measure of clarity and stringency of meaning, our lives will draw yet nearer to chaos" (Steiner 56). There are some who fear a new dark age is upon us, an age entailing the death of literacy. In the words of R. P. Blackmur: "Who knows it may be the next age will not express itself in words … at all, for the next age may not be literate in any sense we understand or the last three thousand years understood" (cited in Steiner 56).

The truth is you cannot read a newspaper or a magazine, or watch a television programme, especially a sportscast, or talk to teenagers without being confronted by atrocious barbarisms of all kinds. Without batting an eyelid people will cheerfully say (or, worse, write) "firstly," "anyways," "would of went," "I seen him yesterday," "between you and I," "myself" (instead of "I" or "me"). They will confuse "much" and "many," "amount" and "number" as well as "can," "may" and "might." They will assume "reticent" means "reluctant," and coerce "fun" and "happening" into serving as awkward adjectives. In their mouths, "issue" becomes the ubiquitous substitute for "concern," "problem," "question" or "topic." They say "jealous" when they really mean "envious," "less" (as in "less calories") when they mean "fewer" and "ironic" when they mean "coincidental." Nothing is ever "unique," always "very unique," and it's never "alike," always "exactly alike". "Neither/ nor" is brushed aside in favour of "not/or." Pairs, as Fowler pointed out, swiftly become snares: "every day" and "everyday," "compose" and "comprise," "flaunt" and "flout," "forbidding" and "foreboding," "ravage" and "ravish," "uninterested" and "disinterested," "alternative" and "alternate," "derisive" and "derisory," "regime" and "regimen," even "grisly" and "grizzly." Perhaps one can forgive a character in *The Sopranos* for saying he is "prostate *with* grief," but when a reputable journalist can refer to a "penile colony" things have come to a pretty pass: we can no longer talk of our well of English undefiled.

Greengrocers are commonly alleged to be very casual in the placing of apostrophes,

> "English is a fundamental thing. And, like, everybody should have a good level of it."
>
> —Attributed to the Chairman of the colleges committee of the Ontario Federation of Students.

as in "banana's" or "tomato'es." In *Eats, Shoots & Leaves*, her popular book on a "zero tolerance approach to punctuation," Lynne Truss takes particular exception to the way people, vaguely suspecting that an apostrophe is called for somewhere, will manage to come up with "it's" or even "its'" when the possessive "its" is all that is required. The rule, she thinks, is absurdly easy to learn, so if you write "good food at it's best," she froths, "you deserve to be struck by lightning, hacked up on the spot and buried in an unmarked grave" (44). It's no surprise that her book has many readers under its spell.

Ungrammatical English has been dubbed "Cringelish" because curmudgeonly sticklers for "proper" usage tend to cringe, twitch, wince or squirm whenever they come across it in written or spoken form. It produces a shuddering physical response, like that elicited when they hear chalk or a sharp fingernail scrape piercingly across a blackboard or even picture in their minds a young boy about to lick the frost off an icy iron railing. A good part of their reaction is caused by their nagging awareness that nobody outside their minority group of fusspots seems to share their reactions, leaving them to man the barricades unaided. For such "sticklers" David Foster Wallace, the renowned American writer who took his own life in 2008, coined the term "snoot," a label he sported as a badge of honour. He revealed that one of his fellow snoots "likes to say that listening to most people's English feels like watching somebody use a Stradivarius to pound nails," but Wallace rejoiced in belonging to a group that cares deeply about the way English is being "manhandled and corrupted by supposedly educated people": "We are the Few, the Proud, the Appalled at Everyone Else" (41).

As a vocal anti-"Trussian," David Crystal would disagree with Wallace's prescriptivist approach. "Every age," he writes, "has its pundits who reflect gloomily on the present state of the language, make dire prophecies about its future, and wish things were like the earlier golden age they remember so well. But there was never any golden age." He notes that "the only people who seem not to have been linguistically downhearted were the Anglo-Saxons," but then "they had other things to worry about, like marauding Vikings" (Crystal 2006, 156, 157). Crystal's view is that "languages do not improve or deteriorate. They just change, like the tides… Words come and go. Grammar fluctuates. Pronunciations alter" (157).

Let's not bother taking issue here with the questionable analogy with the tides, nor with the comparisons he draws in his most recent anti-prescriptivist book *How Language Works* (2007) between language and buildings (both are alleged to have "tolerances" built into them), and between "language maintenance" and "car maintenance," an analogy enabling him to pour triumphant scorn on those middle-class "elitists" and "quacks" who, without qualifications, write "repair manuals about language" and expect other people to abide by their recommendations. Reeling from this untoward onslaught, I would, as I cower, like to issue a modest caveat against Crystal's ultra-liberal stance to linguistic change, enlisting the assistance of two fellow middle-class, elitist quacks: "Not all innovatory practices … have equally valid claims to universal acceptance, and it is up to us, as speakers of a language with a long and noble tradition, to regard as a matter of extreme seriousness our obligation to pass judgement on the merits of the various claimants" (Levin 15). Or, as John Ciardi has written, "resistance may in the end prove futile, but at least it tests the changes and makes them prove their worth" (cited in Bryson 146). Levin and Ciardi appear to be in total agreement with Dr. Johnson's statement in the preface to his famous Dictionary (1755): "Tongues, like governments, have a natural tendency to degenerate…. We retard what we cannot repel, and palliate what we cannot cure."

Mark Twain, who was such a stickler for correct usage that he lugged a heavy dictionary when he and his brother set out for the wide open spaces of Nevada, was never willing to settle for what he called the "approximate" word. The difference, he said, between "the almost-right word and the right word is really a large matter. It's the difference between the lightning-bug and the lightning."

Yet Twain's dictionary probably didn't give him much help when he needed to decide which preposition to use. Modern dictionaries are not of much use either—just try finding out whether "disgusted" is to be followed by *against, at, by, for, toward(s)* or *with* and see how far you get. Largely because up-to-date examples of usage are lacking, even the venerable *OED* is short on practical guidance. The most sophisticated electronic wizardry cannot spare us from inaccuracies. William Safire's candidate, several years ago, for "the most significant solecism written by a piece of software" was this (from AT&T Word Processor): "The built-in spelling dictionary instantly alerts you *of* any spelling errors." Its failure to alert us to "errors" in the use of the preposition may be one reason for their spectacular increase.

A rule of thumb might be: when in doubt, abide by the conventional and traditional. Despite his proclaimed liberal stance on correctness, a stance which is tolerant of usages which don't involve loss of clarity, Crystal would never dream of himself committing the kinds of error—in spelling, grammar and punctuation—that he theoretically condones. His books contain no examples of the misused apostrophe even though, if they did, the misuse would rarely lead to a loss of clarity and understanding. He would never write that he was "bored *of*" the Trussians' authoritarian stance even though, again, no one would be baffled, though they might well be bothered, by the non-standard preposition. He extends to others a leniency he would not accord himself were he tempted to contravene conventional and traditional practice. In his own speaking and writing he implicitly espouses the supreme virtues of convention, clarity, courtesy and convenience, virtues extolled at the end of my earlier chapter on change (Chapter 6).

Nowadays, the conventional and the traditional are scarcely given their due. University teachers are often appalled at how little their students have been taught about English grammar. Since the sixties, stress has been laid, from the primary level upwards, on "creativity" and "self-discovery" and "self-expression," not on fundamental mechanics of the written language—spelling, grammar, punctuation—which are regarded as "too difficult." There is some evidence to show that many teachers lack the ability and the training to inculcate these basic elements in their pupils, who are thus sadly defrauded of their right to learn how their language functions.

In 2005, one observer suggested that educational systems should be putting more emphasis on grammatical structures, not less: "I can't imagine a medical school turning out graduates with no knowledge of basic anatomy, even though learning the parts of the body and their names is 'difficult,' and not very creative" (MacRae

13). Yet a few months later it was reported that the teaching of basic anatomy is so inadequate in some of Australia's medical schools that students are increasingly unable to locate important body parts. According to *The Weekend Australian*, one group of final-year students, when asked by a cardiac surgeon during a live operation to identify a part of the heart that he was pointing to, thought it was the patient's liver.

Granted, distinguishing a preposition from any other part of speech is not as important as not knowing how to tell the heart from another organ. Yet knowing what a preposition is might be seen as a modest step towards using it correctly. Even until mid-twentieth century, students in English grammar schools were still being subjected to an exercise known as "parsing." This almost forgotten term referred to the dissection of an English (and sometimes Latin) sentence into its component parts of speech: nouns, pronouns, verbs, adjectives, prepositions, etc. "At a major American university not long ago," it was reported in early 2007, "incomers into the English department were asked suspiciously by an older scholar to name them, to see whether they were fit to teach. But hardly any of the newcomers could pass the test—it is actually a silly one, in English—and failing was a badge of honour for the young" (Shippey 20). Most students obviously hate parsing. Not so Gertrude Stein, an exception here as in so many of her attitudes. The so-called "mama of Dada" made this admission: "I suppose other things may be more exciting to others when they are at school but to me undoubtedly when I was at school the really completely exciting thing was diagramming sentences and that has been to me ever since the one thing that has been completely exciting and completely completing" ("Poetry and Grammar").

> "I guess it is farewell to grammatical compunction, I guess
> a preposition is the same as a conjunction, I guess an adjective is the same as an adverb,
> And 'to parse' is a bad verb.
>
> —Ogden Nash, "Oafishness Sells Good, like an Advertisement Should" "

Students of Stein's generation were also taught to recognize when a given word was functioning as a noun, verb, adjective, conjunction and so on. In some schools pupils were required to learn all the seventy or so English prepositions by heart just as (in the days before the arrival of the pocket calculator) they learnt their multiplication tables. It is very doubtful that nowadays a majority of secondary-level students in Britain or North America could easily distinguish a noun from a verb, or an adjective from a preposition. If they were taught to do it, they might find the process, if not so "exciting" as Stein did, much less tedious and pointless than they imagined.

The same goes for handwriting. New research has shown that good penmanship is more than a quaint skill, a so-called "relic of a bygone era." The teaching of handwriting helps children learn and facilitates self-expression. Though by no means a hard-and-fast rule, students with good and fluent handwriting tend to produce better written assignments. With the invention of the typewriter in 1873, good penmanship seemed redundant. It may be making a comeback, thanks to the results of this new research.

For the young today, as for many of their elders (many of whom never read a book in any given year), the practice of reading for pleasure and enjoyment has given way to activities which place less emphasis on the written word. Despite the popular success of such works as the Harry Potter books, a culture of words is being gradually replaced, especially for the young, by a culture of images embodied in video and computer games. Digital technology is beginning to revolutionize the way young people think and express themselves. Text messaging and instant messaging, both of which rely on a lingo of codes, symbols, colloquialisms and abbreviations, are now beginning to affect the way young people use English in what is supposed to be formal writing, as in a term paper for example. The neuro-biologist Susan Greenfield is worried that this technology may be changing the way we think. Traditional education, she argues, enables us to "turn information into knowledge" by creating connections which help to establish what she calls "a personalized conceptual framework." "Put like that," one commentator has written, "it is obvious where her worries lie. The flickering up and flashing away of multimedia images do not allow those connections and therefore the context, to build up. In a short attention-span world, fed with pictures, the habit of contemplation and the patient acquisition of knowledge are in retreat" (Ashley 6). New research has shown that over-indulgence in computer games can have a deleterious effect on the young—on their learning abilities, their health and their "sleep efficiency," i.e., the actual time spent sleeping as opposed to the total time spent in bed.

The media, it must be said, are not helping to counteract the steady drift away from idiomatic expression. The other day I heard an eminent newscaster talk about reaction *about* (instead of *to*) a story aired previously. One gets a sinking feeling that any old preposition will do as long as it sounds more or less right. The more widespread this loose or casual approach to language the more, and (because of the speed of technological transmission) the faster, it will be imitated.

Why? Because a kind of Gresham's law operates in language as it does in the world of money: the bad currency drives out the good. If drivers are seen to run red lights, others will follow suit; if people litter public thoroughfares, then littering becomes quite acceptable; if cheating is recognized as a rung on the ladder of upward social mobility, then we all feel licensed to cheat our way to the top. Honesty, truthfulness, integrity seem, increasingly, to be outmoded virtues. As Jacques Barzun has said: "The language has less to fear from the crude vulgarism of the taught than the blithe irresponsibility of the taught" (cited in Nunberg 33)

So, if few of us care about the abuse of language, one can only fear it will go on being abused. When a respectable British newspaper, the *Daily Telegraph* as it so happens, prints "interested *by*"

> What is thought to be a decay of English in our time is, in fact, a decay in the brains of those who have not learned to manipulate English. Worms have made their homes in our brains and have eaten away the power of speech and of our thought. Some highly specialized worms have here and there eaten away the active voice or the prepositional phrase.
>
> —Richard Mitchell,
> *Less Than Words Can Say*

rather than "interested *in,*" some sticklers for "proper" usage may feel what has been aptly described as "a jolt of mental discomfort" (Blamires 2000, 159). The trouble is, not enough of us feel such or jolt, or are bothered by it if we do. It seems that many people are not bothered even when they are baffled by ambiguous or confusing usage. To write in deliberate and ostentatious violation of grammatical rules, to flaunt what is flouted, has, perversely, been defended as a mark of freedom and individuality and even of "being cool." For some (like Stephen Fry) it's fun to commit linguistic transgressions, to kick over the traces.

Citing recent research in the Netherlands, Miller-McCune reports that public signs like "do not litter" and "keep off the grass" can be counter-productive: "If certain rules are clearly spelled out, and you note that others have been disregarding them, you're more likely to break them as well…. It appears antisocial behaviour is contagious, and the more brazen it is, the more power it has to spread."

In any case, the real sense of grammar is perhaps becoming as alien to the contemporary mind as the real sense of sin, the latter as alien, it has been said, "as fetching water from the well or darning socks." Or, in the words of a piece of graffiti, "the days of good English had went." The result of widespread misuse is that even generally careful writers and speakers can easily repeat current errors.

Anything goes. "Coin brassy words at will," Ogden Nash grumbled, "debase the coinage; / We're in an if-you-cannot-lick-them-join age, / A slovenliness-provides-its-own excuse age, / Where usage overnight condones misusage. / Farewell, farewell to my beloved language, / Once English, now a vile orangutanguage." Nash published this poem (the last section of "Laments for a Dying Language") in 1962!

"The true enemy," Bob Blackburn has said, "is not the writer who makes a simple mistake. It is the writer who doesn't give a damn, who is ignorant of his ignorance or simply is comfortable in it, who is unaware of or indifferent to his destructive power" (Blackburn 26). In 1980 Blackburn started writing his columns in *Books in Canada.* They were collections of (and jeremiads about) "errors and practices" in the use of English which, he said, "had offended my eye and ear," describing his castigations of such "linguistic anarchy" as "personal, opinionated, quixotic, and quirky" (Blackburn 11, 13). He reports an eminent film critic, Clyde Gilmour, saying to him: "I suppose you know you are wasting your time, but by all means carry on." Blackburn conceded that Gilmour was probably right. Sticklers for idiomatic usage (whom Stephen Fry, in his famous 2010 video, rather unkindly describes as "pedants" and "a sorry bunch of semi-literate losers") may well be spitting against the wind.

But even though any effort to save our prepositions might also be thought a lost cause or a losing battle, let us not despair. Interest in language is far from moribund: The National Vocabulary Contest, a competition for high-school students, was televised in the US in March, 2007, and spelling bees have become so popular among the young that a documentary film (the Oscar-nominated *Spellbound*) has been made about them. Would a "preposition bee," I wonder, ever catch on? Could software be produced, along the lines of a grammar checker, to alert writers to the misuse of prepositions? Meanwhile, let us continue to encourage that small but stalwart contingent of sharp-eyed language-watchers, like Blackburn, who, standing on guard for beleaguered English, point out errors of grammar and idiom they detect in the newspapers and journals they read, as well as in advertising and the broadcasting media.

Finally, a story I'd like to share. In the spring of 2006, I glimpsed a review of a film entitled *The Preposition*. Heartened and intrigued, I scanned the first paragraph. One comment caught my eye: the picture was described as "frustratingly hard to care about." "Just my point," I said to myself, glad to have some ammunition in the fight to save a cherished part of speech. The bubble burst when I realized that the film was, in fact, called *The Proposition*, a kangaroo western "unfolding in the harsh outback of 19th-century Australia."

CHAPTER 11

WORD PLUS PREPOSITION:
A Tabulated Guide

Perhaps prepositions have always had a tendency to get hopelessly disoriented, losing their way amid larger and more imposing linguistic elements and structures—dynamic verbs, scintillating adjectives, monolithic nouns. One might forgive them the desire to escape from their shackles by gleefully exploiting the general confusion about which preposition is correct.

This chapter is divided into two parts. Part I is an alphabetical list of adjectives (adj.), verbs (v.) and nouns (n.) governed by a preposition (or adverbial particle) forming collocations of the type Noam Chomsky calls "close constructions." It does not, generally speaking, cover collocations (which Chomsky calls "loose associations") that appear to be dictated by the word or adverbial phrase following the preposition (as in "go *against* the grain," "go *by* bus," "go *to* the corner," "learn *by* trial and error," "learn *for* fun," "learn *from* experience"). These Benson (xv) terms "free combinations" which, he notes, "consist of elements that are joined in accordance with the general rules of English syntax and freely allow substitution." Nor does the chapter usually include stock phrases in which prepositions precede nouns (as in "*above* all," "*under* orders," "*within* limits").

Since it concentrates on those collocations which commonly lead to errors, it is not a complete tabulation—a much more comprehensive and detailed list, including useful examples, will be found in Part 2 of Frederick T. Wood's still standard *English Prepositional Idioms* (1967), in the *Oxford Dictionary of Current Idiomatic English* (1975), co-authored by A. P. Cowie and R. Mackin, and in the indispensable *BBI Dictionary of English Word Combinations* (1997) compiled by Morton Benson and others. Again, many verbs, especially those of motion, are followed by so great a number of different prepositions that there is no space to list them all here. A preceding asterisk (*) indicates a prepositional phrase discussed in greater detail in Chapter 8.

My sense, not one, I am sure, shared by everybody, of the currently outlawed preposition (which in time may become, as I have indicated, the generally accepted one) is sometimes noted in parenthesis. All the usages I frown upon, I wish to stress, have been found either documented in written sources or heard spoken by people around me or on radio and television programmes—not one of them has been invented (as is often the case in books on English grammar) for the express (or merely convenient) purpose of illustrating unidiomatic practice.

Part II comprises a list, alphabetically arranged, of those words (mostly verbs) which do not, in most cases, require a preposition but which are often accorded one, sometimes justifiably for stylistic purposes (clarity, emphasis, euphony). The intrusive and usually redundant preposition is provided in parentheses.

~

PART I

Adjectives, verbs and nouns governed by a preposition.

A

abhorrence *of* (violence, not *for* or *to*)
abhorrent *to* (a person)
abide *by* (a rule, a decision, not *with*)
abide *in* (a place)
abide *with* (stay, remain)
ability *at* / *in* (chess, not *with*)
able *to*
abound *in* / *with* (misprints)
abreast *of* (not *about* or *with*)
absolve (a person) *from* / *of* (duty, punishment)
abstain *from* (doing, not *to* do)
abundant *in* / *with*
accede *to* (a demand, the throne)
acceptable *to* (not *by*)
accepted *by*
accessory *to* (the crime)
accommodate (oneself) *to* (a situation)
accommodate (a person) *with* (a thing)
★accompanied *by* (a person)
★accompanied *with* (a thing)
accomplice *in* / *to* (a crime)
accord (v.) *to* (grant)
accord (v.) *with* (match)

account(able) *for* (explain, produce, be responsible)

account(able) *to* (a person) *for* (something)

*accuse(d) *of* (a crime, not *for*, *in* or *with*)

accustomed *to* (not *with*)

acquaint (a person) *with* (something)

*acquiesce *in* / *to* (not *under* or *with*)

acquit *of* (crime, blame)

activated *by* (revenge, not *with*)

adamant *about* / *on*

adapted *for* (purpose, nature)

adapted *from* (based *on*)

adapted *to* (ability, purpose)

addicted *to*

addiction *to* (not *for*)

adept *at* (doing something, not *with*)

adept *in* (an art or practice)

*adequate *for* / *to*

adhere *to*

adherent (adj.) *of* (not *to*)

adherent (n.) *of* (person or party, not *to*)

adjunct *to*

admiration *for* (not *at* or *towards*)

admit *in* / *into* (accept)

admit *of* (a solution, allow)

admit *to* (a crime, confess)

*adoration *for* / *of*

advance (n. v.) *against* / *on* / *to* (enemy troops)

advance (n.) *of* (knowledge, old age)

advance (n.) *in* / *on* (improvement)

*advantage *of* / *to* / *over*

advantageous *for* / *to*

adverse *to* (her wishes, not *against* or *from*)

advise (a person) *of* (inform)

advise (a person) *on* (counsel)

*advocate (n. v.) *for* (human rights)

*advocate (n.) *of* (policy)

affected *by* (her mother's death)

affected *with* (a disease)

*affection *for* (not *towards*)
affectionate *to(wards)*
affiliated *to* / *with*
affiliation *to* / *with*
*affinity *between* / *for* / *with* (liking)
*affinity *with* (kinship, not *about, for* or *to*)
afflicted *with* (leprosy, not *by*)
affront *to* (common sense)
*afraid *for* (a person, a person's safety, the future)
*afraid *of* (the dark, not *at, by* or *for*)
aggravate *by*
agree *on* (a price, a matter or opinion)
agree *on* / *upon* (a plan of action)
agree *to* (a proposal, action, settlement)
agree *with* (a person, proposition)
aggrieved *at* / *by*
agonize *over* (not *about*)
*aim (n.v.) *at* (doing, or a target)
*aim (n.v.) *for* (victory)
*aim (v.) *to* (do)
alarmed *at* / *by*
alert (v.) (children) *to* (dangers, not *about* or *of*)
alien (adj.) *to*
align *against* / *with*
allegiance *to* (not *with*)
*allocate *for* / *to*
allow *for* (make provision *for*)
allow *of* (permit)
aloof *from* / *with* (not *to*)
*alternative *of* (one thing or another)
*alternative *for* / *to* (not *from*)
amazed *at* (surprised)
amazed *by* (bewildered)
ambitious *for* / *of* (fame)
ambivalent *about* (not *to* or *towards*)
amenable *to* (not *by* or *for*)
*amends *by* / *for* / *to*
*amused (adj.) *at* / *by* / *to* (not *about*)

*amused (v.) *by* / *with*
anagram *of* (not *for*)
analogous *to*
analogy *between* (equivalence)
analogy *of* / *to* (simile)
analogy *with* (comparison, resemblance)
anathema *to* (somebody)
ancestor *of*
anger (n.) *about* / *at* / *over* (the incident, not *for*)
anger (v.) (someone) *by* (interrupting, not *for*)
angle (n.) *on* (an issue, not *to*)
angry *about* / *against* / *at* / *over* / *towards* (a thing)
angry *against* / *at* / *towards* / *with* (a person)
animosity *against, between, to*(*wards*) (not *for*)
animus *against* (not *towards*)
annoyed *about* / *at* / *by* (something)
annoyed *at* / *with* (a person)
answer (n.) *to* (not *of* or *on*)
answer (v.) *for* (misdeeds)
answer (v.) *for* (be responsible)
answer (v.) *to* (the voters)
answer (v.) *to* (respond, match)
antagonized *by* (Bob's obstinacy, not *about*)
antagonistic *to* / *towards*
*anticipation *of*
antidote *against* / *to* / *with*
antipathy *to* / *toward*(*s*) (not *against* or *for* or *of*)
antithesis *between* (contrast)
antithesis *of* (opposite, not *to*)
antithetical *to*
anxious *about* / *for* (health, safety, not *of*)
anxious *for* (eager)
anxious *to* (do something)
apathetic *about* / *to* / *towards*
*apathy *toward*(*s*) (something, not *against, for, regarding* or *to*)
apologize *to* (someone) *for* (something, not *over*)
appalled *at* / *by* (the news)
*appeal (n. v.) *against* (a sentence)

*appeal *for* (help)
*appeal (n. v.) *to* (someone) *for* (something)
*appealing (adj. v.) *to* (be attractive, not *for*)
 appetite *for* (winning, not *to* win)
 applicable *to* (not *for*)
 apply *for* (a passport)
 apply *to* (address oneself *to*)
 appoint (someone) *to* (a position, not *for*)
*appreciation *for* / *of* / *to*
 appreciative *of* (not *for*)
 apprehensive *about* (global warming)
 apprehensive *for* (a person's safety)
 apprehensive *of* (danger)
 apprised *of* (the facts)
 appropriate (v.) *for* / *to*
 appropriate (adj.) *for* / *to* (a purpose)
*approve *of* (a decision)
 aptitude *for* (not *about*)
*arbitrate *between* / *in*
 argue *about* / *against* / *with* (a person)
 argue *about* / *against* / *for* / *over* (a proposal)
 argue *for* (*in* support *of*)
 arrival *at* / *in* (London, not *to*)
 arrive *at* / *in* (London, not *to*)
*ashamed *about* / *of* (not *at, by* or *for*)
 ashamed *to* (do)
*ask (a question) *about* / *after* (a subject)
*ask (a favour) *of* (a person)
 aspire *after* / *to* (covet, not *at* or *for*)
 assault (n.) *against* / *on* (not *of*)
 assessment *of* (not *on*)
*assist *at* / *in* / *with* (cooking, not *to* cook)
 assistance *in* (moving house, not *with*)
 associated *with* (not *in* or *to*)
 association *with* (not *in* or *to*)
 astonished *at* / *by*
 astounded *at* / *by*
 astride *of* (not *over*)

attachment *to* (not *for* or *with*)

attack (n.) *by* / *of* / *on* (thing or person, not *against*)

attempt (n.) *against* / *on* (someone's life)

attempt (n.) *at* (climbing a mountain)

attempt (n. v.) *to* (climb a mountain)

attend *on* (a patient)

attend *to* (a patient's needs)

attendant *on* (not *to*)

attended *by* (visitors)

attended *with* (success, fanfare)

★attitude *of* / *to* / *toward(s)* (not *about* or *over*)

★attracted *by* / *to*

★attraction *for* / *on* / *to* (not *towards*)

attractive *to*

attribute (n.) *of* (greatness)

attribute (v.) *to* (good luck)

attuned *to* (not *with*)

atypical *of* (not *for*)

authority *for* (warrant)

authority *on* (expert)

authority *over* (power, control)

avail (oneself) *of* (a thing)

averse *to* (not *against* or *from*)

★aversion *to* (snakes, not *for*)

avert (one's gaze) *from*

aware(ness) *of* (not *about* or *around*)

∿

B

back *out of* (not *out on*)

backed *by* (supported, not *with*)

bad *at* (tennis, not *in*)

balance (v.) *against* / *with* (not *to*)

ban (n.) *on* (insecticides, not *for*)

★bandy (v.) *about* / *around* / *with*

★bargain *for* / *on* / *with*

barren *of* (not *from*)

*base (n. v.) *of* / *on* / *with* (not *around, from* or *in*)
*basis *for* (an allegation)
*basis *in* (fact)
*basis (ingredient) *of*
  ba[u]lk *at* (not *about*)
  bearing (n.) *on* (not *for*)
  begin *by* (doing something)
  begin *from* (a point)
  begin *with* (an act or object)
*behalf *of*
  belief *in* (a creed, not *of* or *toward*)
  beliefs *about* (witches)
  belong *to* (own, be a member)
  belong *with* (same category)
  beneficial *for* / *to* (one's health)
  benefit (n.) *of* (good advice, the doubt)
  benefit (n.) *to* (a person)
  benefit (n. v.) *from* (Yoga, not *by*)
  bent (propensity) *for* (causing mischief)
  bent (determined) *on* (mischief)
  bestow *on* / *upon* (not *to*)
*blame (v.) (a person) *for* (something, not *with*)
*blame (n.) *on* (put blame *on*)
  blind *to* (his wife's faults, not *about*)
  blind *with* (anger)
*blockade *of* (not *against* or *on*)
  boast (n. v.) *about* / *of*
*bored *with* (an activity, not *of*)
*bored *by* (a person, not *of*)
*born *of*
*born *out of* (wedlock)
  borrow (a thing) *from* (a friend, not *of* or *off of*)
  bound *for* (a destination, not *to*)
  boycott (n.) *of* (goods, not *on*)
  brag *about* / *of* (not *on*)
  breach *in* (the wall, not *of*)
  breach *of* (trust, rules, not *in*)
*break *from* / *with*

bridle (v.) *at* (not *over*)
brunt *of* (not *for*)
build *on* (past success, not *off*)
byword *for* (not *in*)

C

campaign (n. v.) *against / for*
capable *of* (not *to*)
capacity *for* (aptitude *for*)
capacity *of* (containing)
★care (v.) *about* (worry)
★care (v.) *for* (like, look after)
★careful *about / of / with*
careless *about / in / of / with*
★cater *for / to*
★cause (n.) *for* (celebration)
★cause *of* (lung cancer)
caused *by* (not *from*)
central *to*
★centre (v.) (*about / around / in / on / round*)
certain *about / of*
champion(ship) *of* (human rights, not *for*)
★chance (n.) *at / for / of / on*
chance (n. v.) *to* (win, not *in* winning))
chance (v.) *on* (happen)
★change (n. v.) *between / for / from / in / into / of / to / with*
characteristic *for / of*
charge(d) *with* (a crime, task, not *for* or *of*)
chary *of*
chat *to / with* (a friend)
cheat (v.) *on / with*
★choose *among / between / from / out of / over*
★clear (adj.) *about / from / of / on / to*
clever *at* (crosswords, not *in*)
★close *about / to / up / with*
cognate *with*

cognizant *of*
★collaboration *with* (a colleague)
★collaboration *on* (a project, not *for*)
collide *with* (not *against*)
collision *between* (two things)
coloured *by* (a dye)
coloured *with* (a prejudice)
combine *with* (not *to*)
comfortable *in* (pajamas)
★comfortable *with* (a proposal)
commensurate *with* (not *to*)
comment (n. v.) *on* (not *about, at* or *to*)
commitment *to* (not *of*)
★common *for* / *in* / *to* / *with*
★compare *to* (note similar)
★compare *with* (note similar and dissimilar)
★comparison *between* / *to* / *with*
★compassion *for* / *on* / *towards*
compatible *with*
compete *against* / *with* (an opponent)
compete *for* (an award, object)
competent *at* (sports)
competent *in* (English)
★complacent *about* (not *over, towards* or *with*)
complain *about* / *against* (something dissatisfying)
complain *of* (a headache)
complement (n.) *of* (a ship)
complement (n.) *to* (addition)
complementary *to* (additional)
complicit *with* (not *to*)
compliment (n.) *to* (somebody)
compliment (v.) (somebody) *on* (an achievement, not *about* or *for*)
complimentary *about* (something, not *of*)
complimentary *to* (somebody)
comply *with* (a request, not *to*)
components *of* (a TV set, not *to*)
composed *of* (consists of, not *with*)
compound (n.) *of* (mixture)

*compound(ed) *of* / *with* (mixed, constituted)
  comprised *of*
  conceive *of*
  concentrate *on* (one's homework, not *about*)
  concern *about* / *over*
*concerned *about* / *at* / / *for* / *over* (worried, not *by*, *of* or *with*)
*concerned *for* (keen to obtain)
*concerned *in* (involved, involving)
*concerned *with* (occupied, related *to*)
  concur *with* (a person) *in* (an opinion, decision)
  condole *with* (a person)
*condolences *on* (a death, not *for*)
*condolences *to* (the bereaved, not *for*)
  conducive *to* (not *of*)
  confer *on* (bestow *upon*)
  confer *with* (discuss)
  confide *in* (trust *in*)
  confide *to* (entrust *to*)
*confident *about* / *in* (one's abilities, not *with*)
*confident *of* (success)
*confident *of* (winning not "*to* win")
  confine *in* (a place)
  confine *to* (restrict)
  conflict (v.) *with* (not *against*)
  conform *to* / *with*
  confront (a person) *about* / *over* (bad manners)
  confront (a person) *with* (the truth)
  confronted *by* (a burglar)
  confronted *with* (the facts)
*confused *about* / *by* / *over* / *with*
  congratulate *on* (a victory, not a*bout* or *for*)
*congratulations *to* (a person) *on* (an achievement)
  coincide *with*
  connected *by* (*by* means *of*)
*connected *to* (linked)
*connected *with* (associated)
  connection *between* (two groups)
*connection *to* (link)

*connection *with* (association)
connive *with* (someone) *at* / *in* (stealing)
conscious *of* (not *about*)
consensus *among* (the experts)
consensus *on* (the best solution, not *for*)
consequence *for* (a person, not *on* or *to*)
consequence *of* (an action, not *from*)
consequent *on* / *upon* (not *to*)
considerate *about* (things)
considerate *of* / *towards* (someone)
consideration *in* / *of* / *to*
*consist *in* (reside *in*, be equivalent *to*)
*consist *of* (part or parts)
consistent *with* (previous reports, not *to*)
*constraint *of* / *on*
consult *about* / *in* (a matter) *with* (somebody)
*consumed *by* (fire)
*consumed *by* / *with* (envy, guilt, desire)
contact (n.) *with* (not *to*)
contemporary (adj.) *with*
contemporary (n.) *of* (not *to*)
contempt *for* (liars, not *of*)
contempt *of* (court or parliament, not *for*)
contemptuous *of* (not *for*)
contend *against* / *with* (struggle)
contend *for* (strive)
content (n.) *with*
content (v.) (oneself) *with* (not *by*)
content (v.) (others) *by*
contiguous *to* / *with*
contingent *on* / *upon*
*continue *by* / *on* / *to* / *with*
continuous *with*
contradictory *of* / *to*
*contrast (n.) *to* / *with* (not *against* or *from*)
*contrast (v.) (one thing) *with* (another, not *against* or *to*)
convenient *for* (person)
convenient *to* (a purpose)

*converge *on* (not *in*)
  conversant *in* (a language, not *about*))
  conversant *with* (an area *of* knowledge, not *about*)
  conversation *with* (my brother) *about* (football)
  converse *about* (a topic)
  converse *with* (a person)
  convict *of* (murder, not *for*)
*convince (a person) *of* (God's existence)
*convinced *by* (an argument)
  cope *with* (not *up*)
  correlate *with* (not *to*)
  correlation *between* / *with*
  correspond *to* / *with* (agree, match)
  correspond *with* (write *to*)
  cost *in* (human lives)
  cost *of* (a house, not *for*)
  count (v.) *on* (rely *on*)
*couple *of*
*courtship *of* (a woman, not *with*)
*covered *in* / *with* (oil)
  crash (v.) *into* (not *against*)
*crazy *about* (a film star)
*crazy *for* (a new house)
*crazy *on* (football)
*credit (n. v.) *for* / *with* (an achievement)
*credit (n. v.) *to* (add money)
*credit (n.) *to* (one's parents)
  critical *for* / *to* (essential)
  critical *of* (hostile)
*criticism *for* (misbehaviour)
*criticism *of* (a plan, not *against* or *for*)
  crucial *for* / *to*
  culminate *in* (not *with*)
*culpable *for*
*culprit
  cure (n.) *for*
  cure (v.) *of* (an illness, not *from*)
  curiosity *about* (not *for*, *in* or *towards*)

*curious *about* (UFOs, not *for, in* or *of*)
  cynical *about* (your motives)
  cynical *toward(s)* (you)
  cynicism *about* / *toward(s)*

D

  dabble *in* (not *at* / *with*)
*date (v.) *back to* / *from* / *to*
  deaf *to* (cries for help)
  deadlock *between* (two warring parties)
  deadlock *over* (whether to raise taxes)
  deal (v.) *in* (doing business)
  deal (v.) *with* (attend *to*)
  debar *from*
  debate (n. v.) *about* / *on* / *over* (an issue, not *around* or *surrounding*)
  debate (n. v) *between* (two sides)
  debate (n. v.) *with* (an opponent)
*decide *about* (a matter)
*decide *against* / *on* (a course *of* action, doing)
*decide *between* (two options)
*decide *to* (get married)
*dedicated *to* (the cause of peace)
*defeat (n.) *of* / *on* / *to* (not *over*)
  defence *against* (attack)
  defence *for* (excuse, justification)
  defence *of* (liberty)
  defend *against* / *from* (not *of*)
  defer *to* (a person) *in* (an opinion)
  defiance *of* (authority)
  defiant *against, of, to, toward(s)*.
  deficient *in*
  definition *of* (a word, not *to*)
*delighted *at* / *by* / *in* / *with*
  demand (n.) *on* (a person) *for* (something)
  demand (v.) (an intangible thing) *of* (a person)
  demand (v.) *of* (a person, ask)

demand (v.) (a tangible thing) *from* (a person)

demanding *on* (onerous, not *of*)

★denouement *of* / *to* (a play or novel)

depart *at* (9 a.m.)

depend(ent) *on* (not *to*)

dependence *of* (one thing) *on* (another)

deprive *of* (not *from*)

derelict *in* (one's duties, not *with*)

★derision *about* / *against* / *for* / *of* / *on* / *on* / *to*(*wards*)

derive (pleasure) *from* (not *in*)

derogate *from* (detract, deviate)

derogatory *of* / *to* / *towards*

description *of* (not *about*)

desire (n.) *for*

desirous *of*

despair *for* (a person)

despair (n.) *of* / *over* (losing)

despair (n. v.) *of* (ever winning, not *for*)

destitute *of*

destructive *of* (not *to*)

details *of* (a policy)

determination *to* excel (not *of* excelling)

deterrent *against* / *to* (not *of*)

detrimental *to*

devastated *at* / *by* (her death)

deviate *from*

devoid *of* (not *from*)

devoted *to* (the welfare of animals, not *for*)

devotee *of* (not *to*)

devotion *to* (not *for* or *in*)

★die *for* (a cause)

★die *from* (an injury)

★die *of* (an illness, not *from*)

differ *about* / *in* / *on* / *over* (an issue)

differ *from* (be different)

differ *from* / *with* (disagree)

difference *between* (two things, not *in*)

difference *in* (age)

difference *to* (me, not *for*)
differences *among* (cultures)
★different *from* / *than* / *to* (not *of*)
differentiate *amongst* (several things)
differentiate *between* (two things)
differentiate (one thing) *from* (another)
★difficult *for* / *of* / *with*
★difficulties *about* / *over* / *with* (an issue)
disabuse (a person) *of* (an idea, not *from*)
★disaffection *for* / *from* / *with* (not *by* or *to*)
disagree *about* / *on* / *over* (things, opinions)
disagree *with* (someone, not *from*)
★disappointed *about* / *at* / *by* / *in* / *over* / *with*
★disappointment *about* / *at* / *for* / *in* / *over* / *to* / *with*
disappointment *to* (somebody)
★disapproval *from* / *of*
discouraged *by* (something)
discouraged *from* (doing, not *in*)
★discrepancy *between* / *in* (not *of*)
discriminate *against* / *in favour of*
discriminate *among* or *between* (alternatives)
discriminate (one thing) *from* (another)
discussion *about* / *on* (not *around*)
disdain *for* / *of* (not *toward*)
disdainful *of* / *towards* (not *about*)
★disgust (n.) *at* / *for* / *with* (not *against* or *toward(s)*)
★disgusted *at* / *by* / *with* (not *against* or *toward(s)*)
disinclination *to*
disincline (a person) *from* (doing)
disinclined *to* (do)
★disinterest *in* (not *for*)
dislike (n.) *for* / *of* (not *at*)
dismayed *at* / *by* (not *with*)
★dispense *with*
★displeased *at* / *by* / *with*
disproportionate *to* (not *with*)
dispute (n. v.) *about* / *over* (a matter)
dispute (n. v.) *with* (somebody, not *against*)

disqualified *for* (a wrongdoing)
disqualified *from* (a race, doing)
disregard *for* / *of*
disrespect (n. v.) *for* (not *of*)
*dissatisfaction *with* (not *about, at, over* or *towards*)
dissatisfied *with*
dissent (v.) *from* (not *on* or *to*)
dissimilar *to* (not *from*)
dissuade *from* (not *against*)
distaste (n. v.) *for*
distinguish *among* (several things)
distinguish *between* (two things)
distinguish (one thing) *from* (another)
distinguished *by* (singled out)
distinguished *for* (eminent)
distracted *from* (one thing) *by* (another)
distraught *about* / *at* / *over* / *with*
distrust(ful) *of*
disturbed *about* / *at* / *over* (perturbed)
disturbed *by* (disrupted)
divest *from* (cease investing)
divest *of* (relinquish)
divide (v.) *into* (six parts, not *in*)
*divided (adj.) *on* / *over* (not *by*)
do (something) *for* (someone, help)
do (something) *to* (someone, hurt)
dominated *by* (an idea, not *with*)
domination *by* (someone) *of* / *over* (another)
*donate *for* / *to*
*doubt (n.) *about* / *of* / *on*
doubtful *about* / *of*
*dream (n. v.) *about* / *of* (entertain a hope/idea)
*dream (v.) *about* / *of* (one's lover)
dressed *in* (red, not *with*)
drive (v.) *into* (a tree, not *against*)
*drunk *from* / *on* / *with*
dubious *about* / *of*
dwell *on* (linger, not *over*)

E

eager *for* (the race to begin)
eager(ness) *to* (begin the race)
*ecstatic *about/ at / over / with*
*effect (n.) *of / on* (not *for* or *to*)
effort *to* (save, not *at* saving)
*either *of*
elaborate *on* (not *about*)
*embargo *against / from / on*
embark *for* (a place)
embark *on* (a ship, career)
*embarrassed *at / by / over* (behaviour, not *of*)
*embarrassed *with* (debts)
emboldened *by* (liquor, not *with*)
embroiled *in* (a dispute)
embroiled *with* (a person or country)
empathize *with* (not *towards*)
empathy *with* (not *towards*)
employee *of* (a company, not *for*)
*enamoured *of* (not *about* or *with*)
*enchanted *by / with*
end (n.) *to* (a problem)
end (v.) *at* (a place, not *up at*)
end (v.) *in / with* (not *by*)
endorsement *of* (a candidate, not *for*)
endowed *by* (fate) *with* (talent)
*endurance *of / for / to*
*enemy *of / to*
*engaged *in / with* (an activity)
*engaged *to* (a person)
engrossed *in* (a book)
engulfed *by* (war)
engulfed *in* (flames, not *by* or *with*)
enmity *against / among / between / towards*
*enough *of* (not *with*)
enquire *about* (fares)

enquire *after* (someone's health)

enquire *for* (look *for*)

enquire *into* (investigate)

enquiry *into* (not *over*)

*enrol *in* (a course, not *for* or *on*)

entangled *in* (one thing)

entangled *with* (two things)

*enter *for* / *in* / *into*

enthralled *by* / *with* (new baby, enchanted)

enthralled *to* (TV, enslaved)

enthused *by* / *over* (not *about*, *for* or *with*)

enthusiasm *for* (not *about* or *over*)

enthusiastic *about* / *over* (the vote, not *for* or *with*)

enthusiastic *about* (competing, not *to* compete)

entrust (something) *to* (someone)

entrust (someone) *with* (something)

*envious *of* (not *about* or *towards*)

equal (adj.) *to* (two things, not *as*, *for* or *with*)

equal (adj.) *to* (the task)

equate *to* (make equal)

equate *with* (consider equal, not *to*)

*equivalent (adj.) *in* / *to*

*equivalent (n.) *of* (not *for*)

*escape (v.) *from* (danger)

essential *for* / *to*

eulogy *of* (not *to*)

euphemism *for* (dying, not *of*)

evidence *for* (a crime or theory, not *of* or *to*)

evidence *of* (human settlement)

example *of* (instance, not *for*)

example *to* (model)

excel *at* / *in* (activity)

excel *in* (ability)

*exception *to* (a rule, statement, not *from* or *with*)

*excited *about* (badminton, not *for*)

*excited *about* / *at* / *by* / *over* (a new baby)

*excitement *about* / *at* / *over* (not for)

excused *for* (pardoned)

excused *from* (released)
exempt(ion) *from* (paying taxes)
★exhausted *by / from* (overwork, not *of*)
★exhausted *of* (emptied)
expect *from / of*
expectation(s) *of* (not *for*)
experience *of* (travel, not *with*)
experience *in* (teaching)
experienced *in* (rock-climbing, not *about*)
explanation *for / of*
explication *of* (a text, not *on*)
extraneous *to* (not *of*
extrinsic *to*
★eye(s) *at / for / off / on / out / over / to*

~
F

facility (skill) *for / in / with* (languages, not *at*)
★familiar *to* (well-known)
★familiar *with* (knowing, friendly)
★fascinated *by / for / with* (not *about* or *in*)
★fascination *for / of* (not *about, in* or *with*)
fatal *for / to* (his hopes)
father (n.) *of* (six children)
father (n.) *to* (me)
father (n. v.) *by / on / with* (a child)
favourable *for* (suitable)
favourable *to* (*in favour of*)
favouritism *towards* (not *of*)
fear (n.) *about / of* (flying)
fear (n. v.) *for* (one's safety)
fear (v.) *to* fly
fear (n.) *of* (God)
★feel(ings) *about / for* (not *toward*)
fight (n. v.) *about / over* (things, opinions)
fight (n. v.) *against* (cancer)
fight (n. v.) *for* (a cause)

fight (n. v.) *with* (a person, not *against*)
fight (n. v.) *with* (a weapon)
filled *by* (agent)
filled *with* (contents, not *by*)
★firm *in* / *of* / *on* / *with*
fixated *on* (not *about* or *with*)
flair *with* (words, not *for*)
flexible *about* (visiting hours, not *over*)
★fob (a person) *off with* (a thing)
focus (n.v.) *on* (not *about*, *around* or *to*)
★foist (a thing) *on* (a person, not *at*)
fond *of*
fondness *for*
forbear (n.) *of*
★forbid(den) *to* (do, not *from* doing)
foreign *to* (way of thinking, not *from*)
forerunner *of* (not *to*)
forge *ahead* (not *on*)
forge *into* (the lead)
★fortunate *in* (one's friends)
★fortunate *with* (investments)
free (adj.) *for* (dinner)
free (adj.) *from* / *of* (pain, debt, bacteria)
free (adj.) *with* (advice, favours)
free (v.) *from* (liberate)
free (v.) *of* (exempt)
free (adj.) *with* (advice, money)
★friend *of* / *to*
★friendly *of* / *to* / *with*
frightened *by* (a recent event)
frightened *of* (general fear)
★frustrated *by* / *with* (not *about*, *at* or *over*)
★full *of* / *with*
fundamental *to* (not *for*)
furious *about* / *at* / *over* (an event)
furious *with* (a person or object)
furnish (someone) *with* (a thing)
fusion *of* (two things, not *between*)

fuss (n. v.) *about / of / over*

G

*generous *in / of / to / with*
*give *for / of / on / onto / to*
 glad *about / at* (an event)
 glad *of* (assistance)
 glad *for* (a person)
*glimpse (n.) *into / of* (not *at* or *from*)
*good *at / for / to / with*
*good luck *on* (your date)
*good luck *to* (your date)
*graduate (n.) *of* (Harvard, not *from*)
*graduate (v.) *from* (Harvard)
 grapple *with*
 grateful *for* (something)
 grateful *to* (somebody)
 gratified *at / by / with* (not *about* or *over*)
 greedy *for* (not *of*)
*grieve *about / at / for / over* (a death)
*grieve *for* (a person)
 guard (v.) *against* (be vigilant, not *from*)
 guard (v.) *against / from* (protect)
 guiltless *of*
 guilty *about* (i.e., feeling guilty)
 guilty *of* (a crime)

H

 habituated *to* (not *with*)
 haggle *with* (a merchant) *about* or *over* (the price)
*hand (v.) *down / up*
 handling (n.) *of* (an affair, not *over*)
 hanker *after / for* (another trip to Africa)
 happen *by* (accident, not *on*)

happen *to* (somebody, not *with*)

*happy *about* / *at* / *for* / *with* (not *over*)

harbinger *of*

*hark *at* / *back to* / *to*

harmful *to* (not *for*)

*hate *for* / *towards* (not *against*)

hateful *to*

*hatred *for* / *of* / *towards* (not *against*)

hats off *to* (someone) *for* (something)

*havoc *with*

hazardous *to* (one's health, not *for*)

*hear *about* / *from* / *of*

heartbroken *about* / *at* / *over* (the loss)

heed *of* (not *to*)

heedful *of* (good advice)

heedless *of* (danger)

heir(ess) *of* (a wealthy man)

heir(ess) *to* (a fortune, the crown)

*hell-bent *for* / *on*

hesitancy *about* / *in*

hesitant *about* or *in* (skydiving)

hesitate *in* (acting)

hesitate *over* (a decision)

hesitate *to* (act)

hesitation *about* / *in* (doing, not *to* do)

*hope (n.) *for* / *of* / *on*

hope (v.) *for* (victory)

hopeful *about* / *of* (victory, not *on*)

*hopeless *about* / *at* / *of* / *with*

hostile *to* / *towards* (not *about* or *against*)

hostility *against* / *to* / *towards*

hunger *after* / *for* (love)

hungry *for* (knowledge, news)

*hysteria *about* (not *for*)

I

*identical *to / with*
 ignorance *about / of* (not *on*)
 ignorant *of* (the facts, not *about* or *to*)
 ill *with* (the 'flu)
 ill-suited *to* (modern life, not *for*)
 imbue (a person) *with* (a quality)
 immaterial *to* (not *for*)
 immersed *in* (not *with*)
 immune *from* (prosecution, not *against*)
 immune *to* (a disease, not *against*)
 immunity *against* (a disease, not *from*)
 immunity *from* (prosecution, punishment)
 immunize *against* (a disease, not *from*)
 impact (n.) *of* (taxes) *on* (taxpayers, not *for* or *to*)
*impact (v.) *on / upon* (not *to*)
 impart (knowledge) *to* (students, not *on*)
 impatient *at / with* (constant delays)
 impatient *for* (news, payment)
 impatient *of* (interruption, rebuke)
 impatient *with* (noisy children)
 impervious *to* (not *of*)
 impinge *on / upon* (one's rights, not *against*)
 implicated *in* (not *for*)
 implication *in* (*robbery*)
 implication *of* (statement)
 implications *for* (not *on*)
*important *for / to*
 impose *on* (not *to*)
*impressed *by / into / on / upon / with* (not *of*)
 inadequate *for / to* (a person, one's needs)
 inadequate *for* (meeting one's needs)
 inadequate *to* (meet one's needs)
 incapable *of* (doing, not *to do*)
 incensed *at / by / over / with*
 incidental *to*

include *among* (two or more)
include *in* (the price)
incomprehension *of* (English grammar, not *for*)
inconsiderate *about* (things or opinions)
inconsiderate *of* (someone's feelings)
inconsistent *with*
increase (n .v.) *in* (energy, not *to*)
increase (n.) *of* (3%)
*inculcate (ideas) *in* / *into* (someone's mind, not *on* or *with*)
*inculcate (someone's mind) *with* ideas
indebted *to* (you) *for* (assistance)
*independent *from* / *of* (not *on*)
indicative *of*
indifferent *to* (not *about, concerning, for* or *on*)
indignant *about* / *at* / *over* (rude remarks)
indignant *with* (a person making rude remarks)
indispensable *for* / *to*
indulge *in* (an activity)
indulgence *for* (toleration)
indulgence *in* (participation)
indulgence (leniency) *to* (a sinner)
indulgent *of* (a person's whim)
indulgent *to* / *towards* (a person)
ineligible *for*
infatuation *with* (not *for*)
infected *with* (disease)
infer(ence) *from*
inferior *to* (not *than*)
infested *with* (vermin)
inflict *on* / *upon* (not *with*)
influence (n.) *on* / *over* / *with* (a person or thing)
influence (v.) *on* / *in* / *upon* (a person or thing)
influenced *by*
influx *of* (immigrants)
influx *from* (China) *into* (Canada, not *in* or *to*)
information *about* / *on* (a subject, not *of*)
information *for* (someone)
*infuse(d) *in* / *into* / *with* (not *by*)

ingratiate (oneself) *with* (the boss, not *to*)
ingredient *of* (not *to*)
inherent *in* (not *to* or *with*)
initiate (v.) *in* (a science)
initiate (v.) *into* (a society)
*injury *on* / *to* (an athlete)
innate *in* (human beings, not *to*)
inscrutable *to* (a person, not *by* or *for*)
insensible *of* / *to* (my feelings)
insight *into* (not *about* or *of*)
insist(ence) *on* (paying, not *about* or *in*)
inspire (a vision) *in* (someone, not *into*)
inspire (someone) *with* (a vision)
inspired *by* / *with*
*instil[l] *in* / *into* (not *towards* or *with*)
instinct *for* / *of* (self-preservation, not *towards*)
insufficient *for* (needs)
insufficient *in* (quantity)
integral *to* (not *with*)
integrate *into* (incorporate *into*, not *in*)
integrate *with* (mix *with*)
intend *to* (not *on*)
intent *on* (something, doing something)
*intention *of* / *to*
intercede *for* (a person) *with* (another person)
*interest (n. v.) *in* (not *around*, *at* or *to*)
interested *in* (not *by* or *of*)
interfere *between* (parent and child)
interfere *in* (intervene, meddle)
interfere *with* (hinder, obstruct)
interfere *with* (sexually molest)
*interested *in* (not *about*)
intrigued *by* (fascinated, not *about* or *with*)
intrigued *with* (plotted)
intrinsic *in* / *to*
intrusion *into* (my affairs, not *of*)
inundated *with* (telegrams, not *by*)
inured *to* (hard work, not *against*)

[205]

invest *in* (stocks, a business, not *into*)
invest *with* (an office) f
investigation *in* / *into* / *of* (not *over*)
★involved *in* (included *in*)
★involved *with* (committed *to*)
★involved *with* (a person)
irrespective *of*
issue (n.) *of* (not *about*)

J

jealous *for* / *of* (my reputation)
jealous *of* (a person, not *about* or *towards*)
jealousy *towards* (a person)
join (v.) *in* (a game)
join (v.) *to* (connect)
join (v.) *with* (a person or thing)
jubilant *about* / *at* / *over* (good news, not *with*)
judged *by* (not *as* or *on*)
★justification *for* (her behaviour, not *of*)
justified *in* (taking action, not *to* take)
justified *in* (opinions, not *of*)
juxtapose(d) *with* (not *to*)

K

keen *of* (hearing)
keen *on* (exams, not *about* of *for*)
keen *on* (passing the exam)
keen *to* (pass the exam)
key *to* (the door, the mystery, not *of*)
kind *to* (not *with*)
knowledge *about* / *of* (a subject)
knowledgeable *about* (not *of* or *on*)

L

labour (n. v.) *at* (a task)
labour (n. v.) *for* (a person, an end)
labour (n. v.) *in* (a cause)
labour (v.) *under* (a disadvantage, difficulty)
*lack (n.) *of* (money)
*lack (v.) *for* (money)
lacking *in* (an attribute, not *of*)
lament (n.) *for* (grief)
lament (n.) *about* (complaint)
lament (v.) *for* / *over* (mourn)
*laugh (n. v.) *about* / *at* / *on* / *over*
*lease *of* / *on* (life)
leisure *to* (do, not *for* doing)
lenient *to* / *towards* (not *with*)
*lesson *for* / *in* / *on*
liable (responsible) *to* (a person) *for* debts
liable *to* (apt, likely, inclined)
liable *to* (dismissal)
libel (n.) *against* / *on*
likelihood *of* (not *for*)
*linger *in* / *over*
link (n.) *between* / *in* / *to* / *with*
link (n. v.) *between* (two things)
link (v.) (one thing) *to* / *with* (another)
listen *for* (a secret signal)
listen *to* (good advice, not *at*)
littered *by* (agent)
littered *with* (substance)
look *after* (care for)
look *at* (fix eyes on)
look *for* (try to find)
look forward *to* (not *for*)
lost *to* (disease, not *by*)
*love (n.) *for* / *of*
*lust *after* / *for*

M

*made *from / of / out of / with*
  mania *for* (crosswords)
  marked *by* (not *with*)
*marriage *of / between* (two bodies)
  marriage *to* (a person, not *with*)
  married *to* (a person, not *with*)
  married *with* (children)
*martyr *for / of / to*
  mastery *of* (an activity)
  mastery *over* (a rival)
  matter *for* (an expert)
  matter *of* (survival)
  meddle *in* (one's affairs)
  meddle *with* (one's things)
  meditate *on / upon* (ponder, not *about* or *over*)
  meet *for* (lunch)
*meet (encounter) *with* (an accident, success)
*mercy *of / on / to*
  mistrust(ful) *of*
*model (oneself) *on* (not *after*)
*money *on / with* (me)
*monopoly *of / on / over*
  mourn *for* (a person)
  mourn *over* (a death)
*muse (v.) *about / over / on / upon*
  mystified *by* (not *over*)

N

*name (n. v.) *after / for*
  name (v.) *to* (appoint)
*native (adj. n.) *of / to* (not *from*)
  necessary *for / to* (happiness, not *of*)
  necessary *to* (live happily)

necessity *for* / *of* (strict measures)
need (n.) *for* / *of*
needed *from* (somebody, not *of*)
negligent *in* (duties, not *about* or *of*)
negligent *of* (fame, not *in*)
negligent *towards* (somebody)
*nervous *about* / *around* / *of* (strangers)
nice *to* (ones wife, not *with*)
north *of* (London, not *from*)
nostalgia *for* (one's native land)
nostalgic *about* (one's schooldays)

O

object (v.) *to* (not *about* or *against*)
*oblivious *of* (not *about* or *to*)
obsess *about* / *over* (one's looks, not *on* or *with*)
*obsessed *about* / *by* / *with* (baseball)
obsession *with* (one's health, not *for*)
obstacle *to* (progress, not *for*)
*offence *against* / *at* / *to* (not *from*)
offend *against* (common decency)
offended *at* / *by* / *with* (his bad language)
offensive (adj.) *to* (visible minorities, not *toward*)
open *for* (business)
open *to* (the public, suggestions)
opinion *about* / *on* (a subject)
opinion *of* (a person)
opponent *of* (not *to*)
*opposite (adj.) *from* / *to* (not *of* or *than*)
*opposite (n.) *of* (not *to*)
*opposite (prep.) *to* (or omit)
opposition *of* (a group, person)
opposition *to* (new policy, not *against*)
*optimism *about* (not *at, for, over* or *toward*)
*optimistic *about* (not *at, for, over* or *toward*)
originate *from* / *in* (a thing)

originate *with* (a person)
outraged *at* / *by* (a suggestion)
overcome *by* (fumes)
overcome *with* (emotion)
*overjoyed *at* / *by* / *with*
overwhelmed *by* (the floods)
overwhelmed *with* (grief)

∼

P

*painting *by* / *from* / *of*
panegyric *on* / *to* / *upon* (not *of*)
parallel (adj. v.) *to* / *with*
parallel(s) (n.) *among* (several things)
parallel(s) (n.) *between* (two things)
parallel(s) (n.) *with* (one thing)
paraphrase (n.) *of* (a lecture, not *on*)
parody (n.) *of* (*Macbeth*, not *about* or *on*)
part (v.) *from* (persons, not *with*)
part (v.) *with* (things, not *from*)
partake *of* (food, quality, not *in*)
partake *in* (participate)
partial *to* (cake, flattery)
participate *in* (not *to*)
passion *for* (not *towards*)
*passionate *about* / *for*
patron *of* (the arts, not *to*)
pay *for* (drinks all round)
penchant *for* (compromise, not *to* compromise)
perpendicular *to* (not *from* or *with*)
persevere *in* / *with*
persist *in* (not *with*)
perspective *on* (not *in* or *to*)
persuade (a person) *of* (the need to save money)
persuade (a person) *to* do (something)
pertain *to* (the issue)
pertinent *to*

*perturbed *about* / *at* / *by* / *over*
*phobia *of* (not *about*, *against*, *towards* or *over*)
  pity (n.) *for* (leniency or mercy *towards*)
  pity (n.) *on* (sympathy *with*)
*place (n.) *for*, *in* or *of*
  plan (n.v.) *for* (the future)
  plan (v.) *on* (early retirement)
  plan (v.) *on* (going to Venice)
  plan (v.) *to* (go to Venice)
  play (v.) *to* (the camera, not *for*)
*pleased *about* / *at* / *by* / *with*
*pleasure *of* / *in*
  point (v.) *at* / *towards* (a thing)
  point (v.) *to* (a fact)
  polite *to* (strangers, not *with*)
*popular *among* / *with* (teenagers, not *to*)
*pore (v.) *over* (documents, not *through*)
  possessed *by* / *with* (an idea, emotion)
  possessed *of* (wealth)
*possibility *for* / *of*
  possible *for* (a person)
  possible *to* (win the race)
*praise (n.) *for* / *of* / *on* / *to*
  praise (v.) (a volunteer) *for* (her efforts)
  precaution(s) *against* (catching a cold, not *for*)
  precursor *of* / *to* (not *for*)
  predecessor *of* (not *to*)
  predilection *for* (not *with*)
  preface (v.) *with* (a remark)
*prefer (one thing) *to* (another, not *above*, *before* or *over*)
*preferable *to* (not *than* or *over*)
*preference *for* / *to* (not *toward*)
  pregnant *by* (a man)
  pregnant *with* (a man's child, not *of*)
  pregnant *with* (possibilities, not *of*)
  prejudice(d) *against* / *in favour of* / *towards* (not *to*)
  premonition *of* (not *for* or *to*)
  preoccupation *with* (fashion, not *by* or *of*)

preoccupied *with* (fashion, not *by* or *of*)

prerequisite *for* (a course, not *of* or *to*)

preside *at* / *over*

prevail *against* / *over* (opposition)

prevail *on* (persuade, not *with*)

prevail *with* (have greater impact)

prevent (someone) *from* (doing, not *to* do)

*pride (n.) *in* (not *about, for* or *toward*)

*pride (v.) (oneself) *on* (one's humility)

principle *of* (not *for*)

*priority *for* / *to*

*privilege (n.) *of* / *to*

*problem *for* / *with*

process *of* / *on* / *to* (not *towards*)

proficient *at* (games)

proficient *in* (surgery)

profuse *in* (one's apologies)

profusion *of* (flowers)

prohibit(ed) *from* (smoking, not *to* smoke)

proof *of* (God's existence, not *for*)

propensity *for* (rudeness, not *in, to* or *towards*)

propensity *to* (be rude)

proponent *of* (a scheme, not *for*)

protect *against* (attack, loss)

protect *from* (harm)

protest (v.) *about* / *against* (not *at* or *to*)

*proud *of* (not *about, at, for* or *with*)

provide *against* (prepare *for*)

provide *for* (supply, the future)

provide (the starving) *with* (food)

proximity *to* (not *with*)

*punctuated *by* / *with*

punish *for* (a crime, not *over*)

punishable *by* (death, not *with*)

*purge (v.) *from* / *of* (not *out of*)

purpose *in* (doing, not *for*)

purpose *of* (this meeting, not *for*)

pursuant *to*

*pursuit *of* (not *for*)

Q

   qualify *for* (the final, not *to*)
   qualify (*to* teach)
   quarrel *between* (two people)
   quarrel *about* / *over* (a matter)
   quarrel *with* (a neighbour)
*question *about* / *of*

R

   rail *against* or *at* (not *about*)
   range (v.) (line up) *against* (enemy forces)
   range (n.v.) *between* (five to ten dollars)
   range(v.) *from* (bad to worse, not *between*)
   react *against* (oppose, not *about*)
   react *to* (respond, not *about* or *on*)
   react *with* (chemical change)
   ready *for* (an exam)
   ready *in* / *with* (an answer)
   reality *of* (child poverty, not *about*)
   reason (n.) *against* / *behind* / *for* (going to war, not *of*)
   reason (v.) *about* (a topic)
   reason (v.) *with* (a person)
   rebel (n.) *against*
   rebel (v.) *against* / *at* (not *from*)
*rebuke (n.) *to* (a lazy student, not *against*)
*rebuke (v.) (a student) *for* (his laziness)
   rebuttal *of* (an argument)
   rebuttal *to* (a person)
   received *by* (jubilation, not *with*)
   received (money) *from* (not *off*)
   receptive *to* (an idea, not *of*)
   reckon *on* (count *on*, expect)

reckon *with* (deal *with*, consider)
*recognition *for* / *from* / *of*
recoil (v.) *at* / *from* (the sight of blood)
recoil *in* (horror)
recommend (a person) *for* (a job)
recommend (a book) *to* (a student)
reconcile *to* (accept a situation)
reconcile (one thing) *with* (another)
reconcile *with* (a person)
recover *from* (all illness, not *of*)
redeem *from* (not *of*)
*reduced *by* / *to*
reduction *from* / *in* / *of* (a price, not *over*)
reduction *in* (salary)
reek *of* (liquor, not *from* or *with*)
reek *with* (sweat)
reference *about* (recommendation letter)
reference *to* (a subject, not *about*)
reflect *on* (not *about*)
reflected (sent back) *by*
reflected (implied) *in*
*reflection *on* (not *of*)
refrain *from* (smoking)
regale *by* (telling funny stories)
regale *on* (strawberries)
regale (an audience) *with* (funny stories)
*regard (n.) *for* / *of* / *to*
rejoice *at* / *in* / *over* (good news, not *for*)
relation (kinship) *of* (not *to*)
relation (connection) *between* / *to*
relevant *for* (a person)
relevant *to* (a debate, not *for*)
*relief *from* / *in* / *to*
*relieve *of* (not *from*)
rely *on* (not *to*)
remark (n.) *about*
remark (v.) *on* (not *about*)
remind *about* / *of*

remonstrate *against* (protest)
remonstrate *with* (reprove)
remorse *for* / *over* (misdeeds, not *about*)
repent *of* (not *for*)
repentance *for* / *of*
*repercussions *for* / *from* / *of* / *on*
*replace *by* / *with*
replenish *with*
replete *with*
report (n.) *of* / *on* (the war, not *about* or *into*)
*report (n. v.) *to* (the boss)
representative (adj. n.) *of* (not *from*)
reproach (n.) *to* (a wrongdoer)
reproach (v.) (someone) *for* (lying)
reproach (v.) (someone) *with* (dishonesty)
repugnance (aversion) *to*
repugnance (inconsistency) *between*
repulsed *by* (not *at*)
required *for* (a purpose)
required *from* (a person, needed)
required *of* (expect of a person, not *from*)
research (n.) *in* / *into* / *on* (not *about*)
resentful *about* / *at* / *of* (harsh treatment)
resigned *from* (the top job)
resigned *to* (one's fate)
*respect (n.v.) *for* / *of* / *to*
response *to* (a person or proposal)
responsibility *for* (the project, not *over*)
responsible *for* (book ordering)
responsible *to* (the head librarian)
restriction *on* (membership, not *of*)
result (n.) *from* (an event)
result (n.) *of* (the poll)
result (v.) (arise) *from*
result (v.) (terminate) *in*
result (v.) *in* (a failure)
retaliate *against* (the enemy, not *to*)
retaliate *by* (throwing punches)

retaliate *with* (punches)
retaliation *against* / *for* (not *to*)
retreat (n.v.) *from* (not *on*)
retribution *against* (an offender)
retribution *for* (an offence)
retroactive *to* (a date, not *from*)
return *from* / *to* (Montreal, not *back* or *back in*)
★revulsion *against* / *at* / *from* / *to*(wards) (not *with*)
rich *in* (oil, possessions, not *with*)
rid (the city) *of* (rats, not *from*)
riddled *with* (scandal, smallpox, not *in*)
rise *to* (the occasion, not *for*)
★risk (n.) *from* / *in* / *of* / *to* (not *for*)
rival (n.) *for* (the job)
rival (v,) *in* (skill)
riveted *by* / *to* (TV programme)
rough *on* (hypercritical, not gentle)
rough *with* (abusive)
rude *to* (not *with*)

~
S

sacrifice (v.) (her life) *to* (her children, not *for*)
safe (adj.) *against* (harm, danger)
safe (adj.) *from* (attack, one's enemies)
salvation *from* (sin, hellfire)
salvation *of* (human souls, not *to*)
★same *for* / *to*
sanguine *about* / *of* (chances of winning)
★satire *of* / *on* (folly, not *about* or *against*)
satisfaction *with* (not *about* or *towards*)
satisfactory *to* (my purposes)
satisfactory *to* (me)
satisfied *of* (convinced)
satisfied *with* (contented, not *about*, *at* or *by*)
★saturated *by* / *in* / *with*
say (n.) *in* (what to do, not *over*)

scared *of*
scathing *about* (not *of*)
sceptical *about* / *of* (not *over* or *toward*)
scepticism *about* (not *over* or *toward*)
*scruple / *about* / *to*
scrupulous *about* (personal hygiene)
scrupulous *in* (cleaning the house)
secret *of* / *to* (success)
secure *about* (the future)
secure *against* (attack)
secure (a loan) *for* (a project)
secure *from* (harm)
secure *in* (a position)
seek *after* / *for* (search *for*)
seek *from* / *of* (request *of*)
seek *out* (hunt *down*)
seized *by* / *with* (fear, illness, remorse)
sensible *about* (doing homework)
sensible (appreciative) *of* (kindness, not *to*)
*sensitive *about* / *to* (not *at*, *of* or *over*)
separate (adj.) *from*
separate (v.) (divide) *into* (three groups)
separate (v.) *from*
*servant *of* / *to*
*shame (n.) *at* / *on* / *to* / *upon*
share (n.) *of* (the profits)
share (v.) *in* (the profits)
*share (v.) (the profits) *with* (friends)
shed light *on* (not *as to*)
shocked *at* / *by* (his arrest, not *about* or *over*)
short *of* (money, not *from*)
short *on* (talent)
shout (v.) *at* (yell aggressively)
shout (v.) *to* (call to)
shrouded *in* (mystery, not *by* or *with*)
shy (wary) *about* / *of* (strangers)
shy (reluctant) *of*
shy (short of) *of* (my target)

shy (deficient) *on*
shy (bashful) *with* (young girls)
sick *at* (heart)
sick *at* (having to leave home)
sick *from* (stress)
sick *of* (tired)
sick *to* (death, one's stomach)
sick *with* (fear, bird flu)
★siege *of* / *to* (a city, not *on*)
★sign (n.) *for* / *of*
★sign *off on* (a report)
similar *to* (not *as*, *between*, *than* or *with*)
similarity *among* (several things)
similarity *between* (one thing and another)
similarity *of* (one thing) *to* (another)
similarity *to* / *with* (a thing)
site *of* (new building, not *for*)
smile (v.) *at* (good or bad news)
smile (v.) *on* (favour, a person)
★soak(ed) *by* / *in* / *into* / *through* / *to* / *up*
solicitous *for* / *of* (not *to*)
solution *of* / *to* (a problem)
sorry *about* / *for* (a terrible mistake)
sorry *for* (feel pity for)
★source *for* or *of* (information)
sparing *of* (praise, not *for, to* or *with*)
★speak *about* / *against* / *of* / *on* (a subject)
speak *from* (the heart, experience)
★speak *to* / *with* (a friend)
★speak *to* (an issue)
specialize *in* (Canadian history, not *for*)
spectator *of* (not *to*)
★spend (money) *for* / *in* / *on* / *upon* (books)
★spend (time) *in* (playing bridge)
spoiled *by* (not *with*)
squabble (n.v.) *about* / *over* (right of way)
squabble (n.v.) *between* / *with* (neighbours)
square (v.) *with* (be or make compatible, not *to*)

stance *on* (attitude, not *towards*)
*star*t (n.) *at / of / on*
startled *at* or *by* (his downfall)
stigma *of* (mental illness, not *around*)
stressed *about* (not *on*)
strive *against / for* (contend, struggle)
strict *about* (punctuality)
strict *in* (one's habits)
strict *with* (prisoners)
strive *after / for* (justice)
subsequent *to*
subsist *on* (not *off*)
substitute (reposition one thing) *for* (another) substitute
(replace one thing) *with* (another)
subtitle *of* (a book, not *for* or *to*)
subversive *of* (not *to*)
succeed *at* (writing novels)
succeed *in* (learning to fly, not *to* learn)
succeed *to* (inherit a fortune, the throne)
sue *for* (peace, damages libel, not *over*)
suffer *for* (one's beliefs)
suffer *from* (an ailment, not *in* or *with*)
suffer *with* (bad feet)
suitable *for / to* (the purpose)
suited *for / to* (the job)
superior *in* (numbers, skill)
superior *to* (other brands, not *than* or *over*)
superiority *to* (not *over*)
supplied *by* (the government)
supply (v.) (books) *for* (the library)
supply (v.) (food) *to* (the starving)
supply (v.) (the army) *with* (tanks)
support (n.) *for* (a policy, not *towards*)
support (n.) *to* (a candidate)
surprised *at* (something astonishing, disappointing)
surprised *by* (something unexpected)
surprised (someone) *with* (something)
surround (oneself) *with* (not *by*)

surrounded *by* (not *with*)
susceptible *of* (explanation, persuasion)
susceptible (liable, sensitive) *to*
suspicious *of* (not *about*)
*swear *at* / *by* / *in* / *off* / *on* / *to*
symbol(ic) *of* (Nazism, not *to*)
sympathetic *to* (person or attitude, not *for*)
*sympathy *for* / *with* (not *to*)
synchronize *with* (not *to*)
synonymous *with* (not *to*)

~
T

*talk *to* / *with* (a friend)
tamper *with* (voting results)
*target (n. v.) *for* / *of*
taste (n.) *for* (liking)
taste (n.) *of* (food)
taste (n.) *in* (art)
tendency *to* / *towards*
tenderness (love) *for* / *towards*
terminate *in* (victory, not *with*)
terrified *at* (a prospect)
terrified *by* (a rifle shot)
terrified *of* (dogs)
terrified *of* (making a mistake, not *to* make)
testament *to* (her abilities, not *of*)
testimonial *to* (her abilities, not *of*)
thankful *for* (the rain, not *to*)
*theory *about* / *of* / *on*
*think *about* / *for* / *of* / *on* / *over* / *to*
thirst (n. v.) *after* / *for* (knowledge)
threat *against* / *to* (not *for*)
threatened *by* (a robber)
threatened *to* (take revenge)
threatened *with* (a gun, an epidemic)
*thrilled *at* / *by* / *to* / *with*

thrive *on* (a vegetarian diet)
throw (n. v.) *at* (aim a missile)
throw (n. v.) *to* (pass a ball)
ties *between* / *to* / *with* (other nations, not *of*)
ties *of* (family history)
tinker (v.) *with* (car engines)
★tired *from* / *of* (not *by*)
token *of* (my lasting affection, not *for*)
tolerance *of* (foreigners, not *for* or *towards*)
tolerant *of* (foreigners, not *towards* or *to*)
★toll *from* / *of* / *on*
★tough (adj.) *for* / *on* / *with*
trade (v.) *for* (exchange)
trade (v.) *in* (barter *with*)
trade (v.) *on* (exploit)
trade (v.) *with* (do business)
tradition *of* excellence (not *in*)
translate *into* (not *in*)
travel *for* (a company)
travel *on* (business, not *for*)
★true *for* (a person)
★true *of* (applicable to, not *for* or *with*)
★true *to* (faithful)
trust (n. v.) *in* (not *for*)
trust (v.) *with* (i.e., "entrust *with*")
typical *of* (not *for*)

U

★umbrage *at* (an insult, not *with*)
unconcerned *about* / *at* / *over* / *with*
unconscious *of* (not *to*)
★understanding *for* (a person's plight)
★understanding *of* (English grammar, not *for*)
unequal *to* (a task, not *for*)
unfair *to* (minority groups, not *for*)
unite *in* (helping, not *to* help)

united *by* (common interests)
united *to* / *with* (joined together)
unsuitable *for* / *to*
unsuited *for* / *to*
update (n. v.) *on* (not *to*)
upset (adj.) *about* / *at* / *by*)

V

vanish *into* (thin air, not *from*)
★variance *with* (not *from*)
variation *in* (colour schemes)
variation *on* (an old folksong)
vary *between* (six and eight degrees)
vary *from* (the norm)
vary *in* (attitude, size)
vary *with* (age)
veiled *in* (secrecy, not *with*)
★veneration *for* / *of*
verdict *of* (not guilty)
verdict *on* (the performance, not *for*)
vexed *about* / *at* / *by* (his harsh criticism)
vexed *at* / *with* (a critic)
★victim *of* / *to*
vie *with* (a rival) *for* (the prize)
★view (n.) *of* (sight *of*)
★view (n.) *on* (opinion *on*)
visited *by* (friends)
visited *with* (afflictions)

W

wait *for* (a friend to arrive)
★wait *on* (a diner in a restaurant)
warn (someone) *against* (doing something, not *about*)
warn (someone) *about* / *of* (a danger, not *on*)

wary *of* (strangers, not *about*)
★watch *for* / *over* (not *on*)
★winnow *out* (not *down*)
★wonder *about* (speculate *on*)
★wonder *at* / *over* (admire, be amazed)
word *to* (the wise, not *for*)
worried *at* (a bone, a knot)
worried (be anxious) *about* / *by* / *for* / *over*
wrangle *with* (someone) *about* / *over* (ownership, not *on*)

Y

yearn *for* (not *after*)

PART II:
Words, mostly verbs, not requiring a preposition.

abdicate (not *from*)
admit (a mistake, not *to*)
answer (not *to*)
ascend (a mountain, not *up*)
attain (not *to*)
calculate (not *out*)
cancel (a booking, not *out*)
catch (fire, not *on*)
chide (not *at*)
circle (not *around*)
combat (not *against*)
compensate (not *to* a person)
comprise (not *of*)
confess (not *to*)
consult (seek advice, not *with*)
crave (not *for*)
culled (not *through*)
debate (not *about* or *on*)
descend (not *down*)
discuss (something, not *about* or *on*)
distribute (not *out*)
divide (not *up*)
dominate (not *over*)

double (adj.) (not *of*)
early (not early *on*)
emphasize (not *on*)
empty (not *out*)
enter (a place, not *in* or *into*)
examine (not *into*)
explain (not *about*)
explore (not *into*)
follow (not *after* or *behind*)
follow *up* (not *up on*)
forward (v.) (not *on*)
free (not *up*)
grieve (protest *against*)
head (v.) (an investigation, not *up*)
help doing (not *from* doing)
hold (the fort, not *down*)
impair
infiltrate (not *through*)
infringe (not *on* or *upon*)
inside (not *of*)
invade (not *into*)
investigate (not *about*, *into* or *upon*)
join (not *together* or *up with*)
jump (v.) (not *up*)
lack (v.) (not *for* or *in*)
lament (v.) (regret, not *about*)
lift (not *up*)
lower (a thing, not *down*)
make good (not *on*)
melt (not *out*)
mention (n. v.) (not *about*)
mock (not *at*)
muster (not *up*)
near (not *to*)
objection *to* (doing, not *toward*)
offend (a person, not *against*)
oppose (not *against*)
outside (not *of*)

penetrate (not *into* or *through*)
permeate (not *through*)
plummet (not *down*)
ponder (a problem, not *about, on* or *over*)
profess (not *to*)
protest (not *against*)
raise (not *up*)
reach (not *to*)
rear (v.) (not *up*)
reconcile (one thing) *with* (another)
reconcile(d) *to* (a person or thing)
refer *to* (not *back to*)
reflect (not *back*)
regress (not back)
reply (not *back*)
request (not *for*)
resign (a post, membership, not *from*)
resemble (not *to*)
resist (not *from*)
respond (not *back*)
return (not *back*)
revert (not *back*)
seek (not *after* or *for*)
segregate (not *out*)
seize (not *upon*)
separate (not *out*)
shunted (not *off*)
sidestep (not *around*)
sift (not *through*)
spare (not *from*)
stress (not *upon*)
study (not *about*)
test (not *out*)
study (not *up on*)
trace (not *down*)
traverse (ski slopes, not *across*)
underneath (not *of*)
until (not *up until*)

watch (not *on*)
win (not *out*)

SELECTED BIBLIOGRAPHY

Abbott. E. A. *A Shakespearian Grammar.* New York: Dover Publications, 1966.

Alford, Henry. *A Plea for the Queen's English.* London: Strahan, 1864.

Algeo, John. *British or American English? A Handbook of Word and Grammar Patterns.* Cambridge: Cambridge University Press, 2006 (esp. 159–97).

Amis, Kingsley. *The King's English.* Hammersmith: HarperCollins, 1998.

Anon. *The Key to English Prepositions.* 2 vols. Toronto: Macmillan, 1964.

Arnason, Eleanor. "The Grammarian's Five Daughters." *Realms of Fantasy* (June, 1999).

Ashley, Jackie. "Your iPod may be changing your brain." *Guardian Weekly* April 28–May 4, 2006.

Benson, Morton et al. *The BBI Dictionary of English Word Combinations.* Revised edition. Amsterdam/Philadelphia: John Benjamins Publishing Company, 1997.

Bernstein, Theodore M. *The Careful Writer.* New York: Atheneum, 1965.

Bierce, Ambrose. *Write It Right: A Little Blacklist of Literary Faults.* New York: Walter Neale, 1909.

Bissell, Clifford H. *Prepositions in French and English.* New York: Richard R. Smith, 1947.

Blackburn, Bob. *Words Fail Us: Good English and Other Lost Causes.* Toronto: McClelland & Stewart, 1993.

Blake, N. F. *Shakespeare's Language: An Introduction.* New York: St Martin's Press, 1983.

--------. *A Grammar of Shakespeare's Language.* New York: Palgrave, 2002.

Blamires, Harry. *The Penguin Guide to Plain English.* Harmondsworth: Penguin, 2000.

--------. *The Queen's English.* London: Bloomsbury, 1994.

Bollinger, Dwight. *The Phrasal Verb in English.* Cambridge, Mass.: Harvard University Press, 1971.

--------. "Reiconization," *World Englishes* VII (1988), 237–42.

Boyd, Charles C. *Grammar for Grown-ups.* London: Allen & Unwin, 1927.

Brians, Paul. *Common Errors in English Usage.* 2nd edition. Wilsonville, Oregon: William, James & Co., 2009.

Brockenbrough, Martha. *Things That Make Us [Sic].* New York: St. Martin's Press, 2008.

Bryson, Bill. *The Mother Tongue.* New York: Perennial, 1990.

Burchfield, R. W. *Fowler's Modern English Usage.* Rev. 3rd ed. Oxford: Oxford University Press, 2004.

Burrow, Colin. "Not for Horrid Profs." Review of Frank Kermode, *Shakespeare's Language*. *London Review of Books* (June 1, 2000), 11–13.

Close, R. A. *Prepositions*. London: Longman's, 1967.

Cochrane, James. *Between You and I*. Cambridge: Icon Books, 2003.

Coffman, Sue. *That's Just the Way it Is: The Amazing English Language*. N. p.: Ist Books Library, [2001].

Cole, Tom. *The Preposition Book: Practice Towards Mastering English Prepositions*. Ann Arbor: University of Michigan Press, 2006.

Connolly, Cyril. *The Unquiet Grave*. Harmondsworth: Penguin, 1967.

Cowie, A. P. and R. Mackin. *Oxford Book of Current Idiomatic English*. London: Oxford University Press, 1975.

Crystal, David. *How Language Works*. Woodstock & New York: The Overlook Press, 2006.

--------. *Words Words Words*. Oxford: Oxford University Press, 2006.

Crystal, David and Ben Crystal. *Shakespeare's Words: A Glossary and Language Companion*. London: Penguin, 2002.

Davies, Hugh Sykes. *Grammar Without Tears*. London: The Bodley Head, 1951.

DuBois, Barbara R. "Preposition Pollution." *Verbatim* 6, #2 (Autumn, 1979), 3–4.

Fernald, James C. *Connectives of English Speech: The Correct Usage of Prepositions etc*. New York: Funk & Wagnalls, 1904.

Fowler H. W. *A Dictionary of Modern English Usage*. Oxford: Clarendon Press, 1926.

Fowler H. W. and F. G. Fowler. *The King's English*, 3rd ed. Oxford: Clarendon Press, 1938.

Garner, Bryan. *Dictionary of Modern American Usage*. New York: Oxford University Press, 1998.

Gooden, Philip. *Faux Pas?* New York: Walker & Company, 2006.

Gowers, Sir Ernest. *The Complete Plain Words*. London: Her Majesty's Stationery Office, 1954.

Greenbaum, Sidney and Janet Whitcut. *Longman Guide to English Usage*. Harmondsworth: Penguin, 1996.

Heaton, J. B. *Prepositions and Adverbial Particles*. London: Longmans, 1965.

Hill, L. A. *Prepositions and Adverbial Particles*. London: Oxford University Press, 1968.

Hitchens, Christopher. *Arguably*. Toronto: Signal/McClelland & Stewart, 2011.

Hitchings, Henry. *The Language Wars: A History of Proper English*. London: John Murray, 2011.

Hodgson, William B. *Errors in the Use of English*. Edinburgh: David Douglas, 1882.

Howard, Godfrey. *The Good English Guide: English Usage in the 1990s*. London: Pan Macmillan, 1993.

Huddleston, Rodney and Geoffrey K. Pullum. *The Cambridge Grammar of the English Language*. Cambridge: Cambridge University Press, 2002.

Humphrys, John. *Lost for Words: The Mangling and Manipulating of the English Language*. London: Hodder & Stoughton, 2004.

Jenkins, Evan. *That or Which, and Why: A Usage Guide for Thoughtful Writers and Editors*. New York: Routledge, 2007.

Kimber, Galina. *Perfect Prepositions: A Real Life Guide to Using English Prepositions*. New York: iUniverse, Inc., 2006.

Lamb, Bernard C. *The Queen's English and How to Use It*. London: Michael O'Mara Books, 2010.

LePan, Don. *The Broadview Book of Common Errors in English*. Peterborough: Broadview Press, 2003.

Lindstromberg, Seth. *English Prepositions Explained*. John Benjamins Publishing Co.: Amsterdam 1998.

Lovinger, Paul W. *The Penguin Dictionary of American English Usage and Style*. Harmondsworth: Penguin, 2000.

Lynch, Jack. *The Lexicographer's Dilemma: The Evolution of "Proper" English from Shakespeare to "South Park."* New York: Walker & Company, 2009.

MacHale, Des. *Wit*. Kansas City: Andrews McMeel Publishing, 2003.

McArthur, Tom. *The Oxford Companion to the English Language*. Oxford: OUP, 1992.

MacRae, Paul. "We're not teaching our children well." *Victoria Times-Colonist,* December 29, 2005.

Michaels, Leonard and Christopher Ricks. *The State of the Language*. Berkeley: University of California Press, 1980.

Nesfield, J.C. *Errors in English Composition*. London: Macmillan, 1903.

Nunberg, Geoffrey. *The Way We Talk Now*. Boston: Houghton Mifflin, 2001.

O'Conner, Patricia T. *Origins of the Specious*. New York: Random House, 2010.

Oxford Phrasal Verbs Dictionary. Oxford: Oxford University Press, 2001.

Partridge, A. C. *Tudor to Augustan English*. London: Andre Deutsch, 1969.

Partridge, Eric. *Usage and Abusage: A Guide to Good English*. New York and London: Harper, 1942.

Pearsall Smith, Logan. *Words and Idioms*. London: Constable, 1925.

Pinker, Steven. *Words and Rules*. New York: Perennial, 2000.

Prieur, Charles N. and Elizabeth Champion Speyer. *The Writer's Guide to Prepositions*. Goodenglish.com, 2000.

Quirk, Randolph et al. *A Grammar of Contemporary English*. London: Longman, 1972.

Rees, Nigel. *Dictionary of Popular Phrases*. London: Bloomsbury, 1990.

Rowe, F. J. and W. T. Webb. *A Guide to the Study of English*. London: Macmillan, 1930 (Ist ed. 1914).

Shakespeare, William. *The Complete Signet Classic Shakespeare*. Edited by Sylvan Barnet. New York: Harcourt, Brace, Jovanovich, 1972.

Shippey, Tom. "I lerne song," *London Review of Books* (February 22, 2007), 19–20.

Simon, John. *Paradigms Lost*. New York: Clarkson N. Potter, 1980.

Sinclair, John (gen. ed.). *Prepositions*. London: HarperCollins, 1997.

Stein, Gertrude. "Poetry and Grammar," in *Lectures in America*. Boston: Beacon Press, 1957 (Ist ed. 1935).

Steiner, George. *Language and Silence*. Harmondsworth: Penguin, 1969.

Strumpf, Michael and Auriel Douglas. *The Grammar Bible*. New York: Henry Holt, 2004.

Swan, Michael. *Practical English Usage*. Oxford: Oxford University Press, 2005.

Swick, Ed. *English Pronouns and Prepositions*. New York: McGraw-Hill, 2005.

Trask, R. L. *Mind the Gaffe*. Harmondsworth: Penguin, 2002.

Truss, Lynne. *Eats, Shoots & Leaves*. New York: Gotham Books, 2004.

Wallace, David Foster. "Tense Present: Democracy, English, and the Wars over Usage." *Harper's Magazine* (April, 2001), 39-58.

Watcyn-Jones, Peter and Jake Allsop. *Test Your Prepositions*. Harlow: Penguin, 2001.

Webb, W. T. *English of To-Day*. London: Routledge, 1925.

White, E. B. *The Second Tree from the Corner*. New York: Harper, 1954.

Wood, Frederick T. *English Prepositional Idioms*. London: Macmillan, 1967.

Yagoda, Ben. *When You Catch an Adjective, Kill It*. New York: Broadway Books, 2007.

NOTE: Bryan Garner's *Dictionary of Modern American Usage* (see above) contains an appendix (pp. 709–19) listing, chronologically, 350 books written between 1786 and 1997 which the author claims constitute "the corpus of literature on English usage."

Printed in Canada